THE BOOK OF AMOS

Jörg Jeremias

THE BOOK
OF AMOS

A Commentary

Westminster John Knox Press
Louisville, Kentucky

Translated by Douglas W. Stott from *Der Prophet Amos*
(Das Alte Testament Deutsch), published 1995 by Vandenhoeck & Ruprecht, Göttingen.

© 1995 Vandenhoeck & Ruprecht, in Göttingen.

English translation © 1998 Westminster John Knox Press

Publisher's Note: The publication of this work was made possible through the assistance of INTER NATIONES, Bonn. / Die Herausgabe dieses Werkes wurde aus Mitteln von INTER NATIONES, Bonn, gefördert.

Book design by Jennifer K. Cox

First American edition 1998

Published by Westminster John Knox Press
Louisville, Kentucky

This book is printed on acid-free paper that meets the American National Standards Institute Z39.48 standard. ∞

PRINTED IN THE UNITED STATES OF AMERICA

98 99 00 01 02 03 04 05 06 07 — 10 9 8 7 6 5 4 3 2 1

Library of Congress Cataloging-in-Publication Data

Jeremias, Jörg.
    [Prophet Amos. English]
    The book of Amos : a commentary / Jörg Jeremias. — 1st ed.
        p.   cm. — (The Old Testament library)
    Includes bibliographical references and index.
    ISBN 0-664-22086-X (alk. paper)
    1. Bible. O.T. Amos—Commentaries. I. Title II. Series.
BS1585.3.J47   1998
224'.8077—dc21   97-28815

To my colleagues in Hermannstadt and Klausenburg

as an expression of gratitude

for bestowing upon me the honorary doctorate

CONTENTS

PREFACE
TO THE GERMAN EDITION

Scholarly interest in the book of Amos has shifted considerably in recent years. During the decades following the Second World War, attention was focused on the prophetic "office" and especially on Amos' social criticism and on a reconstruction of its social background; since the publication of the brilliant commentary of Hans Walter Wolff (1969; 3d ed. 1985; ET 1977), however, the assumption has been that this direction of inquiry was based largely on a naive understanding of the text, one that believed it could hear Amos' oral speech immediately behind the book. The present commentary is shaped by the conviction that the book of Amos in all its parts already presupposes the fall of the Northern Kingdom and over considerable stretches also that of the Southern Kingdom, Judah. Amos' message is delivered as a retrospective, that is, in view of its own (partial) fulfillment and in view of the unwillingness of its contemporaries to be roused by the prophetic word. It is also presented in an artistic form prompting the reader to relate substantively the individual parts of the book to one another. Finally, it has been reworked and updated in a process extending over centuries, a process attesting both the high regard in which the book of Amos was held during the exilic and postexilic periods, as well as the intense interest it prompted during that same time. Reconstruction of Amos' actual oral words is only rarely possible, and even then only with a not inconsiderable degree of uncertainty. To encounter the historical Amos one should start with a reading of the visions, whereas to come to know the book of Amos it is best to start with a reading of Amos 5:1–17. This is a theological book through and through, not a tractate of social criticism, even though social themes do indeed play an important role in it. The book reflects the multilayered history of transmission traversed by Amos' message over the course of numerous centuries. But difficulties attaching to any multilayered textual reading also imply a significant advantage for the contemporary reader: The gulf of history separating us from Amos diminishes; our own updated engagement with this message in sermon and instruction can take as its point of departure the similar updating by later biblical authors, who were themselves already far removed from the historical Amos.

So as not to confuse the reader unnecessarily with different typefaces, I have set off in italics in my translation only the exilic and postexilic redactions (the one exception being Amos 6, in which for the sake of clearer differentiation more recent preexilic passages are also set in italics). In certain instances, discussions of these more recent strata are set apart in the commentary itself by smaller typeface, this, too, for the sake of easier orientation and without implying any theological value judgments—the church fathers, for example, did after all cite the presumably exilic hymns in the book of Amos more frequently than anything else! In the bibliographical offerings concerning the individual pericopes, I have as a rule—as in my commentary on Hosea—restricted myself to two; these are cited in the commentary with a simple "loc. cit.," whereas in the case of familiar commentaries the author's name is followed immediately by the page number or simply "in loc." Wherever the present commentary does not offer enough space for presenting sufficient arguments in support of a particular understanding, I have referred the reader to my volume of essays *Hosea und Amos,* published concurrently.

I would like to thank numerous persons who have assisted me in working on this volume, among whom Annegret Pfirsch and Klaus-Peter Adam may be mentioned as representatives of the many others, as well as my secretary in Munich, Frau Daniela Fischer, for her dependable care in copying a manuscript that underwent multiple modifications.

J. J.

Marburg
February 1995

BIBLIOGRAPHY

1. Text Editions

Biblia Hebraica, ed. R. Kittel, 3d ed. (Stuttgart: Deutsche Bibelgesellschaft, 1933); Librum XII Prophetarum, ed. O. Procksch.

Biblia Hebraica Stuttgartensia, ed. K. Elliger and W. Rudolph (Stuttgart: Deutsche Bibelgesellschaft, 1970); Librum XII Prophetarum, ed. K. Elliger.

Ziegler, *Duodecim prophetae*
   Duodecim prophetae. Septuaginta. Vetus Testamentum Graece, auctoritate Soc. Litt. Gott., ed. J. Ziegler, vol. 13, 2d ed. (Göttingen: Vandenhoeck & Ruprecht, 1967).

2. Commentaries to the Twelve (*Minor*) *Prophets*
(*dates refer to the commentaries on Amos*)

Amsler, S., "Amos," in Edmond Jacob, Carl A. Keller, and Samuel Amsler, *Osée, Joël, Amos, Abadias, Jonas,* Commentaire de l'Ancien Testament 11a (Neuchâtel: Delachaux & Niestlé, 1965), 157–291.

Andersen, F. I., and D. N. Freedman, *Amos: A New Translation with Notes and Commentary,* Anchor Bible 24A (New York: Doubleday, 1989).

Auld, A. G., *Amos,* Old Testament Guides (Sheffield: JSOT Press, 1986).

Deissler, A., *Zwölf Propheten,* Neue Echter Bibel 4/4 (Würzburg: Echter, 1981).

Delcor, M., Les petits prophètes, SB(PC) (Paris: Letouzey & Ane, 1964).

Duhm, B., *The Twelve Prophets: A Version in the Various Poetical Measures of the Original Writings,* trans. A. Duff (London, 1912) [*Die Zwölf Propheten, in den Versmassen der Urschrift übersetzt* (Tübingen, 1910)].

———, "Anmerkungen zu den Zwölf Propheten," *ZAW* 31 (1911): 1–43; 81–110; 161–204.

Frey, H., *Das Buch des Ringens Gottes um seine Kirche: Der Prophet Amos,* Botschaft des Alten Testaments 23/1 (Stuttgart: Calwer, 1958; 3d ed. 1988).

Gelderen, C. van, *Het boek Amos,* Commentaar op het Oude Testament (Kampen, 1933).

Gressmann, H., *Die älteste Geschichtsschreibung und Prophetie Israels* (*von Samuel bis Amos und Hosea*), SAT 3/1, 2d ed. (Göttingen, 1921).

Harper, W. R., *A Critical and Exegetical Commentary on Amos and Hosea,* ICC (Edinburgh: T. & T. Clark, 1905).

Hitzig, F., *Die zwölf kleinen Propheten,* KEH 1, 4th ed. (with H. Steiner) (Leipzig, 1881).

Hoonacker, A. van, *Les douze petits Prophètes,* EtB (Paris, 1908).

Marti, K., *Das Dodekapropheton erklärt,* KHC 13 (Tübingen, 1904).

Mays, J. L., *Amos, A Commentary,* OTL (Philadelphia: Westminster Press, 1969).

McKeating, H., *The Books of Amos, Hosea and Micah,* Cambridge Bible Commentary on the New English Bible (Cambridge: University Press, 1971).

Nötscher, F., *Zwölfprophetenbuch oder Kleine Propheten,* Echter Bibel (Würzburg: Echter, 1948).

Nowack, W., *Die kleinen Propheten übersetzt und erklärt,* HK 3/4, 3d ed. (Göttingen, 1922).

Paul, S. M., *Amos: A Commentary on the Book of Amos,* Hermeneia (Minneapolis: Fortress, 1991).

Procksch, O., *Die kleinen Prophetischen Schriften vor dem Exil,* Erläuterungen zum Alten Testament 3 (Calw/Stuttgart: 1910).

Rinaldi, G., *I Profeti minori,* vol. 1, La Sacra Bibbia (Torino/Rome: Marietti, 1952).

Robinson, T. H., and F. Horst, *Die Zwölf Kleinen Propheten,* HAT 1/14, 3d ed. (Tübingen: Mohr [Siebeck], 1964).

Rudolph, W., *Joel—Amos—Obadja—Jona,* KAT 13/2 (Gütersloh: Gütersloher Verlagshaus Gerd Mohn, 1971).

Sellin, E., *Das Zwölfprophetenbuch,* KAT 12/1, 2d/3d ed. (Leipzig, 1929/30).

Stuart, D., *Hosea-Jonah,* WBC (Dallas: Word, 1987).

Theis, J., "Der Prophet Amos," in J. Lippl and J. Theis, *Die Zwölf Kleinen Propheten,* vol. 1, HSAT 8/3/1 (Bonn, 1937).

Weiser, A., [and K. Elliger], *Das Buch der zwölf Kleinen Propheten,* Das Alte Testament Deutsch, 8th ed. (Göttingen: Vandenhoeck & Ruprecht, 1985).

Wellhausen, J., *Die kleinen Propheten übersetzt und erklärt,* Skizzen und Vorarbeiten 5, 4th ed. (Berlin: Georg Reimer, 1898; repr. 1963).

Wolff, H. W., *Joel and Amos,* trans. Waldemar Janzen, S. Dean McBride, Jr., and Charles A. Muenchow, Hermeneia (Philadelphia: Fortress, 1977).

3. *Individual Commentaries to the Book of Amos*

Cripps, Richard S., *A Critical and Exegetical Commentary on the Book of Amos,* 2d ed. (London: SPCK, 1955–1969).

Hammershaimb, Erling H., *The Book of Amos: A Commentary* (Oxford: Basil Blackwell, 1970).

Hayes, J. H., *Amos* (Nashville: Abingdon, 1988).
Martin-Achard, R., and Re'emi, S. P., *God's People in Crisis: A Commentary on the Book of Amos and on the Book of Lamentations* (Edinburgh: Handsel, 1984).
Smith, G. V., *Amos*, Library of Biblical Interpretation (Grand Rapids: Regency Reference Library, 1989).
Snaith, Norman H., *The Book of Amos*, 2 vols. (London: Epworth, 1945–46).
Soggin, J. A., *The Prophet Amos* (Brescia, 1982 [Italian]; London: SCM, 1987).
Ward, J. M., *Amos and Isaiah: Prophets of the Word of God* (Nashville/New York: Abingdon, 1969).

4. *Abbreviations for Works Cited*

Barstad, *Religious Polemics*
Barstad, H. M., *The Religious Polemics of Amos*, VTSup 34 (Leiden: E. J. Brill, 1984).
Barthélemy, *Critique textuelle*
Barthélemy, D., *Critique textuelle de l'Ancien Testament*, vol. 3: *Ezéchiel, Daniel et les 12 Prophètes*, OBO 50/3 (Fribourg, Switzerland: Editions universitaires; Göttingen: Vandenhoeck & Ruprecht, 1992).
Bjørndalen, *Allegorische Rede*
Bjørndalen, A. J., *Untersuchungen zur Allegorischen Rede der Propheten Amos und Jesaja*, BZAW 165 (Berlin/New York: Walter de Gruyter, 1986).
BRL/BRL² Biblisches Reallexikon, ed. K. Galling, HAT 1/1 (Tübingen: Mohr [Siebeck], 1937; 2d ed. 1977).
Brockelmann, *Syntax*
Brockelmann, C., *Hebräische Syntax* (Neukirchen: Verlag der Buchhandlung des Erziehungsvereins, 1956).
Coote, *Amos*
Coote, R. B., *Amos among the Prophets: Composition and Theology* (Philadelphia: Fortress, 1981).
Dalman, *Arbeit und Sitte*
Dalman, Gustav, *Arbeit und Sitte in Palästina*, 7 vols. (Gütersloh: C. Bertelsmann; [1/1, 2] 1928, [2] 1932, [3] 1933, [4] 1935, [5] 1937, [6] 1939, [7] 1942; repr. Hildesheim: Georg Olms, 1964).
Ehrlich, *Randglossen V*
Ehrlich, Arnold B., *Randglossen zur hebräischen Bibel*, vol. 4: *Ezechiel und die kleinen Propheten* (Leipzig, 1912; repr. Hildesheim: Georg Olms, 1968).
Fendler, "Sozialkritik"
Fendler, M., "Zur Sozialkritik des Amos," *EvT* 33 (1973): 32–53.

Fey, *Amos und Jesaja*
  Fey, R., *Amos und Jesaja, Abhängigkeit und Eigenständigkeit des Jesaja*,
  WMANT 12 (Neukirchen-Vluyn: Neukirchener Verlag, 1963).
Fleischer, *Menschenverkäufer*
  Fleischer, G., *Von Menschenverkäufern, Baschankühen und Rechtsver-
  ehrern: Die Sozialkritik des Amos in historisch-kritischer, sozialgeschicht-
  licher und archäologischer Perspektive*, Athenäums Monografien Theolo-
  gie 74 (Frankfurt am Main: Athenäum, 1989).
Gese, "Komposition"
  Gese, H., "Komposition bei Amos," *VTSup* 32 (Leiden: E. J. Brill, 1981):
  74–95 = idem, *Alttestamentliche Studien* (Tübingen: Mohr [Siebeck],
  1991) 94–115.
Ges.-B
  Gesenius, W., *Hebräisches und aramäisches Wörterbuch über das Alte Tes-
  tament*, 17th ed., ed. F. Buhl (Berlin/Göttingen/Heidelberg: Springer, 1915;
  repr. 1962).
G-K²⁸
  Gesenius' Hebrew Grammar, ed. E. Kautzsch, trans. and rev. A. E. Cowley
  (Oxford: Clarendon Press, 1910). [*W. Gesenius' Hebräische Grammatik*, ed.
  E. Kautzsch, 28th ed. (Leipzig, 1909; repr. Hildesheim: Georg Olms, 1962).]
HAL
  Hebräisches und aramäisches Lexikon zum Alten Testament, eds. L. Köhler
  and W. Baumgartner, 3d ed., rev. W. Baumgartner (Leiden: E. J. Brill, 1990).
Jeremias, *Kultprophetie*
  Jeremias, J., *Kultprophetie und Gerichtsverkündigung in der späten Königszeit
  Israels*, WMANT 35 (Neukirchen-Vluyn: Neukirchener Verlag, 1970).
Jeremias, *Hosea und Amos*
  Jeremias, J., *Hosea und Amos: Studien zu den Anfängen des Do-
  dekapropheton*, Forschungen zum Alten Testament 13 (Tübingen: Mohr
  [Siebeck], 1995).
Joüon, *Grammar*
  Joüon, P., *A Grammar of Biblical Hebrew*, trans. and rev. T. Muraoka, Sub-
  sidia Biblica 14 (Rome: Editrice Pontificio Istituto Biblico, 1991) [= *Gram-
  maire de l'Hébreu biblique* (Rome: Institut Biblique Pontifical, 1923; repr.
  1965)].
KAI 1–3
  Donner, H., and W. Röllig, *Kanaanäische und aramäische Inschriften*, 3
  vols. (Wiesbaden: O. Harrassowitz; [1] 1962, [2, 3] 1964).
Koch, *Amos*, part 2
  Koch, K., et al., *Amos, untersucht mit den Mitteln struktularer Form-
  geschichte*, 3 vols., Alter Orient und Altes Testament 30 (Kevelaer: Butzon
  & Bercker; Neukirchen-Vluyn: Neukirchener Verlag, 1976).

Krause, "Soziale Kritik"
Krause, M., "Das Verhältnis von sozialer Kritik und kommender Katastrophe in den Unheilsprophezeiungen des Amos" (Ph.D. diss., Hamburg, 1972).

Maag, *Text*
Maag, V., *Text, Wortschatz und Begriffswelt des Buches Amos* (Leiden: E. J. Brill, 1951).

Markert, *Scheltwort*
Markert, L., *Struktur und Bezeichnung des Scheltworts: Eine gattungskritische Studie anhand des Amosbuches*, BZAW 140 (Berlin/New York: W. de Gruyter, 1977).

Melugin, "Formation of Amos"
Melugin, R. F., "The Formation of Amos: An Analysis of Exegetical Method," in P. Achtemeier, ed., *SBL Seminar Papers* (Missoula, Mont.: Scholars, 1978), 369–92.

Reventlow, *Amt*
Reventlow, H. Graf, *Das Amt des Propheten bei Amos*, FRLANT 80 (Göttingen: Vandenhoeck & Ruprecht, 1962).

Schmidt, *Deuteronomistische Redaktion*
Schmidt, W. H., "Die deuteronomistische Redaktion des Amosbuches," *ZAW* 77 (1965): 168–93.

TGI²
Galling, K., ed., *Textbuch zur Geschichte Israels*, 2d ed. (Tübingen: Mohr [Siebeck], 1968).

de Vaux, *AncIsr*
de Vaux, R., *Ancient Israel: Its Life and Institutions*, trans. John McHugh (New York: McGraw-Hill, 1961; 2d ed. 1965).

Vermeylen, *Isaïe*
Vermeylen, J., *Du prophète Isaïe à l'apocalyptique*, vol. 2, EtB (Paris: Gabalda, 1978).

Vollmer, *Geschichtliche Rückblicke*
Vollmer, J., *Geschichtliche Rückblicke und Motive in der Prophetie des Amos, Hosea und Jesaja*, BZAW 119 (Berlin: W. de Gruyter, 1971).

Weimar, "Schluss des Amos-Buches"
Weimar, P., "Der Schluss des Amos-Buches. Ein Beitrag zur Redaktionsgeschichte des Amos-Buches," *BN* 16 (1981): 60–100.

Weippert, "Amos—seine Bilder"
Weippert, H., "Amos—seine Bilder und ihr Milieu," in H. Weippert, K. Seybold, and M. Weippert, *Beiträge zur prophetischen Bildsprache in Israel und Assyrien*, OBO 64 (Freiburg, Switzerland: Universitätsverlag, 1985): 1–29.

Weiser, *Profetie*
Weiser, A., *Die Profetie des Amos*, BZAW 53 (Giessen: A. Töpelmann, 1929).

Willi-Plein, *Schriftexegese*
Willi-Plein, I., *Vorformen der Schriftexegese innerhalb des Alten Testaments: Untersuchungen zum literarischen Werden der auf Amos, Hosea und Micha zurückgehenden Bücher im hebräischen Zwölfprophetenbuch*, BZAW 123 (Berlin/New York: W. de Gruyter, 1971).

Wolff, *Amos' geistige Heimat*
Amos' geistige Heimat, WMANT 18 (Neukirchen-Vluyn: Neukirchener Verlag, 1964); ET, *Amos the Prophet: The Man and His Background*, trans. F. R. McCurley (Philadelphia: Fortress, 1973).

Würthwein, "Amos-Studien"
Würthwein, Ernst, "Amos-Studien," in idem, *Wort und Existenz* (Göttingen: Vandenhoeck & Ruprecht, 1970), 68–110 (= *ZAW* 62 [1950]: 10–52).

ABBREVIATIONS

AB	Anchor Bible
ADPV	Abhandlungen des deutschen Palästina-Vereins
AOAT	Alter Orient und Altes Testament
ATANT	Abhandlungen zur Theologie des Alten und Neuen Testaments
ATD	Das Alte Testament Deutsch
ATD.E	Das Alte Testament Deutsch Ergänzungsheft
ATSAT	Arbeiten zu Text und Sprache im Alten Testament
BASOR	*Bulletin of the American Schools of Oriental Research*
BAT	Botschaft des Alten Testaments
BBB	Bonner biblische Beiträge
BEAT	Beiträge zur Erforschung des Alten Testaments und des antiken Judentums
BET	Beiträge zur biblischen Exegese und Theologie
BEvT	Beiträge zur evangelischen Theologie
BHK	*Biblia Hebraica*, ed. R. Kittel
BHS	*Biblia Hebraica Stuttgartensia*
Bib	*Biblica* (Rome)
BiBe	Biblische Beiträge
BibS(N)	Biblische Studien (Neukirchen, 1951–)
BK	Biblischer Kommentar
BN	*Biblische Notizen*
BRL	*Biblisches Reallexikon,* ed. K. Galling, HAT 1/1 (Tübingen: Mohr [Siebeck], 1937)
BRL[2]	Biblisches Reallexikon, ed. K. Galling, 2d ed. (Tübingen: Mohr [Siebeck], 1977)
BThSt	Biblisch-theologische Studien
BWAT	Beiträge zur Wissenschaft vom Alten Testament
BZAW	Beihefte zur Zeitschrift für die alttestamentliche Wissenschaft
CBC	Cambridge Bible Commentary on the New English Bible
CB.OT	Coniectanea biblica. Old Testament series
CBQ	*Catholic Biblical Quarterly*
COT	Commentaar op het Oude Testament

CAT	Commentaire de l'Ancien Testament
CRAI	Comptes rendus des séances de l'académie des inscriptions et belles lettres
EB	Echter Bibel
ET	English translation
EtB	Études bibliques
EvT	*Evangelische Theologie*
ExpTim	*Expository Times*
EzAT	Erläuterungen zum Alten Testament
FAT	Forschungen zum Alten Testament
FRLANT	Forschungen zur Religion und Literatur des Alten und Neuen Testaments
HAT	Handbuch zum Alten Testament
HDR	Harvard Dissertations in Religion
HKAT	Handkommentar zum Alten Testament
HSAT	Die Heilige Schrift des Alten Testaments
HUCA	*Hebrew Union College Annual*
ICC	International Critical Commentary
IEJ	*Israel Exploration Journal*
Int	*Interpretation*
JBL	*Journal of Biblical Literature*
JETS	*Journal of the Evangelical Theological Society*
JNES	*Journal of Near Eastern Studies*
JPOS	*Journal of Palestine Oriental Society*
JSOTSup	Journal for the Study of the Old Testament—Supplemental Series
JSS	*Journal of Semitic Studies*
JTS	*Journal of Theological Studies*
KAI	H. Donner and W. Röllig, *Kanaanäische und aramäische Inschriften*
KAT	Kommentar zum Alten Testament
KEH	Kurzgefasstes exegetisches Handbuch
KuD	*Kerygma und Dogma*
KHC	Kurzer Hand-Commentar zum Alten Testament
LXX	Septuagint
MT	Masoretic Text
NAWG	Nachrichten (1941–1944: von) der Akademie der Wissenschaften in Göttingen
NEB	Neue Echter Bibel
NRSV	New Revised Standard Version
N.S.	new series
OBO	Orbis biblicus et orientalis
OrAnt	*Oriens antiquus*

OTGui	Old Testament Guides
OTL	Old Testament Library
OTS	*Oudtestamentische Studiën*
OTWSA.P	(Papers read at) Ou testamentiese werkgemeenskap in Suid-Afrika
PEQ	*Palestine Exploration Quarterly*
RB	*Revue biblique*
RLA	*Reallexikon der Assyriologie,* ed. E. Ebeling and B. Meissner (Berlin, 1932f.)
SAT	Schriften des Alten Testaments in Auswahl
SBLDS	SBL Dissertation Series
SB(PC)	Sainte bible: Publ. sous la direction générale de Louis Pirot et continuée par A. Clamer
SB(F)	Sacra bibbia (Firenze)
Sem	*Semitica*
TB	Theologische Bücherei
TDOT	*Theological Dictionary of the Old Testament*
TGI2	Textbuch zur Geschichte Israels, ed. Kurt Galling (Tübingen: Mohr [Siebeck], 1950; 2d ed. 1968)
THAT	*Theologisches Handwörterbuch zum Alten Testament,* ed. E. Jenni and C. Westermann, 2 vols. (Munich: C. Kaiser, 1971–79)
TLZ	*Theologische Literaturzeitung*
TQ	Theologische Quartalschrift (Tübingen)
TRE	*Theologische Realenzyklopädie*
ThWAT	*Theologisches Wörterbuch zum Alten Testament*
TZ	*Theologische Zeitschrift*
UF	*Ugarit-Forschungen*
VT	*Vetus Testamentum*
VTSup	Vetus Testamentum, Supplements
WBC	Word Biblical Commentary
WD	*Wort und Dienst*
WMANT	Wissenschaftliche Monographien zum Alten und Neuen Testament
WO	*Die Welt des Orients*
ZA	*Zeitschrift für Assyriologie*
ZAW	*Zeitschrift für die alttestamentliche Wissenschaft*
ZDMG	*Zeitschrift der deutschen morgenländischen Gesellschaft*
ZDMGSup	*Zeitschrift der deutschen morgenländischen Gesellschaft— Supplemental Series*
ZDPV	*Zeitschrift des deutschen Palästina-Vereins*
ZST	*Zeitschrift für systematische Theologie*
ZTK	*Zeitschrift für Theologie und Kirche*

INTRODUCTION

1. Period and Person

According to the book's superscription, Amos appeared as a prophet during the reign of Jeroboam II (usually dated 787–747 B.C.E., and almost simultaneous with the reign of Uzziah over Judah, who is also mentioned). His words as passed down to us are directed almost without exception against, and delivered in, the Northern Kingdom (1:1b), presumably above all in the capital Samaria (3:9–4:3; 6:1–11) and in Bethel (7:10–17; cf. 4:4f.; 5:4f.). If one takes the concluding date of the superscription ("two years before the earthquake") literally, he was only briefly active as a prophet, at most about a year.

The main accomplishment of Jeroboam II was to conclude victoriously the bloody wars waged for decades between the Northern Kingdom and the Arameans for possession of the central lands of east Jordan; one result was that in this region the expansion of the kingdom under David was apparently almost restored in full (2 Kings 14:20).[1] Among Amos' oracles against the nations, the first against the Arameans (1:3ff.) still reflects the temporal proximity to these gruesome battles, as does also the quotation of the boasting victors in 6:13. On the other hand, the corpus of Amos' sayings presupposes a time of economic prosperity in the Northern Kingdom, concentrated in the capital Samaria, of the sort conceivable only during a time of peace; excavations in Samaria as well as, for example, in Hazor, Megiddo, and Dan have provided graphic evidence illustrating this background to the texts. By the same token, however, Amos' words do not yet exhibit any direct evidence of the rumblings characterizing the final years of the reign of Jeroboam II in the form of the awakening of the Assyrian high power, which was soon to ascend to a position of world power; in contrast to his slightly younger contemporaries Hosea and Isaiah, Amos never mentions the Assyrians, at least not by name, but speaks rather only generally of "a nation" that Yahweh will use in inflicting punishment (6:14, et passim). Hence the traditional dating of Amos' sayings in the second half of the reign of Jeroboam II is probably correct, even though precise evidence for such

1. Cf. in this regard esp. H. Donner, *Geschichte des Volkes Israel und seiner Nachbarn in Grundzügen*, vol. 2, ATD.E 4/2 (Göttingen: Vandenhoeck & Ruprecht, 1986), 282f.

a determination is lacking. The most likely period is the decade between 760 and 750 B.C.E.; no more precise determination is possible.

Although Amos prophesied in the Northern Kingdom, he actually came from the Southern Kingdom Judah (1:1; 7:12).[2] This presumably explains the striking differences between Amos and his only slightly later contemporary Hosea, who grew up in the Northern Kingdom, and—vice versa—his in part noteworthy similarity to the even younger Jerusalemite Isaiah (see discussion below). His hometown of Tekoa is located a good fifteen kilometers south of Jerusalem, at the extreme edge of the cultivated land that drops off abruptly to the wilderness of Judah; this locale possibly also explains the agricultural double occupation that made him an economically independent prophet. On the one hand, he owned oxen (and—if 7:14 is not drawing on proverbial sayings[3]— possibly also small livestock); on the other, he cultivated mulberry figs, which flourished in the warm climate of the Jordan plain (7:14f.). Amos' language also reflects this rural milieu of his surroundings.[4] Amos 7:10–17 suggests that his prophetic activity in the Northern Kingdom ended as abruptly as it began. We do not know, however, whether Amos was genuinely expelled or even deported from the Northern Kingdom, as has often been suspected, nor whether he died a martyr's death in Bethel (so the *Vitae Prophetarum* from the first century C.E.).

2. His Message

The oldest material we possess from Amos is his visionary accounts, which suggest that his prophetic activity underwent an incisive transformation. Although through prophetic intercession on behalf of the guilty people of God he was initially able to avert the catastrophe Yahweh had planned for Israel, he soon had to learn that there are limits to divine patience in the face of excessive guilt, limits prompting such prophetic intercession to fall silent; Amos was obliged to take the side of God as a messenger of the divine retribution leading to the "end of Israel" (8:2).[5] All the texts in the book of Amos outside the visions already presuppose this change in the understanding of the prophetic commission; this is most clearly the case in the oracles against the nations, which allude in several respects to the visions. We can no longer determine

2. Scholars have often without justification tried to circumvent this genuine puzzle in Amos' biography by searching for an (unknown) Tekoa in the Northern Kingdom; cf. the discussion of 1:1.

3. Cf. the commentary. The more recent indication of occupation in 1:1 ("shepherd") does in any case interpret 7:14 in the literal sense.

4. Cf. H. Weippert, "Amos—seine Bilder," 1–29.

5. E. Würthwein has presented the most intensive study of this change in the understanding of the prophetic office ("Amos-Studien," esp. 86–93).

whether individual oral sayings extend back to the period before the change just described. This might apply to sayings that, instead of condemning Israel as a whole (so the context), from the very beginning condemned in the name of God specific, brutal groups of wealthy men and women (e.g., 3:12; 4:1–3; 5:11; 6:1ff., etc.). In any event, Amos himself (or at least someone close to him) apparently wrote down the visionary accounts to document, over against his critics, the fact that he did not voluntarily become a messenger of this God who was set upon severely punishing his own people; other texts in the book of Amos similarly emphasize the coercive element attaching to the divine word (of judgment; 3:3–8; 7:14f.). Because these visionary portrayals presuppose that Amos had already functioned as a prophet previously, however, they do not represent an account of prophetic calling; neither do they contain any commission for proclamation.

Whereas Israel's guilt is merely presupposed in the visionary accounts without actually being specified, all the more vehemently does that guilt come to expression in the concluding strophe of the oracles against the nations. The horrible war crimes perpetrated against the weak and defenseless by Israel's neighbors—whom Yahweh harshly calls to account—are mentioned in the oracles against the nations only because, in a surprising about face and intensification, Israel's own social violence against the poor, the indebted, women, and so on, is revealed as the far more grievous guilt, perpetrated as it is against one's own people; even though it occurs within the external framework of legality, it nonetheless abuses the spirit of the institutions themselves. At the same time, the secret, central theme of Amos appears for the first time—one the tradents of his sayings ardently emphasized—namely, the special responsibility the people of God bear based on their special experience of God in history (2:9).

In the superscription-like introduction to the collection of sayings occupying the middle part of the book of Amos (chaps. 3–6), the tradents define this particular theme as that of election, which, though separating Israel from the other nations, simultaneously imposes different standards of behavior upon it (3:2). Amos finds that his own generation fails miserably when measured against these standards, and fails especially in three areas. First of all, it fails because of its religiously embellished (6:1–7) sumptuous life of luxury in the capital Samaria (3:9–4:3; 6:1–11), not because luxury as such is deleterious, but because it derives from violence against the weak (3:10; 4:1; cf. 5:11) and results in indifference toward the distress of others, as well as in the repression of any notion of a disastrous future (6:3, 6; cf. 5:18–20). Second, it fails by abrogating justice through bribery (5:7, 10–12, 14f., 24; 6:12). Justice, as God's special gift to Israel, should have functioned to settle disputes and to uncover and eliminate injustices. The prophet considers a people of God lacking a functioning system of justice to be incapable of life (5:15). Finally, his own generation fails because of its misguided trust in pilgrimages and elaborate worship services (4:4f.; 5:4f., 21–24). Because these activities fail to promote justice, they are no longer able to reach Yahweh in the first place, and are thus ineffectual ("your festivals," 5:21; "for so you love to do, O people of Israel!" 4:5). By lulling the guilty into a false sense of security, they lead directly to ruin; by providing a good conscience to accompany evil deeds, they prevent one from acknowledging one's own guilt (4:4; 5:24). Because sanctuaries—which really should have been places of intimate encounter with God—have through such perversion become places of "transgression" (4:4), Yahweh himself will actualize "Israel's end" (8:2) by destroying these houses of God, thus cutting off all possible contact between Israel and himself (9:1–4; 5:5; cf. 3:14). The result is that lengthy portions of chaps. 5–6 (cf. 8:3ff.; 9:2–4) are characterized by lament for the dead.

It comes as no surprise that this excruciatingly harsh message delivered by Amos was attacked on several fronts; indeed, his own argumentation betrays this situation again and again. The point of many of his words is that they turn ideas and expectations of his own contemporaries upside down (most clearly in 5:18–20; cf. 3:2, 12; 4:4f.; 9:7, et passim), and his tradents followed Amos' lead in this regard.[6]

One cannot fail to notice how very different is Amos' justification of "Israel's end" from that of his slightly younger contemporary Hosea, who also was active in the Northern Kingdom and predicted Israel's fall with comparable severity.[7] The themes of such central importance for Amos, namely those of social and legal criticism, play only a marginal role in Hosea. In their (in principle shared) criticism of the cult, the accentuation is quite different. For Amos, the disparity between sin as practiced in daily life and (pretended) harmony with God in worship is central; by contrast, for Hosea the substantive question of the adulteration of the cult through alien ideas drawn from the Canaanite Baal belief is central. For Hosea, Israel's history as the locus of the experience of God plays a central role and is explicated in a plethora of details (Hos. 9–13); for Amos, this is true only in a very general sense. Hosea becomes passionately enraged over the image of the calf in Bethel (8:4–6; 10:5f.; 13:2); Amos does not even mention it. These differences apparently derive from the fact that Hosea grew up in the Northern Kingdom, Amos in Judah. The history of influence also took remarkably different shape in each case. Amos shares many themes with the slightly younger Jerusalemite Isaiah, whose message was

---

6. Cf. esp. S. Gillingham, "Der die Morgenröte zur Finsternis macht," *EvT* 53 (1993): 109–23.

7. Concerning these differences, cf. esp. H.-J. Zobel, "Prophet in Israel und Juda," *ZTK* 82 (1985): 281–99, reprinted in *Altes Testament: Literatursammlung und Heilige Schrift: gesammelte Aufsätze zur Entstehung, Geschichte, und Auslegung des Alten Testaments*, ed. J. Mannchen and E.-J. Waschke; BZAW 212 (Berlin/New York: W. de Gruyter, 1993), 77–96; Jeremias, *Hosea und Amos*, 35–57.

demonstrably influenced by Amos; this applies especially to the emphasis on "justice and righteousness" (Isa. 1:21ff.; 3 and 5), the character of his cult criticism (Isa. 1:10ff.), the theme of the "day of Yahweh" (Amos 5:18–20; Isa. 2:10ff.), and so on.[8] Hosea's theology had a far more profound effect on the young Jeremiah[9] and on Deuteronomy and the Deuteronomistic history.

Amos was the most severe of all the biblical prophets of judgment insofar as it is in his work that traces of any proclamation of salvation are most difficult to adduce, if such is possible at all. The salvific conclusion to the book (9:8–15) in all probability derives only from an updating of his message for the postexilic period. Prior to that, it is only in 5:15 that an extremely reserved element of salvific hope resonates, and even this is subject to the condition of a decisive turn "to the good," and is doubly restricted: Deliverance from catastrophe will come about only "maybe"; that is, it is not the prophet's commission to predict this. Such initiative is shifted back to God's own will. In any case, it would apply only to a "remnant of Joseph," and thus by no means to the people of God as a whole. As H. W. Wolff has shown,[10] even this extremely reserved element of hope itself already represents the exegesis of an older saying of Amos by his tradents, more specifically an exegesis of the only extant admonitory saying we have from Amos that because of its brevity and quotation-like character cannot be understood unequivocally: "For thus says Yahweh to the house of Israel: 'Seek me and live.'"

3. The Book

To be sure, Amos' message as just described can be recovered only through complicated, and in many instances only hypothetical, reconstruction. The book of Amos itself by no means reflects this message directly, but represents rather the precipitate of this message's history of reception and influence; it was not transmitted as the result of any historical interest in past history, but rather was written down and at the same time continually updated on the basis of its meaning for an ever new and changing present. In its present form, the book of Amos comes from the (late) postexilic period (9:11–15; cf. 9:7–10). It underwent its constitutive formation after the fall of Jerusalem during the exilic–early postexilic period. Even the "first edition" of the book, appearing after the fall of Samaria, underwent considerable expansion approximately a century later, during the age of Jeremiah.

a. It is essential to understand that even the first tradents of Amos' words had incomparably more in mind than merely the preservation of some of Amos' important sayings. In contrast to the (probably older[11]) core of the book of

8. Cf. Fey, *Amos und Jesaja* (1963).
9. Cf. Jeremias, "Hoseas Einfluss auf das Jeremiabuch," loc. cit. (note 7), 122ff.
10. Wolff, in loc.
11. Cf. Jeremias, loc. cit. (note 7), 34ff., esp. 41, 52f.

Hosea (Hosea 4–11*), with its almost seamless sequence of individual sayings rendering a continuous overall portrayal, the oldest book of Amos is the result of an artistic composition that no attentive reader can fail to notice. Four characteristic features stand out.

1. The oldest book of Amos was framed by two compositions—oracles against the nations (Amos 1–2*) and visions (Amos 7–9*)—of five strophes each, each composition containing two strophic pairs and then one concluding strophe of intensification; the two compositions were variously linked with each other thematically.[12] The oracles against the nations contain numerous allusions that the reader of the book cannot understand fully until Amos' last vision is reached. At the same time, the sayings against Israel in chaps. 3–6 are to be read within the horizon of this framework. It is possible that the oracles against the nations on the one hand, and the visionary accounts on the other, initially constituted a separate collection (as did chaps. 3–6* as well; cf. the discussion of 1:1).

2. The parallel section superscriptions in 3:1 and 5:1 divide the middle section of the book (Amos 3–6*) into two parts of approximately equal length, the first of which is introduced as a divine oracle against the people of God, and the second as a prophetic discourse against the state. Internally, both parts contain divine and prophetic discourse. They are not, however, to be understood from the perspective of this split, but rather from that of the superscriptions themselves, the order of the two sections being irreversible.

3. A different organization runs hand in hand with this double division of the middle chapters. The book's central chapter 5 (more exactly 5:1–17) is organized in a highly artificial fashion as a concentric figure or ring composition: the (extremely reserved) offer of life intervenes twice between the context of the most grievous sin of the people on the one hand, and resultant death on the other, interrupting thus the logic of culpability and punishment. Apparently this represents a further reflection on Amos' harsh message of death for the survivors in the catastrophe of the Northern Kingdom.

4. Both these compositional principles—the linear and the concentric—are also discernible in what follows. First, the two oracles of woe (deriving from the lament for the dead) in 5:18–27 and 6 are structured exactly parallel with one another, whereby the questions in 5:25 and 6:12 with their lingering hope for understanding are especially noticeable. In a fashion comparable to the offer of life in 5:1–17, these once again interrupt the logic of the message of death governing the context as a whole. Second, the two collections with accusations against the upper classes in the capital Samaria (3:9–4:3; 6) are grouped as a framework around the central chapter 5.

12. Ibid., 157ff.

The artistic composition variously links the individual sayings of Amos with one another. Theologically these are modified especially in three respects.

1. Those particular sayings originally directed against limited groups (e.g., 3:12; 4:1–3, etc.; see discussion above) are placed into a context that speaks throughout about the people of God as a whole (cf. esp. 3:2). This renders impossible any distinction among the people of God between those who are primarily or partially guilty or not guilty at all.

2. At hermeneutical key points, the tradents formulated sayings strongly influenced by the language and conceptual world of Hosea (3:2; 5:25*; 6:8; cf. from a more recent period 2:8; 7:9). Through this device, they wanted to prompt the readers of the book of Amos to associate Amos' own accusations with those of Hosea and thereby to relate the sayings of the two prophets. They together constitute the one truth of God for Israel, a truth decisively confirmed by the fall of Samaria.

3.1 The central position of the ring composition in 5:1–17 reveals that the real heart of Amos' message is the legal theme, which appears only in chapter 5 (and in 6:12). In contrast to Amos' social criticism, the theme "justice and righteousness" is not limited to accusation (5:7, 10, 12). Some of the "open" sayings of the older book of Amos yet envision—in however reserved a fashion—the possibility of repentance on the part of the survivors of the military catastrophe of the Northern Kingdom; without exception, every such saying specifies that the unalterable presupposition of life is the actualization of "justice and righteousness," either in the form of imperatives (5:4f., 14), jussives (5:24), or questions (5:25*; 6:12).

3.2 In the following century, the age of the prophet Jeremiah, these theological tendencies in Judah were considerably amplified, with older texts of Amos being combined with one another for the sake of mutual interpretation (6:8ff.; 8:3ff.). That all Israel is doomed to death (6:9f.; 8:3, 9f.) is now portrayed in great detail; accusations of Hosea are combined anew with those of Amos (2:8; 7:9), and Amos' own social criticism is applied to the sphere of commerce (8:4–7). Above all, however, Amos' reflections concerning his own office (cf. 3:3–8* as well as the visions) are heightened to such an extent in anticipation of Deuteronomistic theology that the inexorable prediction of destruction is now issued to an Israel that listens more to the state than to the prophetic word (7:10–17).

3.3 The older book of Amos underwent its most incisive alteration after the fall of Jerusalem in the sixth century B.C.E. During this period, those who had proven themselves in the catastrophe were urgently warned—with the help of the book of Amos—that they should not understand their mere physical survival as deliverance. Two linguistically different, albeit substantively related, theological trends can be distinguished.

a. In the passages of so-called Deuteronomistic theology,[13] the guilt of the people of God is substantiated in the history of salvation; that is, it is heightened by being juxtaposed with the experiences of the saving acts of God and is thus related directly to God (2:10; 3:1b). At the same time, this guilt is related to God's overall will, a will already known to Israel and whose rejection actually constitutes a rejection of God himself and an exchange of God for idols (2:4). In the more recent book of Amos, the prototype for these idols and for the faulty worship services they prompt is the cult in Bethel (3:14; 5:6) together with the syncretistic tendencies in Samaria (as well as in Dan and Beer-sheba: 5:26; 8:14). Hand in hand with this, the high estimation of the prophetic word itself is heightened: It is not yet because of their immeasurable guilt that the people of God are lost, but rather because they have rejected the prophetic word, since prophets like Amos are, after all, God's most extreme means of bringing the threatening catastrophe to Israel's attention in the eleventh hour and thus of bringing Israel itself to its senses (2:11f.; 3:7). The prophetic word is Israel's most precious possession, yet one it can easily lose through inattentiveness (8:11f.).

b. The other—actually more significant—reworking, one easily identifiable linguistically through its hymnic diction, drew its theological leitmotifs from exilic services of penance; Amos 4:6–13 is modeled after such a worship liturgy, as the parallel in 1 Kings 8:30ff. shows. In this liturgy, the hymns occupied the role of "judgment-doxologies" (F. Horst); that is, they served to acknowledge the catastrophe that befell Judah as a justly deserved judgment of God. In the exilic book of Amos, the hymns constitute both the book's broadest framework—that is, beginning and end (1:2; 9:5f.)—and its substantive center as well (4:13; 5:8f.).[14] They do not, to be sure, function primarily as a retrospective on the destruction of Jerusalem, but rather praise God's creative power for the sake of enticing Israel, with the help Amos' own words, to turn anew to God (and to turn away from the error of syncretistic worship in Bethel[15]). They do this with all the seriousness of a last chance. Whoever loses the impending encounter with God, one repeating the new beginning at Sinai (4:12), is lost forever.

---

13. Cf. the summary of W. H. Schmidt, *Deuteronomistische Redaktion,* as well as Wolff, 112f. This is primarily a question of Amos 1:9–12; 2:4f., 10–12; 3:1b, 7; 5:25 (in its final form), as well as—in close proximity to these texts—2:7b, 9; 3:13f.; 5:6, 26; 8:11–14. Many of these texts can be shown to derive from different authors, though present scholarly tools still do not allow any clear differentiation (e.g., into subgroups of Deuteronomistic theology).

14. A more detailed discussion can be found in Jeremias, "Die Mitte des Amosbuches," loc. cit. (note 7), 198ff. At the same time, in the later period the accumulation of predicates—one without analogy in the Old Testament—"Yahweh, God of hosts" (cf. Wolff's excursus, 287f.) repeatedly alludes to the content of the doxologies, in which it appears twice in a programmatic fashion (4:13; 9:5).

15. The two theological trends coincide in this theme; see discussion above.

3.4 We find the postexilic period concerned with the question of just how Amos' harsh message of judgment can be reconciled with the old traditions of salvation, and who is actually affected by it (Amos 9:7–10). The answer to the latter question is: Irretrievably lost are both the autocratic state that places itself above the prophetic word, as well as all those indifferent people who do not take that word seriously. No salvation is possible independent of the prophetic word. Only on the basis of this theological clarification did later redactors dare to portray the divine salvation in the form of a newly established kingdom of David with its attendant element of security (9:11–15*). In the final, latest stratum, this new salvation—and with it the entire message of Amos—is related as part of the book of the twelve prophets to analogous statements of the preceding book of Joel and the following book of Obadiah (9:12f.).

The growth of the book of Amos over many centuries reflects the high estimation it enjoyed already during the biblical period itself, as well as the lively engagement it elicited—engagement now constituting a considerable portion of its richness. This state of affairs implies that within the book of Amos itself the modern exegete must deal first of all with the exilic/postexilic history of transmission of Amos' message. Any attempt to get back to earlier strata of the book, not to speak of Amos' actual words themselves, is necessarily burdened by a (variously differing) degree of uncertainty.

Superscription and Leitmotif
Amos 1:1–2

1 The words of Amos *who was among the shepherds* of Tekoa, which he saw concerning Israel *in the days of King Uzziah of Judah and in the days of King Jeroboam son of Joash of Israel,* two years before the earthquake.
2 *And he said:*

> *Yahweh roars from Zion,*
> *and utters his voice from Jerusalem;*
> *the pastures of the shepherds mourn,*[1]
> *and the top of Carmel dries up.*

Bibliography: H. F. Fuhs, "Amos 1,1: Erwägungen zur Tradition und Redaktion des Amosbuches," in H. J. Fabry, ed., *Bausteine biblischer Theologie: Festschrift G. J. Botterweck* (Cologne/Bonn: Hanstein, 1977), 271–89; J. Jeremias, " 'Zwei Jahre vor dem Erdbeben' (Am 1,1)," in *Hosea und Amos,* 183–97; M. Weiss, "Images: Amos 1:2," in idem, *The Bible from Within: The Method of Total Interpretation* (Jerusalem: Magnes Press, Hebrew University, 1984), 194–221.

[1:1] The superscription to the book of Amos reflects the history of its growth. The first thing one notices is that the unusual and extremely precise dating "two years before the earthquake" is preceded by an even more extensive one mentioning the reigns of kings. The Judean king Uzziah (presumably 787–736 B.C.E.) stands before Jeroboam II, the king of the Northern Kingdom (presumably 787–747 B.C.E.), even though Amos—as the superscription itself attests—prophesied in the Northern Kingdom and came into conflict with Jeroboam II (Amos 7:10–17); this sequence clearly has later Judean readers in mind. Together with analogous information in Hos. 1:1; Micah 1:1; Zeph. 1:1 (cf. Isa. 1:1; Jer. 1:2), Amos 1:1 in its final form suggests that the Twelve Prophets were collected and redacted in all probability during the exilic period.

The inserted indication of Amos' occupation comes presumably from the same period. It awkwardly separates the prophet's name and hometown and

---

1. This somewhat artificial translation (instead of wither, become desolate) is intended to provide a bridge to the identical verb in 8:8 and 9:5, where it refers to human behavior; cf. the analogous juxtaposition of mourning human beings and "mourning" nature in Joel 1:9f. E. Kutsch, " 'Trauerbräuche' und 'Selbstminderungsriten' im Alten Testament," *Kleine Schriften zum Alten Testament,* BZAW 168 (Berlin/New York: W. de Gruyter, 1986), 88f., following J. Scharbert, *Der Schmerz im Alten Testament,* BBB 8 (Bonn: P. Hanstein, 1955), 47ff., has shown convincingly that Hebrew attests only one root *'bl.*

clashes especially with the earlier, second relative clause referring to Amos'
words (Wolff). Its content alludes to Amos 7:14f. with a term borrowed from
Akkadian *nāqidu,* referring to the flock owner in contrast to the employed shepherd (cf. King Mesha of Moab in 2 Kings 3:4).[2]

Yet even the earlier, preexilic superscription "the words of Amos of Tekoa,
which he saw concerning Israel, two years before the earthquake" is itself full
of tension. Although other prophetic books similarly attest a "seeing of words"
(Isa. 2:1; Micah 1:1; cf. Hab. 1:1), they always refer to Yahweh's words. The
unique formulation in Amos 1:1 can probably best be explained as a result of
two different, partial superscriptions ("the words of Amos of Tekoa" and something to the effect of "the word that Amos saw concerning Israel . . . ") having
been fused together (Wolff, Fuhs). In that case, the latter superscription probably referred primarily to the visionary accounts, even though these use the
verb *r'h,* "to see," one not customary in superscriptions,[3] whereas the former
more likely refers to the sayings collection in chaps. 3–6 (cf. Amos in the first-
person in 5:1). The collection of oracles against the nations exhibits several literary connections with the visionary accounts;[4] this is commensurate with the
fact that the earthquake, mentioned in the dating and in 1:1 related to this activity of seeing, is mentioned outside the visionary accounts only in the oracles
to the nations (Amos 2:13), and not in chaps. 3–6. In this way, Amos 1:1 shows
that the book of Amos was formed from two partial collections: chaps. 3–6 and
the chapters framing them, namely, chaps. 1–2 and 7–9.

Compared with the superscriptions of other prophetic books, Amos 1:1 contains especially two unusual pieces of information. The first is the reference to
"the words of Amos" instead of to "the word of Yahweh" as in other prophetic
books. The closest analogy are the collections of sayings attributed to wisdom
teachers such as "the words of Agur" (Prov. 30:1) or "the words of Lemuel"
(Prov. 31:1). This observation suggests that this piece of information is extremely old, deriving from a period predating the emergence of any specific
form of prophetic superscription; it also betrays a highly developed self-
consciousness on the part of the prophet, who is also mentioned emphatically
by name in the visions (Amos 7:8; 8:2). The name Amos is presumably the abbreviated form of a thanksgiving name whose full form is Amasiah, "Yahweh has
carried, supported," that is, has preserved the child from harm (2 Chron. 17:16).

---

2. The cultic interpretation of this term, popular during the 1950s and based on Ugaritic texts,
has been variously refuted and is no longer advocated.

3. Perhaps one should follow Rudolph's conclusion that this refers to the visions expanded
by the (later) narrative 7:10–17, since the priest Amaziah addresses Amos with the root *ḥzh* "seer."
Concerning the distinction between the verbs ("to see" for punctiliar vision, and "to view" for basic legitimation), cf. H. F. Fuhs, "Sehen und Schauen," *Forschungen zur Bibel* 32 (1978): 177ff.,
305ff.

4. Cf. the continuation of the views of Wolff and H. Gese (*Komposition,* 74ff.) by J. Jeremias,
"Völkersprüche und Visionsberichte im Amosbuch," in *Hosea und Amos,* 157–71.

This context also includes the prophet's place of origin, which is just as important for understanding his message as is the unmistakable name. For Amos comes from the Southern Kingdom, more specifically from a place a good fifteen kilometers south of Jerusalem, where the land drops off to the Judean wilderness (modern Khirbet Teqûʻ). His vocation as livestock herder becomes especially comprehensible here, and above all it best explains the striking differences between his proclamation and that of Hosea.[5] Not least for this reason, the search for a locale with the name Tekoa in the Northern Kingdom,[6] a search repeatedly undertaken from rabbinic exegesis up till the present, is futile from the very outset.

The second unusual piece of information is the precise date "two years before the earthquake." Although the reference here is no doubt to an especially serious earthquake (cf. Zech. 14:5), the frequency of earthquakes in Palestine[7] has rendered impossible all attempts to draw historical conclusions.[8] This information does, however, show that in contrast to Hosea and Isaiah, Amos prophesied for only a very brief period, probably hardly more than a single year. This information was committed to writing above all, however, because for the tradents the experience of that earthquake itself demonstrated the truth of Amos' words, though one must point out that this confirmation is not meant primarily as fulfillment, and certainly not at all as fulfillment in the full sense of that word. What this earthquake means for the book of Amos—from the quaking of the temple in Bethel to the quaking of the cosmos itself—is shown by passages such as 2:13 and 9:1, and later specified more closely by 8:8 and 9:5f. The reader is, however, very much encouraged to understand the experience of the earthquake as a first step toward the actualization of the word of God as proclaimed by Amos. It is one of the secret themes of the book of Amos which are resolved only from the perspective of the end, that is, from the perspective of chapter 9, and which expect the reader to read the book carefully all the way to this end.

[**1:2**] The hymn in v. 2 offers an initial aid to understanding for those reading the book later, after the fall of Jerusalem. It draws on the form of theophany portrayals of the sort Israel used in the earliest period to celebrate its victories as Yahweh's deeds, who—like the weather god in the surrounding areas—powerfully intervened against his enemies amid the quakings of nature (Judg. 5:4f.; Ps. 68:8f. [7f.E], et passim).[9] Amos 1:2 gives the impression of a

---

5. Cf. in this regard Jeremias, *Hosea und Amos*, 35–57.

6. Cf. esp. H. Schmidt, "Die Herkunft des Propheten Amos," in *Beiträge zur alttestamentlichen Wissenschaft: Festschrift K. Budde,* ed. Karl Marti, BZAW 34 (Giessen: A. Töpelmann, 1920), 158ff., and most recently K. Koch, *Amos,* part 2.2.

7. D. H. Kallner-Amiran, "A Revised Earthquake-Catalogue of Palestine," *IEJ* 1 (1950/51): 223–46; 2 (1952): 48–65, offers an earthquake catalog for the period since 64 B.C.E.

8. Cf., e.g., J. A. Soggin, "Das Erdbeben von Am 1,1 und die Chronologie der Könige Ussia und Jotham von Juda," *ZAW* 82 (1970): 117–21.

9. Cf. J. Jeremias, *Theophanie,* WMANT 10, 2d ed. (Neukirchen-Vluyn: Neukirchener Verlag, 1977).

completely contrary experience of God. The traditional statement about the powerful, thundering voice of the weather god is immediately understood as the frightening roar of the lion; the attendant deadly associations (especially the confluence of terrible divine speech and action) are made even more clear in Amos 3:4, 8, 12. This mortal danger, however, is not directed at enemies. Rather, in the following clause the divine roar of the lion directly causes the withering and drying up of the most fertile regions in the Northern Kingdom.[10] Amos' own vocation perhaps prompted the allusion to the shepherds' vitally important pasturelands, whose desolation often represents the most terrible disaster during the later period (usually as "pastures of the wilderness," Jer. 9:9 [10E]; 23:10; Joel 1:19, 20, et passim);[11] during this period Mount Carmel, with its dense forests, together with Bashan (cf. Amos 4:1), Lebanon, or the plain of Sharon, stands representatively for the most fertile regions of Palestine (cf. Isa. 33:9; 35:2; Jer. 50:19; Nahum 1:4). The expression "top of Carmel" in particular, however, provides the bridge to the fifth vision (Amos 9:3). Together, these two poetic sentences circumscribe the end of all vegetation (Wolff, Weiss). It is not, however, some foreign power that brings about this devastation—this is the most important statement of the entire verse—but rather "Yahweh of Zion," who in judgment on his own people demonstrates his power (cf. Ps. 50:2). This prepares the reader for the hymnic sections of the book of Amos (4:13; 5:8f.; 9:5f.) and for the numerous divine predicates such as "Yahweh, God of hosts." This applies especially, however, to the book's former concluding doxology in 9:5f. (cf. the introduction), in which the "mourning" of the shepherds' pastures becomes the "mourning" of human beings in the face of the God who through the destruction of the temple withdraws his own presence from them and yet is still recognized and praised as the Lord of the world.

The introductory hymn thus emphasizes the enduring validity of Amos' message—even after the destruction of Samaria and of Jerusalem—and by mentioning the "top of Carmel" and the "mourning" of nature creates a bridge to the former conclusion to the book in 9:6. Later redactors, by prepositioning the book of Joel and the close parallel in Joel 4:16 (cf. Amos 9:13 with Joel 4:18), created an additional context prompting the reader to understand not only the book of Amos, but also the book of the Twelve Prophets (or a prior stage of that book) as a whole, that is, as the one word of God delivered through different prophetic witnesses.

10. It is worth noting that in the other two passages in which the verbs "mourn (= wither)" and "dry up" stand parallel (Jer. 12:4; 23:10), this natural occurrence is prompted by Israel's guilt. I think this association is probably being presupposed among the readers and contributed to the disharmonious proportion of the metaphor (the divine roaring of the lion causes something to dry up).

11. K. Koch, "Die Rolle der hymnischen Abschnitte in der Komposition des Amos-Buches," *ZAW* 86 (1974): 33, understands the "shepherds" as the "kings" of the following verses, but in so doing destroys the statement's poetic nexus.

Part I

ORACLES
AGAINST THE NATIONS
(AMOS 1:3–2:16)

The Guilt of Neighboring Peoples
Amos 1:3–2:3

1:3 Thus says Yahweh:
For three transgressions of Damascus,
and for four, I will not revoke it:[1]
because they have threshed Gilead with threshing sledges of iron.
4 So I will send a fire on the house of Hazael,
and it shall devour the palaces of Ben-hadad.
5 I will break the gate bars of Damascus,
and cut off the ruler[2] from the Valley of Aven ("sin valley"),
and the one who holds the scepter from Beth-eden ("house of
delight");
and the people of Aram shall go into exile to Kir,
says Yahweh.

6 Thus says Yahweh:
For three transgressions of Gaza,
and for four, I will not revoke it;
because they carried into exile entire communities,
(merely) to hand them over to Edom.
7 So I will send a fire on the wall of Gaza,
fire that shall devour its palaces.
8 I will cut off the ruler[2] from Ashdod,
and the one who holds the scepter from Ashkelon;
I will turn my hand against Ekron,
and the remnant of the Philistines shall perish,
says *the Lord*[3] Yahweh.

9 *Thus says Yahweh:*
For three transgressions of Tyre,

1. Concerning the question of the antecedent, cf. the commentary.
2. All the versions understand *yôšēb* as a collective singular, "the inhabitants." The *parallelismus membrorum* and especially the last sentence in v. 5 and v. 8, however, support the translation "the enthroned one."
3. This additional divine predicate occurs only here in the oracles against the nations; the LXX does not yet seem to be familiar with it. As in 7:6, its intention is probably to mark a stronger caesura (Gese, "Komposition," 87, n. 41); elsewhere in the book of Amos as well, it is often added to the formula of the divine oracle. Cf. note 1 to Amos 7:1ff., and V. Maag, *Text*, 118f.

and for four, I will not revoke it;
because they delivered entire communities over to Edom,
and did not remember the covenant of kinship.
10 *So I will send a fire on the wall of Tyre,*
fire that shall devour its palaces.

11 *Thus says Yahweh:*
For three transgressions of Edom,
and for four, I will not revoke it;
because it pursued its brother with the sword
and cast off all pity;[4]
and his anger tore perpetually,
and his wrath kept forever.[5]
12 *So I will send a fire on Teman,*
and it shall devour the palaces of Bozrah.

13 Thus says Yahweh:
For three transgressions of the Ammonites,
and for four, I will not revoke it;
because they have ripped open pregnant women in Gilead
(merely) in order to enlarge their territory.
14 So I will kindle a fire against the wall of Rabbah,
fire that shall devour its palaces,
with shouting on the day of battle,
with a storm on the day of the whirlwind;
15 then their king[6] shall go into exile,
he and his officials together,
says Yahweh.

2:1 Thus says Yahweh:
For three transgressions of Moab,
and for four, I will not revoke it;
because it burned to lime the bones of the king of Edom.
2 So I will send a fire on Moab,
and it shall devour the palaces of Kerioth,

4. LXX* reads: "and violated his (own) womb (*raḥmô*)."
5. A (slight) textual emendation according to Jer. 3:5 is popular: "it maintained its anger continuously and its wrath remained ever alert." This is not necessary, as esp. Wolff, 130f., and Barthélemy, *Critique textuelle*, 642f., have shown. The vocalization of the verb in the last stich is probably an instance of *nĕsîgâ* (recessive tone) (Wolff).
6. Later tradents (LXX partim; Aquila, Symmachus, Vulgate) vocalize the consonants differently and understand this as an allusion to the Ammonite deity Milcom; cf. the similar case in Zeph. 1:5.

and Moab shall die amid uproar,
amid shouting and the sound of the trumpet.

3 I will cut off the ruler from its[7] midst,
and will kill all its[7] officials with him,
says Yahweh.

Bibliography: P. Höffken, "Untersuchungen zu den Begründungselementen der Völkerorakel im Alten Testament" (Dissertation, Bonn, 1977), 46ff., 102ff.; J. Barton, *Amos' Oracles against the Nations,* Society for Old Testament Study Monograph Series 6 (Cambridge /New York: Cambridge University Press, 1980); J. Jeremias, "Zur Entstehung der Völkersprüche im Amosbuch," in *Hosea und Amos,* 172–82.

No other prophetic book in the Bible begins, as does the book of Amos, with oracles of judgment against foreign nations (1:3–2:3). Usually—as in the final form of the books of Isaiah, Jeremiah (here only in the Greek version), Ezekiel, and Zephaniah—a collection of oracles to the nations stands in the middle between the initial words of judgment and the concluding words of salvation to Israel. Through this medial position, the oracles to the nations attest two things: first, that the nations are also guilty before God and, like Israel, must expect Yahweh's punishment; second, that this judgment on them prepares the future age of salvation for the people of God. This latter point is commensurate with the fact that oracles to the nations during the period prior to Amos implicitly represented words of salvation for Israel, since they announced God's punishment on its enemies.[8] Obviously, Amos' words against foreign nations have been collected together and positioned with a different intention. In Amos 1–2, the entire emphasis is on the comparative. Horrible things have happened among Israel's neighbors, especially also against Israel, but the people of God itself is incomparably more guilty than all these neighboring peoples; hence much more must be said about its transgressions and about the punishment coming to it (2:6–16). It is certainly not salvation that follows for Israel from these oracles to the nations.

The question has been raised whether the oracles against the nations in the book of Amos were from very outset intended to function as a foil to Israel's own more comprehensive guilt. From the differences in form between the actual oracles against the nations and the concluding strophe concerning Israel,

7. The feminine suffixes refer presumably to Kerioth, since Moab is used as a masculine (Amsler, Wolff, Rudolph).

8. Cf. J. Jeremias, *Kultprophetie,* 149, 178; regarding the conceptual background, cf. J. H. Hayes, "The Oracles against the Nations in the Old Testament" (Ph.D. diss., Princeton University, 1964); D. L. Christensen, *Transformations of the War Oracle in Old Testament Prophecy: Studies in the Oracles against the Nations,* HDR 3 (Missoula, Mont.: Scholars Press [for Harvard Theological Review], 1975); esp. P. Höfken, loc. cit.

K. Koch has concluded that the two units initially existed independent of one another,[9] a suspicion that E. Würthwein anticipated a quarter century earlier based on considerations of content. By separating the oracles against the nations in 1:3–2:3 from the Israel-strophe, and interpreting these in connection with the first two visions (7:1–6)—which he similarly isolated from the following visions—he reconstructed an initial salvific-prophetic stage in Amos' proclamation deriving from a period prior to that in which Amos denounced Israel's transgressions so severely.[10]

A more likely explanation of the differences between the oracles against the nations on the one hand, and the concluding Israel-strophe on the other—despite simultaneously and clearly shared features at their beginnings—is that the Israel-strophe with its formal variations should be understood in every respect as a heightening of the preceding strophes. A whole series of indicators suggest that it was not an originally independent Israel-strophe that in Amos 2:6 was accommodated subsequently to the oracles against the nations (Koch); quite the opposite seems to have been the case, namely, that the literary formation of the oracles against the nations was undertaken from the perspective of the Israel-strophe as their intensification.[11] Specifically, two formal devices within the stereotypical framework of the oracles against the nations (see discussion below) are conceived entirely from the perspective of the Israel-strophe: the graded numerical sequence ("for three transgressions of . . . and for four"), and the formula of irrevocability (" . . . will not revoke it"). The graded numerical sequence is not rendered fully until the Israel-strophe, where—as the formula leads one to expect—four transgressions are enumerated, whereas the oracles against the nations are content with mentioning but a single one, to wit, the most grievous among several. The negative aspect of the formula of irrevocability excludes one possibility for influencing the divine will of the sort that before the exile the Old Testament attests only for Israel, namely, prophetic intercession. Third, the category of guilt *peša'*, "transgression," is frequently a political category referring to revolts against or apostasy from a superior entity.[12] In the

9. K. Koch, *Amos,* 2.68 et passim; similarly also G. Fleischer, *Menschenverkäufer,* 18ff.

10. E. Würthwein, "Amos-Studien," 93ff.

11. So already Höffken, loc. cit., 56, 65; and recently H. M. Niemann, "Theologie in geographischem Gewand," in H. M. Niemann et al., eds., *Nachdenken über Israel: Festschrift K.-D. Schunck,* BEAT 37 (Frankfurt am Main/New York: Peter Lang, 1994), 177–96. The latter assumes that the cycle of oracles against the nations originated (and underwent several stages of growth) only after the fall of Samaria; this continues a thesis presented by V. Fritz, "Die Fremdvölkersprüche des Amos," *VT* 37 (1987): 26–38, who views the oracles against the nations as a retrospective interpretation of history.

12. Cf. R. Knierim, *Die Hauptbegriffe für Sünde im Alten Testament,* 2d ed. (Gütersloh: Gütersloher Verlagshaus Gerd Mohn, 1967), 113–84; idem, *"peša'* Verbrechen," *THAT* 2.488–95; H. Seebass, *ThWAT, "pāša',"* vol. 6 (Stuttgart: W. Kohlhammer, 1988), 793–810; esp. E. Beaucamp, "Le pesha' d'Israël et celui des nations," *Science et esprit* 21 (1969): 435–41.

metaphorical sense, it is designed primarily for Israel (cf. Amos 4:4; 5:12), and only afterward is applied to the nations as well.

Indeed, these conclusions can be taken even further. For every attentive reader of the book of Amos, the formula of irrevocability provides the substantive bridge to the concluding visionary accounts. It is hardly an accident that these, like the oracles against the nations in their original form (which we will soon discuss), are organized in five strophes; in both instances, the first four strophes constitute two strophic pairs, while the last one stands apart and is emphasized by itself. The visionary accounts, however, maintain from the first to the second pair of visions the path along which God guided the prophet Amos. This path led from God's willingness, prompted by the prophet's intercession, to delay or even to suspend Israel's punishment, thence to an announcement of the end of the divine patience: "I can no longer pass them (i.e., Israel) by (and spare them) (7:8; 8:2). This path obviously has already been traversed prior to the oracles against the nations. Not only does the formulation "I will not revoke it" in the oracles against the nations accordingly presuppose in substance the Israel-strophe, since (at least for all preexilic occurrences in the Old Testament) a "revocation" of divine punishment or of the announcement of such punishment for grievous past guilt is conceivable only on the basis of prophetic intercession for Israel, but the Israel-strophe in its own turn in substance also presupposes the visionary accounts, which describe the end of this sort of intercessory possibility for the prophet Amos.[13]

Hence Amos' oracles against the nations cannot be interpreted apart from the Israel-strophe as their eclipse, a strophe to which the framing formulae of the oracles against the nations are already pointing, and which here (together with the substantively related Judah-strophe) is separated out only for the sake of an external overview. We will discuss below how the oracles against the nations function in Amos' oral proclamation.

Leaving in abeyance for a moment the peculiarities of the Israel-strophe as the culmination of the larger composition, the *formulaic character* of the structure in the remaining seven strophes emerges clearly from five recurring statements:

1. The messenger formula, deriving from the language of diplomacy, stands at the beginning in each instance. Whereas emissaries of a king in the ancient orient normally identified themselves with this formula ("thus says king X"), in prophetic contexts it serves to legitimize the prophets' divine commission before their listeners.

2. As an introduction of the various addressees and their transgressions, there then follows a consistently identical, so-called graded numerical sequence; within the parallelism of the poetic sentence parts, a number x appears first (here:

---

13. For a more detailed discussion, cf. J. Jeremias, "Völkersprüche und Visionsberichte im Amosbuch," in *Hosea und Amos,* 157–71.

three), then the next higher number $x + 1$ (here: four). From the very outset, the last number in the chain, that is, the one surpassing x itself, bears the main emphasis. This form was presumably at home primarily in instruction in Israel, serving as a mnemonic aid in virtually all areas of learning; it is no accident that it occurs more frequently in the book of Proverbs and later in the book of Sirach.[14]

3. Immediately thereafter stands the aforementioned, terminologically consistent formula of irrevocability, that is, Yahweh's solemn declaration that in view of the severity of past sin it is impossible for him to forego punishment. Here it is substantively of almost no consequence whether the anticipatory, indefinite "it" in the sentence " . . . will not revoke it" is referring to the announcement of punishment (so, e.g., Wolff), or to the punishment itself (e.g., Rudolph and the majority of exegetes); it is of decisive significance, to be sure, that the latter understanding is supported by the analogy in the visionary accounts already mentioned.[15]

4. Immediately thereafter, and in a consistently analogous construction (Hebrew *'al* with infinitive), the concrete transgressions of the various nations are mentioned, or more precisely: the most grievous transgression, which in view of the graded numerical sequence refers to transgression "$x + 1$" (Wolff, Haran), or—following the great Jewish exegetes of the Middle Ages—to that particular transgression that causes God's patience to run out. Up till the Judah-strophe (2:4f.), these are always war crimes, though no specific historical circumstances are ever mentioned (with the exception of the Aramean-strophe at the beginning).

5. The following announcement of punishment initially states in all cases that Yahweh "will send a fire" ("kindle" only in 1:14[16]), which more specifically will "devour the palaces." Just as the sin itself is political, so also is punishment visited primarily on those who are politically responsible.

Through the formulaic character of its parts, this text prompts the reader to relate the individual strophes closely to one another and—together with the Israel-strophe, which similarly attests features 1–4—to understand them as a literary unit.

---

14. Cf., e.g., Prov. 6:16–19; 30:15f., 18f., 21ff., 29ff.; Sir. 25:7–11; 26:5f., 28, and in this regard—among others—W. M. W. Roth, "The Numerical Sequence $x/x+1$ in the Old Testament," *VT* 12 (1962): 300–11; H. W. Wolff, *Amos' geistige Heimat*, 24–30 (see also ET, *Amos the Prophet*); M. Weiss, "The Pattern of Numerical Sequence in Amos 1–2," *JBL* 86 (1967): 416–23 (with the improbable interpretation that Amos was referring to $3 + 4 = 7$ transgressions); M. Haran, "The Graded Numerical Sequence," *VTSup* 22 (1972): 238–67.

15. Other, more oblique interpretations of the formula are mentioned in Wolff, 128, and in M. L. Barré, "The Meaning of *l' 'šybnw* in Amos 1:3–2:6," *JBL* 105 (1986): 611–31, 611f. (whose own interpretation—Yahweh prevents a return to him as ruler ["I will not let him/it return (to me) (or: I will not take him back)"]—I find misdirected with regard to the nations).

16. The striking variant presupposes perhaps some influence from Jer. 17:27; 49:27 (Wolff, 131, 161; Gese, "Komposition," 87n40).

At the same time, *traces of growth* become discernible. Whereas the four older strophes add to the announcement of fire a portrayal (with varying details) of the taking of the capital city, the imprisonment or killing of the king, the exile of the people, and so on, the three younger strophes contain no more specific explication of the effects of this "fire." Although this observation in and of itself need not yet reveal anything, it does coincide with analogous features. The four older strophes round off the initial "thus says Yahweh" with " . . . says Yahweh"; the three younger strophes do not. Above all, however, the relative disinterest the younger strophes exhibit in the form of the divine punishment corresponds to a heightened interest in the sin of the various nations. Not only is the demonstration of guilt more extensive than in the older strophes—which despite the numerical sequence mention only *one* transgression each—independent narrative sentences (in the perfect or imperfect consecutive) are also added formally to the infinitives mentioned above, and categories of sin with different content are used. To the statements in the older strophes attesting soberly brutal cruelty are added an emotionally charged terminology ("brother," "pity," "wrath," etc.) referring to specific historical or political ties, and serving to describe "motives and subjective attitudes" (Wolff, 140); in the Judah-strophe (2:4f.) this flows seamlessly into specifically theological terminology. In this latter and doubtless most evident case, it is not difficult to specify the locus of these categories within the history of the theology. Here linguistic features drawn almost exclusively from what is known as the Deuteronomistic history, which during the exilic period portrayed Israel's history from Moses to the fall of the state as one of increasing sin, are picked up to show how little Judah can claim to have been better than Israel (2:6–16). In addition to the formal features they already share with the Judah-strophe (see discussion above), the strophes concerning Tyre and Edom (1:9–12) are related inextricably with the Judah-strophe insofar as they too employ categories of sin pointing to the exilic period. Thus it is no accident that their later origin was discerned on the basis of content long before scholars became aware of the previously discussed formal peculiarities.[17]

Only when the evidence of growth in these strophes has been reviewed does the *structure* of the larger unit become discernible. The search for an organizational principle has frequently taken as its point of departure the assumption

---

17. Among earlier scholars, cf., e.g., K. Marti, "Zur Komposition von Amos 1,3–2,3," in *Abhandlungen zur semitischen Religionskunde und Sprachwissenschaft: Festschrift W. W. Graf Baudissin*, ed. W. Frankenberg and F. Küchler; BZAW 33 (Giessen: A. Töpelmann, 1918): 323–30 (though he eliminates the Philistine-strophe), and in the current discussion, cf. the careful argumentation by W. H. Schmidt, *Deuteronomistische Redaktion*, 174–78, and esp. Höffken, loc. cit., 46ff., 112f. More recent scholarship is presented virtually in full by Gese, *Komposition*, 86, and Fleischer, *Menschenverkäufer*, 19. The few dissenting voices come above all from the U.S.A. and from Israel (one exception being W. Rudolph).

that the sequence of nations stems from some geographical order. Without exception, however, the manifold attempts at discovering this order—at least for the age of Amos—must be viewed as failures.[18] This also applies to the most influential of these attempts, namely that of A. Bentzen, who tried to explain Amos 1–2 from the perspective of an Egyptian ritual during which earthen vessels, inscribed with countries and cities, were dashed to pieces in order through imitative magic to effect an analogous fate for the hostile lands and cities.[19] The sequence of the nations is based rather on *pairs,*[20] which in 1:9–12 (Tyre and Edom) were also complemented by pairs or, in the case of Judah (2:4f.), complemented in such a way that together with the Israel-strophe (2:6–16) a new, fourth pair emerged. This ordering in pairs becomes discernible above all from the perspective of content and tradition history, as we will soon show, though it also comes to expression in an external-formal fashion, specifically in an extremely artistic double fashion.

First, two strophes in immediate succession are related closely through stylistic and terminological features restricted to them alone. The strophes against Damascus and Gaza are related especially through their use of the consciously identical announcement "I will cut off the ruler from X and the one who holds the scepter from Y" (1:5, 8), an expression not occurring elsewhere; the strophes against Ammon and Moab share a plethora of formal features (see discussion below). Second, the strophic pairs emerging through these devices are in their own turn related to one another. Their demonstrations of sin proceed in parallel insofar as each initial strophe (Damascus, Ammon) denounces extreme cruelties perpetrated against "Gilead," while each second strophe directs attention southward, to Edom. The announcements of punishment are structured analogously insofar as each initial strophe announces exile (of the population in the first pair, of the officials in the second), while each second strophe announces death. Exile and death together designate hopeless ruin, thus are not intended to be viewed separately such that exile taken in and of itself might constitute a fate less harsh.

What can the *intention* have been of this artistic ordering in pairs, one

18. A different situation obtains regarding the (earliest) exilic final form of the cycle of oracles against the nations, where geographical considerations may very well have played a role; cf. A. S. Steinmann, "The Order of Amos' Oracles against the Nations 1:3–2:16," *JBL* 111 (1992): 683ff.; 687, and most recently Niemann, loc. cit. (note 11).

19. A. Bentzen, "The Ritual Background of Amos 1:2–2:16," *OTS* 8 (Leiden: E. J. Brill, 1950), 85–99. Bentzen and many of his followers suspect not only that the order of the nations in Amos 1–2 derives from the "pattern" of the Egyptian execration texts, but also that Amos himself used this sequence in what was in the widest sense an analogous situation. Cf. the refutation by, e.g., Wolff, 144ff., as well as M. Weiss, "The Pattern of the 'Execration Texts,'" *IEJ* 19 (1969): 150–57.

20. Cf. in this regard Wolff ("seriatim structure"), 148, 151, et passim, and, following him, the extensive discussion in Gese, *Komposition*, 88f.; Jeremias, "Völkersprüche und Visionsberichte im Amosbuch," in *Hosea und Amos,* 157–71.

prompting the reader to relate so closely in each case the sin and punishment of two different nations? The (previously given) analogy of the visionary accounts, whose ordering in pairs is quite tangible, does not suffice as an explanation, since it follows the completely different intention of demonstrating the change in Amos' prophetic function. Rather, the meaning of this ordering in pairs is that each initial strophe mentions cruelties affecting the Northern Kingdom directly, while by contrast each second strophe mentions those either affecting Judah (Philistine-strophe: 1:6) or convulsing at least primarily the Judeans as neighbors of Edom (Moabite-strophe: 2:1). As I have tried to demonstrate elsewhere,[21] this likely derives from the fact that Amos probably compared the transgressions of the Arameans and Ammonites with Israel's sin in his oral proclamation, and the Judeans associated these transgressions in their own experience with the horrifying and infuriating transgressions of their neighbors—only to have their own sin then put into a separate category altogether as being incomparably worse. The precondition for this progressive actualization was the fact that the oracles against the nations (with the exception of the prepositioned Aramean-strophe) do not mention any specific historical background, but rather war crimes of a completely general nature whose typical feature is cruelty perpetrated against the defenseless.[22]

If this reconstruction attempt is correct, then we are dealing with two stages of growth. Amos himself compared two nations with Israel in this entanglement in sin, the oldest book of Amos four nations, the exilic book of Amos—and thus the present text—seven nations. Be that as it may, it is certain that the oracles against the nations are ordered in literary pairs and thus should be interpreted from the perspective of these pairs.

Damascus and Gaza
(1:3–5, 6, 8)

Arameans and Philistines introduce the series of nations as the first pair presumably because they were Israel's archenemies from the very beginning of its statehood. The Arameans stand first with good reason, since they had for decades been the main enemy of the Northern Kingdom. It was only Jeroboam II, under whose reign Amos prophesied, who in the middle of his long reign (787–747 B.C.E.) finally put an end to the wars with the Arameans, wars lasting almost an entire century and in which Israel was more frequently the vanquished than the victor (cf. the people's sense of triumph behind Amos 6:13). These wars were fought primarily for possession of the middle and northern part of East Jordan, especially for possession of "Gilead," that is, the forested

---

21. Cf. the essay mentioned at the beginning of the chapter.
22. So Höffken, loc. cit., 105f., 109.

area south and above all north of the Jabbok. The Philistines played the central role as Israel's enemy during the period prior to this, more exactly in the waning years of the period of the judges and during the early formation of the state. At that time, they occupied broad stretches of Israel and exacted tribute before David received his military training among them and then conquered them with their own weapons. But they did remain natural enemies after that as well, though now less enemies of Israel — which fought boundary conflicts with them shortly after the division of the kingdom (1 Kings 15:27; 16:15–17)—than of Judah, which was concerned first with possession of the northern Shephelah, that is, of the fertile hill country between the mountain ranges and coastal plain. Amos 9:7 shows how closely associated the Arameans and Philistines were for Amos (or for the Judean readers of the book of Amos) as a result of the experiences of the Aramean wars (cf. 2 Kings 12:28) and despite their geographical separation. For the slightly younger contemporary Isaiah, Israel's most acute distress came when Yahweh stirred up these two archenemies: "the Arameans on the east and the Philistines on the west" (Isa. 9:11).

[1:3–5] Verse 3 accuses the Aramean army of gruesome excesses. The image of threshing is occasionally used elsewhere as well to refer metaphorically to the crushing of a conquered population,[23] and in 2 Kings 13:7 already in reference to (earlier) actions by the Arameans. This horror is heightened through the notion of iron threshing sledges, composed of thick wooden boards with iron teeth on the underside on which the farmer stood during threshing.[24] As in all of Amos' earlier oracles against the nations, Yahweh's punishment is directed first against the rulers as those bearing primary responsibility, along with their palaces (cf. the discussion of 3:9). The state itself is designated as the territory of the reigning dynasty, which in its own turn is named after its founder (here "house of Hazael" corresponds to the designation "house of Omri" for the Northern Kingdom in Assyrian inscriptions).[25] Ben-hadad is mentioned as the current ruler, referring presumably to Hazael's son, Ben-hadad III, who ascended the throne in 802 B.C.E.[26] In what follows, the fall of the Aramean kingdom is described in a highly artistic fashion. Between the announcement of the conquest of the capital Damascus and the banishment of the population (it is presumably

---

23. Also in boastful battle accounts of the Assyrians; cf. Höffken, loc. cit., 449–51, n. 342.

24. H. Weippert, "Dreschen und Worfeln," *BRL²,* 64; Gustaf Dalman, *Arbeit und Sitte in Palästina,* 3.88–91, with illustrations 21–23 (cf. s.v. "Dreschen," *BRL,* 137–39), refers to Isa. 28:27f. and suggests the reference is to a threshing cart with sharpened rollers.

25. Cf. in this regard Höffken, "Eine Bemerkung zum 'Haus Hasaels' in Amos 1,4," *ZAW* 94 (1982): 413–15.

26. There was, however, presumably also a later ruler by this name; cf. S. Timm, *Die Dynastie Omri,* FRLANT 124 (Göttingen: Vandenhoeck & Ruprecht, 1981), 242–45. D. Vieweger, "Zur Herkunft der Völkerworte im Amosbuch," in *Festschrift H. Graf Reventlow* (Frankfurt am Main/New York: Peter Lang, 1994), 103–19, has recently shown anew that the reign of Ben-hadad III was probably associated with a strengthening of the Aramean kingdom.

the Assyrians who are conceived as God's instrument) two partial states are mentioned that were either allies with or subordinated to Damascus, and that here represent others as well. They were chosen not for historical reasons, but rather because their names were evocative for every reader. The first is referring geographically probably to the fertile valley between the Lebanon and Anti-Lebanon ranges, called el-Beqaʿ today; since E. Sellin, the second has often been identified with the state on the two sides of the middle Euphrates, which in Assyrian is called Bit-adini, though by 855 B.C.E. this had already become an Assyrian province.[27] The names were chosen, however, primarily as derogatory designations, something coming to expression particularly in the addition of *'āwen*, "nothingness, sin," to the first name. The divine punishment ends with the exile of the population. The goal Kir, the place of origin and starting point for the Arameans (cf. Amos 9:7), makes it clear that the history of the Arameans will come to a definitive end (Hosea's analogous threat that Israel must "return to Egypt" [Hos. 8:13; 9:3] probably served as the model here[28]). 2 Kings 16:9 confirms the fulfillment of this prediction by the Assyrians in the year 732 B.C.E.

[1:6–8] The charge against the Philistines, who like the Arameans are represented by their most significant city, is more difficult to interpret. When during the border conflicts with Judah (cf. 2 Kings 12:18 [17E]; 2 Chron. 26:6) they (literally) "exiled a complete group of exiles" in order "to deliver them to Edom," this probably is not referring to deportations within the framework of territorial expansion, but rather more likely to slaving expeditions involving smaller border locales. The verb *sgr* hiphil is usually used in reference to the life-threatening act of handing over escaped slaves (cf. the prohibition in Deut. 23:16); in Obadiah 14 it refers to the Edomites handing over fleeing Jerusalemites to the hostile Babylonians. Amos 1:6 is most likely referring to the greed of the Edomites, who needed slaves for the expansion of their extensive copper industry. The significance of the trade route from Gaza and Ashkelon (via Kurnub) to the northern Wadi Arabah and from there to the eastern high plateau is broadly attested during the golden age of the Nabateans, though it probably existed long before this.[29]

---

27. Shortly after 800, however, the Assyrian province Bīt-adini was ruled for five decades by an extremely confident Assyrian governor, Šamši-ilu, who at the same time was the commander in chief of the Assyrian army (turtānu) and whom many exegetes, following A. Malamat, "Amos 1:5 in the Light of the Til Barsip Inscriptions," *BASOR* 129 (1953): 35f., consider to be the ruler mentioned in Amos 1:5. Concerning this figure, cf. esp. E. Lipiński, "Jeroboam II et la Syrie," in *Storia e tradizioni di Israele: Festschrift J. A. Soggin,* ed. D. Garrone and F. Israel (Brescia: Paideia, 1991), 171–76.

28. Cf. Niemann, loc. cit. (note 11), 180f.

29. Because the conjecture "Aram" instead of "Edom" (P. Haupt, "Heb. *galût šôlĕmâ,* a peaceful colony," *JBL* 35 [1916]: 288; M. Haran, "Observations on the Historical Background of Amos 1:2–2:6," *IEJ* 18 [1968]: 201–12; 206f.) is not supported by any ancient textual witnesses, its discussion is superfluous.

The announcement of judgment includes in addition to Gaza also three other cities of the Philistine pentapolis; it is uncertain whether the fifth, namely Gath, is omitted for historical reasons (had it in the meantime again become Judean? was it already destroyed? In that case, the oracle would have to be dated after 711) or for poetical reasons. In consciously identical formulations with 1:5, it is again the rulers who are affected first, and the end of the kingdom is proclaimed; in conclusion, the announcement is then made that the rest of the population as well, to the extent that they survive the battle, will perish.

Ammon and Moab
(1:13–2:3)

The second pair of nations in the older text, now introduced by the ethnic name rather than by the capital city (though cf. 1:14: Rabbah, "the Great," modern Amman, and 2:2: Kerioth, modern *Qurēyāt 'Alēyān*), is linked by both literary and substantive features. The reference is to the neighbors in East Jordan in Israel's south. These border one another and, according to Gen. 19:30ff., were considered closely related; again, the sin of the second, more southerly one (perpetrated against an Edomite king) affects the Northern Kingdom Israel much less than it does Edom's neighbor Judah. Several shared literary features emerge in the announcements of punishment for these two peoples: (1) an indication of the circumstances amid which fire is kindled against the palaces; the asyndetic enumeration of the same preposition (four or three times *b*, "with, amid" in 1:14b; 2:2b) emphasizes the suddenness of the events;[30] (2) conscious repetition of words in connection with the loud outcry that, accompanied by the blast of trumpets, opens every battle as a signal of attack (1:14b; 2:2b); and (3) the emphatic inclusion of officials in the fate of the rulers as those bearing the primary responsibility, whether this fate implies exile as in the case of the Arameans (1:15) or death as in the case of the Philistines (2:3); only in the case of Moab is it explicitly stated that the population will perish.

[1:13] Links to the first pair of nations are found not only in the announcement of punishment, but also in the accusation. As in the sequence of 1:3–8, the first strophe (here the Ammonites) again mentions merciless horrors perpetrated against the population of "Gilead" (1:13 has the territory south of the Jabbok in mind), now explicitly for the sake of territorial expansion, though we cannot say whether the two activities were connected—for example, whether the Ammonites used the Arameans' victories to their own advantage. As is so

30. As 1:14 with its pronounced elements of theophany shows ("with a storm on the day of the whirlwind"; cf. Isa. 29:6; Ezek. 1:4; Job 38:1, et passim), it is more than the usual battle that is taking place here.

frequently the case (cf., e.g., 2 Kings 15:16; Hos. 14:1 [13:16E]), these horrors culminate in the massacre of nascent life.

[2:1] Again, the second strophe (here the Moabites) directs attention to a crime in which the locale plays no significant role; attention is, however, directed to the fact that Edom is affected, though in 2:1b it is envisioned only passively. The Moabites have committed a shocking cultic sacrilege on their king. (Is this a reference to corpse violation? Or does the emphasis fall, as the Targum understands it, on the material "lime," such that the sacrilege consisted in using the ashes? The understanding of the Vulgate is probably closer to the mark [*usque ad cinerem*] in suggesting that the bones — and thus the person's existence — were totally destroyed.[31]) As has often been correctly emphasized, this charge shows that the God of Amos did not concern himself with war crimes perpetrated only against his own people; but it also implicitly reveals the special connection (Israel and) Judah had with Edom, since the references are primarily to transgressions of neighboring peoples in the past or present certain to elicit strong emotions among the listeners or readers. The younger Edom-strophe picks up on this special relationship.

Tyre and Edom
(1:9–12)

The later oracles against the nations completely shift the reader's interest from the announcement of punishment to the demonstration of guilt, and they mention the coming disaster now only in the stereotypical formula of the devouring fire; these strophes are probably already looking back at the experiences of the destruction of Jerusalem.

[1:9–10] Such applies at least to the Edom-strophe, while the Tyre-strophe is historically more difficult to interpret because it constantly engages in citation.[32] The latter is formulated even in its details after the model of the Philistine-oracle; this applies both to the accusation, which though abbreviated is picked up in the same sense, as well as to the announcement of punishment (v. 10 corresponds exactly to v. 7), while the idea of the "covenant of brothers" with Israel is formulated in connection with the Edom-strophe. Such a citation does not necessarily mean that the

---

31. The desecration of royal graves and the pulverization of the bones of a hated enemy are also attested among the Assyrians; cf. Höffken, loc. cit., 452, note 351.

32. Wolff, 158, correctly points out that analogous words against the island fortress Tyre are attested the Old Testament only after 604 B.C.E., and for the most part considerably later. The most careful attempt at a historical interpretation has been presented by H.-P. Müller, "Phönizien und Juda in exilisch-nachexilischer Zeit," *WO* 6 (1970/71): 189–204.

sin is identical, but rather that it is of equal severity.[33] Since trade relations between Tyre and Edom are not historically attested and are rather
improbable,[34] the quoted "Edom" to whom the Tyreans deliver over the
abducted slaves may also be meant typologically, similar to "Assyria" in
many late Old Testament texts. In the ancient oriental language of diplomacy, contractual partners are called "brothers." In the case of Tyre, this
probably refers to the alliance between (David and) Solomon and Hiram
of Tyre (1 Kings 5:15ff.; 9:10ff., esp. 9:13), an alliance carried on in the
marriage between Ahab and the Tyrean princess Jezebel. Precisely this
reference to Israel's distant past suggests that the choice of this particular notion was influenced by the parallel Edom-strophe.

[**1:11–12**] In the case of Edom, the category of "brother" was familiar
to every reader on the basis of shared earlier history, something attested
not only by the Jacob-Esau narratives, but also by decrees such as Deut.
23:8f. [7f.E] or Deut. 2:4f. (cf. Num. 20:14). All the more horrific then
was the experience of Edom's active participation in taking and destroying Jerusalem (in the form of plundering, the handing over of refugees,
etc.), which Obadiah 10–14 (cf. Ps. 137:7; Lam. 4:21) describes, and the
occupation of southern Judah in the following period,[35] to which the image of the pursuing sword may be alluding. Both these experiences led to
a deep hatred of Edom in the late Old Testament texts (e.g., Ps. 137; Isa.
34; Jer. 49:7ff.; Ezek. 25:12–14; Obad.). They also provide the background to the emotional charges here in v. 11, a verse emphasizing the enduring quality of this hostility (cf. Ezek. 35:5) and the utter lack of
compassion characterizing Edom's actions, which are compared with the
wild fury of a predatory animal. Whereas the transgressions of those mentioned in the older oracles against the nations clearly lay in the past, those
in the Edom-strophe are oppressively present. And how different is the
prophetic empathy for Edom in 2:1! The time lapse is also reflected by the
fact that the territory of Teman and Bozrah (modern Buṣeirah) as the capital is mentioned as the recipient of Yahweh's punishment, which is the
case otherwise "only in exilic and postexilic literature" (Wellhausen),
rather than the older Sela (Judg. 1:36; 2 Kings 14:7).

33. The abbreviation of the accusation may indicate that Tyre is being charged as a middle-
man in the slave-trade; so U. Kellermann, "Israel und Edom" (Ph.D. diss., Münster, 1975), 39f.

34. Müller, loc. cit. (note 32), 194, suggests the reference may be to intermediary business
with the goal Sheba (the Sabeans), following Joel 4:8 (a text from the fourth century).

35. Cf. the summary of historical findings in H. Wildberger, *Jesaja,* BK 10/3 (Neukirchen-
Vluyn: Neukirchener Verlag, 1982), 1335–39; M. Weippert, "Edom und Israel," *TRE* 9 (1982):
291–99 (with bibliography); J. R. Bartlett, *Edom and the Edomites,* JSOTSup 77 (Sheffield: JSOT,
1989).

Hence the two later oracles against the nations, which (together with Israel) bring the number of nations to (the symbolically complete number) "seven," show that later redactors read Amos' words not out of historical interest, but rather with an eye on their own situation; during the exile, this interest was directed above all to the theme of guilt.

Beginning with the two initial strophic pairs, the older train of thought proceeded quite consciously toward the goal of the Israel-strophe as their intensification. The oracles against the nations, however, are more than merely a foil for the Israel-strophe. Although they do not yet show that Yahweh is a God of the whole world—this was not yet a theme for Amos' generation—they do show that Yahweh is more and something different than a national God; they show rather that he punishes not only Israel's sin, but that of Israel's neighbors as well. This acknowledges that they—like Paul's nations in Romans 1–3— have a consciousness of justice attributable to them quite independent of any specific experience of God, and which we today would circumscribe with the concept of human rights.[36] To that extent, as the common form of the oracles already indicates, they are basically put on the same level as Israel. The nations, too, commit *peša‛*, that is, "transgressions" in the sense of a revolt against their superior (see discussion above), and, as the charge in 2:1 shows, not just because the victims were Israelites. On the other hand, this standard reveals anew that Amos is not proceeding conceptually from the general, namely, the notion of a universal knowledge of God, to the particular, namely, Israel's own specific experience of God. Rather, he commences with Israel's own particular experience of God and fathoms its universal consequences.

(Judah and) Israel: Guiltier than the Nations Amos 2:4–5, 6–16

2:4 *Thus says Yahweh:*
For three transgressions of Judah,
and for four, I will not revoke it;
because they have rejected the law of Yahweh,
and have not kept his statutes,

---

36. Cf. S. Amsler, "Amos et les droits de l'homme," in *De la Torah au Messie: Festschrift H. Cazelles,* ed. M. Carrez, J. Doré, and P. Grelot; AOAT 212 (Paris: Desclée, 1981), 181–87; J. Barton, loc. cit., 39ff.

but they have been led astray by their (gods of) lies
after which their ancestors (already) walked.
5 *So I will send a fire on Judah,*
and it shall devour the palaces of Jerusalem.

6 Thus says Yahweh:
For three transgressions of Israel,
and for four, I will not revoke it;
because they sell the righteous for silver,
and the needy for a pair of sandals—
7 they who trample the head[1] of the poor *into the dust of the earth,*[2]
and bend the way of the afflicted;[3]
father and son go in to the same girl,
so that my holy name is profaned;
8 they lay themselves down[4] on garments taken in pledge
beside every altar;
and in the house of their God
they drink wine bought with fines they imposed.

9 Yet I destroyed the Amorite before them,
whose height was like the height of cedars,
and who was as strong as oaks;
I destroyed his fruit above,
and his roots beneath.
10 *Also I brought you up out of the land of Egypt,*
and led you forty years in the wilderness,
to possess the land of the Amorite.
11 *And I raised up some of your children to be prophets*
and some of your youths to be nazirites.

---

1. As the LXX and the identical parallel in 8:4 show, the verb is not derived from *š'p* ("snatch at"; so MT), which otherwise is never used with the preposition *'al*, but rather from the less frequently attested root *šūp* I, "trample" (*haššā'pîm*). Cf. the wordplay with the two roots in Gen. 3:15.

2. The intention of this variously superfluous addendum is to heighten the older accusation.

3. This is a presumably elliptical expression for "bend the way of justice"; cf. Prov. 17:23 and the numerous occurrences of *nṭh* hiphil together with *mišpāṭ* as object or place designation (G. Liedke, *Gestaltung und Bezeichnung alttestamentlicher Rechtssätze*, WMANT 39 [Neukirchen-Vluyn: Neukirchener Verlag, 1971], 93); cf. Wolff, 133, 166, and in connection with the "way" of justice also I. L. Seeligmann, "Zur Terminologie für das Gerichtsverfahren im Wortschatz des biblischen Hebräisch," in *Hebräische Wortforschung: Festschrift W. Baumgartner*, VTSup 16 (Leiden: E. J. Brill, 1967), 268f.; M. Schwantes, *Das Recht der Armen* (Frankfurt am Main/Las Vegas: Peter Lang, 1977), 90f.

4. This is a presumably elliptical expression for *nṭh* hiphil + *miṭṭâ*, "to spread out a bed [place for lying down]"; cf. *HAL*, 655. The translation can hardly even suggest that the Hebrew uses the same verb as in the second sentence of v. 7 ("to bend the way").

Is it not indeed so, O people of Israel?
says Yahweh.

12 *But you made the nazirites drink wine,*
and commanded the prophets,
saying, "You shall not prophesy."[5]

13 Behold, I will split open (the ground) beneath you,[6]
as the cart splits (it) open
when it is overloaded[7] with sheaves.

14 Flight shall perish from the swift,
and the strong shall not retain his strength,
nor shall the mighty save his life;

15 he who handles the bow shall not stand,
and he who is swift of foot
shall not save himself,[8]
nor shall he who rides horses save his life;

16 and even he who is stout of heart among the mighty
shall flee away naked in that day,
says Yahweh.

Bibliography: G. Fleischer, *Menschenverkäufer* (1989), 18–79 (esp. concerning vv. 6–8); M. Köckert, "Das Gesetz und die Propheten in Amos 1–2," in J. Hausmann and H.-J. Zobel, eds., *Alttestamentlicher Glaube und Biblische Theologie: Festschrift H. D. Preuss* (Stuttgart: W. Kohlhammer, 1992), 145–54 (concerning vv. 9–12).

[2:6–16] The Israel-strophe (like the prepositioned, later Judah-strophe as well, which will be interpreted at the end) differs in several different and profound ways from the preceding oracles against the nations, from which it is separated here only for the sake of overview. Since both formally and substantively it surpasses everything that has been said to this point, it is in every respect the culmination of the composition. Let me start by pointing out only the four most significant differences.

The first immediately apparent feature is that (1) the "three, indeed four transgressions," which in the stereotypical introductory formula of the divine discourse are charged to all the enumerated nations, are actually explicated in full only here (vv. 6–8), though one can indeed argue whether the sequence of

5. An amplified negation of the imperative (so-called prohibitive), as is customary with commandments, probably following Amos 7:16; cf. *G-K*[28], sections 107o; 109c; 152b.

6. Cf. the commentary. The address "you" presumably accommodates the older v. 13 to the later verses 10–12.

7. *lāh* is the so-called *dativus commodi*, which according to the sense becomes the *dativus incommodi* (so Rudolph and others).

8. This is to be vocalized as niphal, following the majority of versions.

transgressions is meant to underscore a continual increase or decrease in culpability.[9] In any event, (2) it is quite clear that Israel's transgressions are directed inward, toward its own fellow Israelites, rather than toward foreign
nations, whereby the circle of perpetrators is simultaneously expanded from
those who are politically responsible (in the oracles against the nations) to include anyone with any influence at all. Accordingly, (3) God's judgment is
portrayed in a much broader and more comprehensive fashion. It involves
God's direct intervention (v. 13), and is no longer mediated by fire, as in the
case of the nations; the consequences affect not only largely capital cities and
"those who hold the scepter," but rather all the inhabitants (vv. 14–16). Above
all, however, (4) an intermediary reflection is inserted in v. 9 between the accusation and the announcement of punishment; this recalls God's salvific acts
on Israel's behalf, thus making both accusation and announcement of judgment equally more incisive. It is no accident that it was precisely this notion
that later redactors expanded and deepened (vv. 10–12): By virtue of its experience of God, Israel is subject to different standards of justice than are the
nations, and for that reason also becomes guilty in a different way and is punished in a different way. (Concerning the formation of this complex composition, see the introduction.)

Israel's Sin
2:6–8

The "transgressions of Israel" (concerning this concept, see the discussion
above, pp. 20f.) enumerated in vv. 6–8 stand *pars pro toto* for a thoroughly
selfish society. Because of strictures of form already in effect from the oracles against the nations, these transgressions are concentrated into the briefest
possible literary form; Amos probably explicated them much more broadly
in oral discourse. In this concise written version, these verses present considerable difficulties for later exegetes precisely because they are obviously
referring to such concrete individual examples, something only very few
other verses in the book of Amos do. In any event, these transgressions were
committed by various circles of perpetrators, something already indicated by
the transition from the singular object ("the righteous [one]," "the needy
[one]," v. 6b) to the plural ("the poor [people]," "the afflicted [ones]," v. 7),
and by the alternating syntactical structure in the description of sin. At the

---

9. The answer to this question depends essentially on whether one understands the cultic concepts in vv. 7–8 as an expansion (so esp. Wolff) or as an intentional high point (so esp. H. Gese,
"Komposition," 90ff.). In my opinion, Gese is correct with regard to the present text (see the discussion of v. 8), and Wolff with regard to the actual discourse of Amos lying behind the text; see
the discussion below.

beginning (v. 6b), as in the oracles against the nations, stands an infinitive; v. 7a—the first verse to do so—uses the participle, until finally vv. 7aβ–8 shift to the imperfect, which in Hebrew signals repetition and duration. The temporal sequence implied by the infinitive and participle is unspecific; by contrast, the imperfects show that—differently than in the oracles against the nations (where the later strophes appropriately continue the infinitives with perfects)—no particular, exceptional, one-time deeds are being portrayed, but rather the typical, enduring behavior of the inhabitants. This complicated syntactical structure suggests that the tradents summarized several of Amos' discourses here.

[2:6] Probably the most severe reproach for Amos himself is found right at the beginning—analogous to the oracles against the nations, which mention only the most serious transgression in each instance. Verse 6 addresses the issue of the sale of human beings, that is, the ending of a farmer's independent existence. This is referring to the institution of a (temporally restricted; cf. Ex. 21:2ff.; Lev. 25:39ff.; Deut. 15:12ff.) debt slavery into which an impoverished farmer had to sell himself or one of his family members if he was unable to settle a large debt (not even by selling his possessions could he pay the debt). This long established institution was originally conceived as a way to keep body and soul together for a hopelessly impoverished person in a status of dependency, and to provide that person with a way to rebuild an independent existence (cf. esp. Deut. 15:12ff.). What Amos is attacking here is its grotesque abuse. It is unclear, though, whether "they sell" is used technically or merely imprecisely. The subject of such selling is customarily the *pater familias,* who in distress sells either family members (Neh. 5:2) or himself (Lev. 25:39, 47f.; Deut. 15:12; Jer. 34:14). In imprecise usage, the expression "they sell" would have to mean that the creditors force the debtors to sell themselves. In technical usage, the expression would have to mean that the creditors sell debt slaves to a third party, the way Joseph's brothers sell him to the Midianites (Gen. 37:28), that is, probably into slavery (cf. the distinction between the two in Lev. 25:39ff.).[10] More specifically, two different kinds of abuse are distinguished. In the first case, the goal of the transaction stands in the foreground: The sale of an indebted person is made for the sake of profit alone, and quite independent of any real-life circumstances, that is, independent of the degree to which the affected person is or is not responsible for his or her own distress. In the second case, the actual debt situation is more likely present: Creditors ruthlessly proceed to sell the debtor even in the case of the most trifling debt (cf. 1 Sam. 12:3 LXX; Sir.

---

10. In contradistinction to debt slavery, normal slavery was possibly valid for an unlimited period, which would explain the higher profit; cf. G. Fleischer, *Menschenverkäufer,* 50ff.

46:19).[11] In both instances, human beings become calculable goods, and become such under the cloak of legality. The nations treat foreigners as if they were goods (Amos 1:6, 9); the Israelites treat their own fellows and neighbors this way!

[**2:7**] The second charge (in v. 7a) initially describes in a general statement the brutal treatment of human beings; the parallel characterization then makes this more concrete. Dependent persons are humiliated in an insulting fashion; the proverbial trampling of a person's head was long a familiar symbol on illustrations of Mesopotamian kings for the subjugation of enemies. After this introduction, the more precise charge of "bending the way" is not a reference to the comparatively harmless gesture of jostling a person on the street (Rudolph), but rather to the violent obstruction of justice through the bribing of judges—as the analogous verb in 5:12b shows and as especially Wolff, Seeligmann, and Schwantes have demonstrated on the basis of parallel passages (cf. note 3 above). Here the term *'ānî/'ānāw,* "needy," occurring especially in the Psalms, quite frequently implies a claim for help. Thus are desperate persons robbed of their only means of defending themselves against injustices they may have suffered. As Amos 5:7–15 will explicate in more detail, this simultaneously strikes at the nerve of collective life in Israel, since the processes of justice were charged with eliminating all disputes and disturbances within the community, guaranteeing thereby the order of cooperative life. Where those who have no means to defend themselves through bribery are denied their rights, the community as a whole is destroyed.

The third charge (in v. 7b) contrasts with the others insofar as it is expressed in only a single sentence. Here one must try to sense how the prophet's outrage comes to expression in the *ritardando* of the four-stress bicolon rhythm (previously a three-stress bicolon). The concise manner of expression does, however, make interpretation more difficult, particularly since unequivocal parallels are

11. It is considerably more improbable that the two cases are dealing with the same accusation, i.e., that in the original text the two different prepositions (the so-called *b pretii* and the *ba'ăbūr* designating purpose) were semantic equivalents. In this understanding, either *bksp* would have to mean—as is nowhere else the case in the Old Testament—"because of a money debt" (so B. Lang, "Sklaven und Unfreie im Buch Amos (II 6, VIII 6)," *VT* 31 [1981]: 482f.), or, in a reverse fashion, the pair of sandals mentioned here would have to refer to the goal for the sake of which the sale is made. With reference to Ruth 4:7 and Ps. 60:10 (8E) (cf. Deut. 25:9), some have suggested the presence of a symbolic act at which a shoe could count as a legal claim for possession; cf. esp. E. A. Speiser, "Of Shoes and Shekels," *BASOR* 77 (1940): 15–20; repr. in idem, *Oriental and Biblical Studies,* ed. J. J. Finkelstein and M. Greenberg (Philadelphia: University of Pennsylvania, 1967), 151–59. The passages adduced, however, by no means attest that the simple mention of a pair of sandals—the symbolic acts mentioned in the Old Testament always speak of *one* shoe—could express a claim to possession. Cf. the discussion of this complex of questions most recently in Åke Viberg, *Symbols of Law: Contextual Analysis of Legal Symbolic Acts in the Old Testament,* CB.OT 34 (Stockholm: Almqvist & Wiksell, 1992), 157f.

lacking. The only thing virtually certain here is that the verb "go in to" is meant in the sexual sense.[12] The general expression "girl"—this term suggests youth and someone who is a minor, or is personally dependent on a master—might in a general fashion be alluding to the disintegration of cooperative cohabitation within the extended family, as described in a basic fashion in Leviticus 18; Lev. 18:8, 15, for example, forbid a son from having sexual relations with the wife of his father, or the father with the wife of his son. In this context, however, the reference is more likely to some form of dependency, though probably not to a female slave, who is generally designated more precisely[13]; rather, this is probably a maid belonging to the family. The closest substantive parallels in the Old Testament are those texts that speak of rape. A case of violent (Deut. 22:28f.) or even consensual (Ex. 22:15 [16E]) sexual intercourse with an unbetrothed girl establishes a marriage which, according to Deut. 22:29, cannot be dissolved, and the forceful invasion of a second man into a marriage begun thus (or in some other way) results in the death penalty (Deut. 22:23–27). In this way, the law tried to protect the woman's dignity as well as the obligation implied by the love between man and woman; by contrast, Amos sees before him a society in which sexual desire determines a person's actions, desire shamelessly selecting socially dependent persons as its victims.

[2:8] The concluding, fourth charge returns to the initial theme of social criticism in the narrower sense. Again, the focus is on the ruthless treatment of the indebted in two variations, and again, the problem is the excessive abuse of what in and of themselves are actually legal ordinances. In this instance, however, it is not profit that occupies the foreground as in v. 6b, but rather the luxurious lives of the creditors; at stake are the vitally important possessions of the debtors rather than persons. In the first case, Amos does not attack the institution of taking pledges as such, but rather the pledging of clothes for the purpose of reclining on the pledged garment (in celebration) instead of on one's own (according to Ex. 22:25 [26E] and Deut. 24:12f., the poor person's cloak may not be kept overnight, since it serves as a cover; and the widow's garment may not be taken in pledge at all [Deut. 24:17][14]). Just as little does Amos in v. 8b attack the collection of fines as such, as provided by law especially in the case of violence

12. Akkadian occurrences are adduced by S. M. Paul, "Two Cognate Semitic Terms for Mating and Copulation," *VT* 32 (1982): 492f. A different view is taken by Barstad, *Religious Polemics,* 18ff., though with rather unpersuasive reasons.

13. Cf. H. P. Stähli, "Knabe—Jüngling—Knecht," *BET* 7 (1978): 244; Fleischer, loc. cit., 61ff., esp. 67. Following Maag, *Text,* 174ff., Rudolph, in loc., and others, Stähli also shows that the meaning "(temple) prostitute" often suggested earlier is to be rejected (238–41).

14. Cf. the desperate petition of a Judean harvest worker from the seventh century, who could not recover his pledged cloak (*TGI²,* 70f.). One cannot exclude the possibility that the garment served as a security pledge. In that case, a debtor who could not discharge his debts would have to sell himself (de Vaux, *AncIsr,* 171ff.; Fleischer, loc. cit., 74).

against women as compensation for damages (Ex. 21:22; Deut. 22:19). Here, too, he is not discussing the appropriateness of compensatory payments—at most, one might conclude the presence of particular severity from the analogy with v. 8a[15]—but instead puts all emphasis on the purpose and goal of such coercive measures, namely, to enhance one's own revelry and drinking.

It is not only when they are without debt in the first place (v. 6b), but also when they have indeed incurred debt of some sort that the prophet takes the side of the impoverished and indebted, that is, for those members of Israel who are least able to help themselves. It is for just that reason that for him they become the standard of the people of God and of their community life.

The two specifications of place in v. 8 shift the reproof of Amos' oral discourse in the sense of Hoseanic theology, and show that the tradents of Amos viewed his message together with that of Hosea as a matter of course.[16] This presupposes the typically Hoseanic condemnation of the proliferation of cultic sites and priests (Hos. 4:7f.; 8:11–13; 10:1f., et passim), which in Amos is otherwise found only in Amos 7:9 (to be evaluated analogously). The expression "the house of their God"—in divine discourse!—presumably indicates a distancing from the imperial sanctuary in Bethel of the sort again characteristic of Hoseanic theology (Hos. 8:5f.; 10:5f.; 13:2). In its final form, v. 8 is focused entirely on the places at which believers worship. The charge of a lack of social compassion has become that of having misused worship services for excessive celebrations. Verse 7bβ, composed more than a century later, continues this tendency and intensifies one of Amos' social criticisms—following language typical of Ezekiel and the Holiness Code—into a religious accusation.[17]

God's Intervention for Israel
in Its Weakness (2:9–12)

Verses 9–12 function as a hinge in this text. On the one hand, they intensify the accusation by confronting the behavior of the Israelite leaders toward those dependent on them with Yahweh's own intervention for Israel in its

15. The text offers no grounds for assuming that these debtors were necessarily vintners whose very basis of existence is taken (Rudolph, in loc.; M. Fendler, "Sozialkritik," 36).

16. With regard to Amos 2:7f., cf. already A. Alt's letter to K. Galling, "Bethel und Gilgal II," *ZDPV* 67 (1944): 37f., and, following him, Wolff and Soggin in loc.; also J. L. Sicre, *"Con los pobres de la tierra": la justicia social en los profetas de Israel* (Madrid: Cristiandad, 1984), 110; regarding parallel passages for the appropriation of Hoseanic theology in the book of Amos, cf. J. Jeremias, "Die Anfänge des Dodekapropheton," in *Hosea und Amos*, 34ff.; 41–52.

17. W. Dietrich, "JHWH, Israel und die Völker beim Propheten Amos," *TZ* 48 (1992): 321, levels these differences by declaring vv. 7b–8 (together with vv. 9–12) without hesitation to be Deuteronomistic.

helplessness during the land conquest. Israel has learned nothing from its own history. On the other hand, they intensify the pronouncement of judgment against Israel in vv. 13–16 by juxtaposing Yahweh's intervention *for* Israel in the form of the total annihilation of mighty adversaries with his imminent intervention *against* Israel, which will be just as thoroughgoing and comprehensive.[18] Strictly speaking, this double contextual link and intensification applies only to v. 9. Verses 10–12 are already set apart by the transition to elevated prose and to the device of direct address, something one does not expect stylistically until the pronouncement of punishment in v. 13; their recollection of the exodus introduces the basic salvific-historical event of Israel's confession, and the theme of the rejected prophets and nazirites introduces a new, substantively quite different accusation than in vv. 6–8. Scholars have long recognized that these verses derive from what is known as Deuteronomistic theology, and thus belong to the new edition of the book of Amos during the exilic period.[19]

[2:9] The language and conceptual disposition of v. 9, however, are probably also not those of the historical Amos.[20] In current scholarship, though, v. 9 is still extremely disputed.[21] I personally consider it inconceivable that the Israel-strophe ever existed in a literary form without v. 9; the contextual relationships discussed above are too tight for this to have been the case (relationships characteristically absent in vv. 10–12). On the other hand, the language of v. 9 is clearly different from that in vv. 6–8; with the term "Amorite" it picks up on traditions from the Northern Kingdom, and

---

18. Both the verb *šmd* hiphil, "exterminate," in v. 9 and the statements in vv. 14–16 derive from the tradition of the wars of Yahweh, or "holy war."

19. Cf. the proof provided by W. H. Schmidt, *Deuteronomistische Redaktion,* 178–83, as well as Wolff, in loc., and most recently esp. Köckert, loc. cit., 147ff.

20. The Hebrew term *šmd* hiphil, "exterminate," with an entire people as its object, is common only after the seventh century (cf., however, Deut. 33:27; 2 Sam. 14:7, 11; Isa. 10:7, etc., as well as several earlier niphal occurrences); the designation "Amorites" for the previous inhabitants of the promised land occurs for the most part in Deuteronomy, though certainly also prior to this (in isolated traditions such as Judg. 1:34ff.; 2 Sam. 21:2 [1E], and in what are normally called "Elohistic" texts of the Northern Kingdom: Gen. 28:22; Num. 21:21, 25f., 31; 22:2); cf. M. Noth, "Num. 21 als Glied der 'Hexateuch'-Erzählung," *ZAW* 58 (1940/41): 181–89; repr. in *Aufsätze zur biblischen Landes- und Altertumskunde,* 2 vols., ed. H. W. Wolff (Neukirchen-Vluyn: Neukirchener Verlag, 1971), 1.94–101.

21. The extreme age of the verse has been defended esp. by H. W. Wolff, in loc.; A. J. Bjørndalen, *Allegorische Rede* (1986), 135ff., and M. Köckert, "Jahwe, Israel und das Land bei den Propheten Amos und Hosea," in *Gottesvolk: Beiträge zu einem Thema Biblischer Theologie: Festschrift S. Wagner,* ed. A. Meinhold and R. Lux (Berlin: Evangelische Verlagsanstalt, 1988), 69n39; a different position is taken, e.g., by J. Vermeylen, *Isaïe* 2.536f.; L. Perlitt, "Riesen im Alten Testament," *NAWG* (1990), no. 1, 22f.; repr. in *Deuteronomium-Studien,* Forschungen zum Alten Testament 8 (Tübingen: Mohr [Siebeck], 1994), 221f.

with images such as that of a tree's "root" and "fruit" as an expression of the totality and finality of destruction it draws possibly from Hos. 9:16.[22] Amos 2:6–16 is just as little a tape recording of Amos' actual speech as are any other texts from Amos. Rather, the tradents concentrate various sayings of Amos into a single discourse and in the process draw relationships with the book of Hosea already available to them (cf. the discussion of v. 8), as well as with other texts from the Northern Kingdom. In passing down Amos' words, their primary concern is that Israel's guilt become fully revealed in its entire severity only when it is viewed together with the special experiences of the people of God, a people whom God saved in times of distress when all seemed hopelessly lost. In this regard, we find in v. 9 the proverbial gargantuan dimensions of the previous inhabitants, who as such, however, are normally called Anakites.[23] And yet these giants were completely destroyed for Israel's sake. The people of God, through its particular experience of God, has other standards of justice than do the nations, and for that reason it becomes more guilty than they; it is also, however, called to account much more harshly (cf. 3:2). Only through this justification does Israel's sin in the strict sense become sin against God; only through this accounting does the sum of fortuitous individual deeds in vv. 6–8 become the sin of the people of God as a collective. At the same time, the retrospective on the total annihilation of the Amorites takes on a threatening character (vv. 13–16).

[2:10] During the exile, it is made clear to the survivors of Jerusalem's fall that the people of God have had far more experiences with their God—experiences that should have served as a standard for their behavior—than merely this deliverance from the giant original inhabitants of Palestine. The preeminent position is occupied (as is always the case in such enumerations at latest after the exile) by the original experience of liberation from Egypt (cf. already Hos. 12:10 [9E]; 13:4), one that became the central content of hope precisely for this generation of the exile: "To bring up" (instead of "to lead out") "is employed where the gift of the land is included within a retrospective view of the exodus" (Wolff,

---

22. So Vermeylen, ibid. However, cf. also the similar imprecatory formula from Sidon, three centuries after Amos (*KAI*, no. 14, lines 11f.) and Isa. 14:29; Ezek. 17:9. On the other hand, it is worth considering how for Hosea's theology the experiences of God in history play a constitutive role, serving several times to intensify an accusation by introducing an adversative divine "I, by contrast . . . ," something occurring in Amos only in 2:9; cf. Hos. 7:13, 15 (8:12; 9:10); 10:11; 11:3 (4); 13:4f., and in this regard K. Koch, *Amos*, part 2.12.

23. The reference is to a local tradition originally associated with Caleb and Hebron (Num. 13:22; Judg. 1:20), but later expanded to include the previous inhabitants as a whole (Num. 13:28; Deut. 9:2; Josh. 14:12, et passim).

169f.).[24] When v. 9 formulates the meaning of the divine victory over the Amorites in the traditional fashion as an occupation of the land, however, it is not recollecting merely the goal of this act of liberation; it is also drawing attention to the long delay in attaining this goal that resulted from the journey through the wilderness. When the wilderness wanderings are recalled as having lasted forty years (as is continually the case in Deuteronomistic writings, e.g., Deut. 1:3; 2:7; Josh. 5:6) and P (Ex. 16:35; Num. 14:33f.), this also implicitly recalls God's own patience with his dissatisfied and complaining people.

[**2:11f**] Although it may seem surprising that vv. 11f. shift to Yahweh's actions concerning specially authorized persons, for exilic theology this was not a different kind of theme (cf. Judg. 6:8–10; 1 Sam. 12:6ff.; Jer. 7:22–26). When v. 10 offered what might be called a Pentateuch *in nuce,* the intention was to recall the foundations of Israel's faith. No Israelite could formulate that faith without knowing the content of v. 10. By contrast, v. 11 is referring to the measures God took in order to preserve that faith in history through the gifts bestowed on special persons. For the sake of this goal, nazirites and prophets performed quite different functions. Nazirites, about whom especially Numbers 6 speaks and whose best-known representative was Samson (Judg. 13:5, 7; 16:17), functioned as models by abstaining from alcohol, ritual impurity, and hair cutting for the sake of honoring God. As persons "consecrated" to God in this way (this is what the term means) and dedicated to him, they "put themselves at the disposal of the deity as a special instrument."[25] In the view of Deuteronomistic theology, when Israel was in danger of incurring guilt it was the task of prophets to warn Israel of God's judgment by confronting it continually with the will of God. "Early and late" (Jer. 7:25; 25:4; 26:5, et passim; cf. 2 Kings 17:13), Yahweh sent prophets, because Israel was not yet completely lost in his eyes as a result of sin; only when it no longer listened to his prophets, prophets who sought to move it to repent, would it be lost.[26] But this is precisely what it has done

---

24. Cf. the proofs presented in J. Wijngaards, "*'yxwh* and *hleh*: A Twofold Approach to the Exodus," *VT* 15 (1965): 91–102, 99; H. J. Boecker, *Die Beurteilung der Anfänge des Königtums*, WMANT 31 (Neukirchen-Vluyn: Neukirchener Verlag, 1969), 39–43; E. Zenger, "Funktion und Sinn der ältesten Herausführungsformel (Nu 23,22; 24,8)," *ZDMGSup* I (1969): 334–42; G. Wehmeier, "*'lh* hinaufgehen," *THAT* 2.289; W. H. Schmidt, *Exodus,* BK 2 (Neukirchen-Vluyn: Neukirchener Verlag, 1974), 152f.

25. G. von Rad, *Old Testament Theology,* vol. 1 (New York: Harper & Brothers, 1962), 63; cf. M. Noth, *Numbers: A Commentary,* trans. J. D. Martin; OTL (Philadelphia: Westminster Press: 1968), on Num. 6:1–21; de Vaux, *AncIsr,* 466f. Rudolph (147) sketches in a plausible development of the institution of the nazirites.

26. Concerning this view of the prophets, cf. O. H. Steck, *Israel und das gewaltsame Geschick der Propheten,* WMANT 23 (Neukirchen-Vluyn: Neukirchener Verlag, 1967), esp. 60ff.

by forbidding prophets to prophesy—an allusion to Amos 7:10ff. (and perhaps also to Jer. 11:21)—and by not allowing the nazirites to fulfill their exemplary functions. The artificial language of commandments (see note 5 above) is used to express the irreconcilability between stiff-necked Israel and the salubrious words of the prophets. With that, Israel has wasted its last chance for deliverance; to force acknowledgment of this state of affairs, v. 11b confronts the readers with a question demanding assent. For the generation of the exile as well as for all later generations, the book of Amos is of preeminent importance because without its prophets, Israel in all its sin—sin presupposed as being constant—is hopelessly lost, as the fall of Jerusalem showed. Only the disclosure of that sin by the prophets and their call to repentance can save Israel. "One cannot think more highly of prophecy than this."[27]

Israel's Punishment
(2:13–16)

Israel's punishment is already much more severe than that of the nations; rather than sending fire (or the Assyrians) as his instrument, Yahweh now intervenes personally. Verses 14–16 suggest that the result of this action is a devastating military defeat ending in panic-stricken, futile flight. Verse 13, however, which actually describes this activity, uses the metaphor of an earthquake. This association of an earthquake with the consequences of war is unusual. As I have explicated more fully elsewhere, it is probably to be understood as a prelude to the final vision. Not only does Amos 9:1–4 include substantively the same association of quaking with hopeless flight (v. 1a), but also the same stylistic form of priamel (see discussion below) and the same conceptual devices in its description of the impossibility of flight (vv. 1b–4).[28] The tradents of Amos were not anticipating readers with short attention spans who would focus merely on individual pericopes, but rather with persons who would take the time to observe the substantive relationships within the book of Amos and to reflect on their mutually complementary explanatory value.

[2:13] Israel's punishment is introduced with a call to attentiveness standing outside the (three-stress colon) meter, one prompting the reader to expect

---

27. Köckert, loc. cit., 149.

28. Cf. J. Jeremias, "'Zwei Jahre vor dem Erdbeben' (Am 1,1)," in *Hosea und Amos,* 183ff.; cf. "Völkersprüche und Visionsberichte im Amosbuch," ibid., 172ff. By contrast, the unique metaphor of the harvest cart in v. 13 hardly permits the interpretation of the earthquake as Yahweh's weapon of war (Wolff).

something extraordinary. Instead of what in Hebrew is the customary *futurum instans* (*hinnĕnî* with participle: "I am about to do the following"), the emphatic "I" of God (with participle) creates a bridge to the equally emphatic initial "I" in v. 9 (and v. 10). Both acts are typical for this "I," that is, they are possible only for God, though they bear a completely different premonitory sign. The utter annihilation of the Amorites for Israel's sake turns into the utter annihilation of Israel itself, with no hope of flight (vv. 14–16); and the land for the sake of which the Amorites were destroyed (v. 10b) becomes ground unable to provide any support at all. Israel plunges into the abyss when the ground of life quakes "beneath you." Both an unusual verb as well as an unusual metaphor are chosen to express what is in itself an unusual statement. H. Gese, drawing on post-biblical Hebrew, has shown[29] that the verb *'wq* hiphil, occurring only here in the Old Testament, like Arabic (and Ugaritic) *'qq,* is to be understood in the sense of "split, cleave open (the ground)," yielding the image of a heavily-laden harvest cart[30] that tears open the earth in a field softened by rain. The furrows and fissures this creates provide the comparison with the earthquake, an earthquake signifying incomparably more than merely a natural phenomenon. It rescinds the gift of the land, as the connection with v. 9 (and 10) makes clear. And even more: As the aforementioned connection with the fifth vision shows, this also portends the collapse of the cosmic order itself, though Amos 2 remains yet completely focused on Israel's own sphere. Perhaps Gese is correct in suspecting that beyond this, the harvest metaphor is alluding to the fourth vision (Amos 8:1f.) and its announcement of "Israel's end."

[2:14–16] The futile flight described in vv. 14–16 as the consequence of the earthquake is not to be understood primarily as an attempt of some survivors of the natural catastrophe to save their own lives. Rather, these refugees are all characterized as splendid warriors. All possibility of flight is excluded in a priamel (from Latin *praeambulum*), a stylistic form listing similar examples one after another (frequently with a concluding point).[31] Verses 14 and 15 address exemplary pairs in which warriors fail precisely where their special strengths ought to lie. Since in v. 15 these are described with functional military designations, the characterizations in v. 14 are probably also to be understood

---

29. "Kleine Beiträge zum Verständnis des Amosbuches," *VT* 12 (1962): 417–23; cf. Wolff, 171. *HAL,* 758 mentions alternative interpretive possibilities ("cause to crack"—as the noise of an earthquake—or "cause to rock, sway," so Targum). Despite a certain element of philological uncertainty, the interpretation as an earthquake is currently not disputed.

30. Concerning the form of the agricultural cart drawn by two oxen (2 Sam. 6:3), cf. H. Weippert, "Wagen," *BRL²,* 356 (with illustration).

31. Cf. W. Bühlmann and K. Scherer, "Stilfiguren der Bibel," *BiBe* 10 (1973): 61f. (with bibliography). W. H. Schmidt drew attention to this in his review of H. W. Wolff, *Dodekapropheton 2: Amos,* BK 14/6–9 (Neukirchen-Vluyn: Neukirchener Verlag, 1967/69) in *TLZ* 96 (1971): 184 in connection with Amos 9:2–4.

technically ("the swift" perhaps as a reference to lightly armed, mobile troops, and "the strong" as a reference to more heavily armed troops).[32] Finally, at the culmination and in an isolated individual example, v. 16 speaks in the superlative of the most heroic warrior, who throws down weapons and equipment ("naked") and runs for his life, here, too—as the context implies—in futility. Although the occasion prompting this flight is not directly specified, it does emerge from the traditio-historical background. Yahweh now fights against his own people with the same intensity and overpowering might with which he once fought against the Amorites. No one can stand up against this warrior. In contrast to the oracles against the nations, it is not only the ruler and the politically responsible who perish, but rather everyone, without exception, because everyone has become guilty (cf. the discussion of v. 9).

Judah's Guilt and Punishment
(2:4–5)

The younger Judah-strophe, with its characteristically Deuteronomistic terminology,[33] is placed before the Israel-strophe. Just as the younger creation story in Genesis 1 interprets the older one in Genesis 2–3, so also does the Judah-strophe seek to show the readers of the book of Amos, after the destruction of Jerusalem, just what the real sin of the people of God was that first prompted the transgressions against their own fellows, transgressions about which Amos spoke in 2:6–8. The central sin was that the people of God rejected the revealed will of Yahweh, a will entrusted only to it (primarily in the expanded book of Deuteronomy; this will is designated in a summary fashion by the most important term of the late period, singular *tôrâ,* "instruction," which is then characterized in its individual parts in the plural form as written "statutes"). Instead, Judah was enticed by the gods of the nations, just as were earlier generations, and in this way exchanged the true God for idols only pretending to have power, idols which are thus really the embodiment of "lies." This is the only place at which Amos 2:4f., which otherwise employs the language of the Deuteronomistic school, uses original formulations in its alteration of 2 Kings 17:13–15. On the whole, the Judah-strophe ensures that the readers of the book understand Amos' reproaches in the strict sense theologically.

---

32. So, e.g., W. Dietrich, "JHWH, Israel und die Völker beim Propheten Amos," *TZ* 48 (1992): 326. As has long been acknowledged, vv. 14b and 15aβ are actually addenda that pick up and combine the conceptuality of the passage. Their function is presumably to increase the present number of designations "five" to the more complete number "seven."

33. Cf. p. 23 above; concerning the terminological analysis, cf., e.g., Wolff in loc. as well as B. Gosse, "Le recueil d'oracles contre les nations du livre d'Amos et l'histoire deuteronomique,'" *VT* 38 (1988): 29f.

Part II

THE COLLECTIONS
OF AMOS' SAYINGS
(AMOS 3–6)

1. Divine Discourse (Amos 3–4)

Justification of the
Message of Disaster
Amos 3:1–8

3:1 Hear this word that Yahweh has spoken against you, O people of
Israel,
against the whole family that I brought up out of the land of Egypt:
2 You only have I known of all the families of the earth;
therefore I will punish you for all your iniquities.

3 Do two walk together unless they have met?[1]
4 Does a lion roar in the forest, when it has no prey?
Does a young lion cry out from its den,[2] unless it has caught
something?
5 Does a bird fall to earth,[3] when there is no trap for it?
Does a snare spring up from the ground, when it has really caught
nothing?
6 Or is a trumpet blown in a city, and the people are not afraid?
Does disaster befall a city, unless Yahweh has done it?
7 *Surely the Lord, Yahweh, does nothing without revealing his secret
to his servants the prophets.*
8 The lion has roared; who will not fear?
The Lord[4] Yahweh has spoken;
who can but prophesy?

Bibliography: S. Mittmann, "Gestalt und Gehalt einer prophetischen Selbstrechtfertigung (Am 3,3–8)," *TQ* 151 (1971): 134–45; B. Renaud, "Génèse et Théologie d'Amos 3,3–8," in *De la Torah au Messie: Festschrift H. Cazelles,* ed. M. Carrez, J. Doré, and P. Grelot; AOAT 212 (Paris: Desclée, 1981): 353–72.

The central portion of the book, containing oracles against Israel, begins with
Amos 3. It encompasses Amos 3–6 and is divided exactly into two sections, as
shown by the two consciously parallel section superscriptions 3:1 and 5:1 (see

1. Concerning this translation, cf. Rudolph in loc.
2. "From its den" transcends the meter and probably represents an addendum indicating place
in accommodating v. 4b to its neighboring stichoi (Wolff, Renaud).
3. So LXX; MT erroneously already includes the additional "snare" here from v. 5b.
4. This addendum probably already presupposes the insertion of v. 7.

discussion below). In its present form, Amos 3–4 is in its own turn divided into three sections. The center is occupied by a collection of individual sayings revealing the sin of influential groups in the capital Samaria (3:9–4:3). The collection is itself doubly framed: at the beginning by the superscription (3:1), a programmatic saying (3:2), and a pericope of legitimation (3:3–8), and at the end by a (probably exilic) penitential liturgy following one of Amos' cult-critical sayings (4:4ff., 6–13). Both parts of this framing structure, each in its own way, prevent the sayings against Samaria from being read as a reproof against certain groups (as was yet the case in the oral discourse); they now name—*pars pro toto*—the sin of all Israel.

The programmatic saying in 3:2 in particular serves as a hermeneutic key to Amos 3–4. That it is more than a merely arbitrary individual saying is shown by the fact that it follows immediately upon the superscription in v. 1 and is thoroughly defended by the argumentative unit comprising vv. 3–8. Put differently: Verse 1 announces Amos' divine discourse; v. 2 names it; and vv. 3–8 legitimize it. The inclusion between v. 1a (" . . . the word that Yahweh has spoken against you") and v. 8 ("Yahweh has spoken . . . ") shows that with v. 8 a certain initial conceptual resolution has been reached.

[3:1a] The superscription in 3:1a must be interpreted together with its correspondence in 5:1. The two superscriptions have been consciously formed parallel,[5] albeit with two characteristic deviations. The imperative "hear this word" is followed in each case by a relative clause with the prepositional specification "against you" and a vocative, though each relative clause introduces a different discourse subject. Whereas it is Yahweh in 3:1, in 5:1 it is Amos. Commensurate with the subjects, the temporal relationships are different: Yahweh has already spoken (to the prophet; 3:1, perfect); Amos' words are issued in the immediate present (5:1, participle). This shows that the tradents considered the sequence of these chapters to be irreversible; Amos' words are the consequence of and reaction to the divine discourse he has received.

The second distinction between the two superscriptions is more difficult to assess. Amos 3:1 addresses the listeners as "people of Israel," 5:1 by contrast as "house of Israel." This distinction apparently possesses programmatic significance, since the expression "people of Israel" governs chaps. 3–4 just as exclusively (3:1, 12; 4:5) as "house of Israel" does chaps. 5–6 (5:1, 3, 4, 25; 6:1, 14); neither expression appears together with its counterpart.[6] "You/people of Israel" (like simple "Israel" and "my people") is most likely a designation of the people of God for whose sake God has acted and yet acts, while "house of Israel" is referring primarily to the state of the Northern Kingdom.[7] Put simply, these two dis-

5. By contrast, 4:1 was only later related to these two superscriptions; cf. the introduction to 3:9–4:3.
6. The LXX was cognizant of this difference and accommodated 3:1 to the linguistic usage of chaps. 5–6 ("house of Israel").
7. Cf. the argumentation in Wolff, 164f.

tinctions between 3:1 and 5:1 taken together suggest that in Amos 3–4 Yahweh is addressing the sin of the people of God, and in Amos 5–6 the prophet is lamenting the imminent fall of the commonwealth. Hence the tradents of Amos were quite conscious in the way they ordered the prophet's sayings, though the individual sayings transmitted down to them do not always fit their ordering principle.

[**3:1b**] The superscription in v. 1a already alludes indirectly to the theme of election in v. 2: The "people of Israel" are the chosen people, though Yahweh must now speak "against" his people. Verse 1b tries to amplify this connection by including the divine discourse already in the superscription itself, by appropriating the concept of "family" from v. 2 into v. 1, and above all by already mentioning explicitly the theme of election, though—in contradistinction to v. 2—in the customary terminology of Deuteronomistic salvific-historical retrospectives (cf. the discussion of 2:10). It thereby makes it clear that the experience of the foundational salvific deed at the exodus constitutes the decisive standard for judging the people of God.

Consequences of Election
(3:2)

[**3:2**] With v. 2, the tradents positioned a summary of the commissioned divine oracle before Amos' own reproofs against individual circumstances of sin in vv. 9ff. Its position between the superscription and the pericope of legitimation shows two things: First, it attests the great import of this divine oracle, which stands representatively for all of Amos' divine oracles—"this also could have served as a motto for the entire book" (Wellhausen); second, it indicates that in the eyes of the readers this oracle will be an extremely unusual, indeed offensive statement in need of special justification. Whoever wishes to understand the book of Amos must above all understand Amos 3:2 in the sense of its first edition. All the more noteworthy is the fact that Amos 3:2 is composed in terminology unique within the book of Amos itself. In this summary of his message, Amos' tradents are consciously creating associations with other texts, in particular with the message of Hosea,[8]

---

8. This is true especially of the concept of "iniquity, guilt" (*'āwôn*), which Amos never uses even though he speaks often enough of Israel's guilt, but which Hosea uses quite frequently (ten times); it also applies to the verb "punish" (*pqd*) with God as the subject (only in Amos 3:14 in dependence on Amos 3:2, though seven times in Hosea); and it applies finally to the verb "know" with God as the subject (Hos. 13:5; there firmly anchored in a wordplay with human knowing, which plays a central role in Hosea). The unusual expression "families of the earth," which avoids customary terminology associated with the state, is alluding perhaps to Gen. 12:3 (28:14), though one might also compare the similar later usage in Jer. 1:15; 2:4; 25:9; Ezek. 20:32, or even later in Pss. 22:28; 96:7. Formal indicators also support the redactional character of Amos 3:2; cf. K. Koch, *Amos,* part 2, 15, and esp. Melugin, "The Formation of Amos," 378, 380f.

since for them both prophets witness to one and the same truth of God, truth applying primarily to the Northern Kingdom, but just as much also to the rest of the people of God (cf. the introduction and analogous situation in Amos 2:8f.; 5:25; 7:9).[9]

Verse 2 thrives on the contrast between the first and second verse halves. The first recalls something already known (if v. 2 were ever an oral saying, one would have seen all the listeners nodding assent); the second then draws completely unexpected conclusions. The people of God have forgotten that election means not only privilege, but also heightened responsibility they have not assumed. Sin weighs more when it occurs in the knowledge of divine salvation (cf. 2:6–9); the "unfaithful servant" (Matt. 18:23–35) cannot expect leniency from the judge, since he has misused God's undeserved kindness by treating his own fellow human beings severely. Israel experienced God's proximity in a unique way whose exclusivity Amos 3:2 doubly emphasizes through the initial "alone" and through reference to Israel's difference from all other nations.[10] At the same time, the intensity of this relationship is emphasized. In Hebrew, the verb "know" (yd') means far more than cognitive understanding; among human beings, it circumscribes the most intimate fellowship extending even into the sexual sphere (Gen. 4:1 et passim), and refers to the ideal fellowship between Israel and God for which Hosea hopes (cf. Hos. 2:22 [21E]; 4:1; J. Jeremias, *Der Prophet Hosea,* ATD 24/1 [Göttingen: Vandenhoeck & Ruprecht, 1983], 51, 61). When God is the subject, as in Amos 3:2 and Deut. 9:24, both the unique favor he at his own initiative shows to Israel as well as his care for Israel are meant. The term *yd'* aims more strongly than does the *terminus technicus* "elect" (*bḥr*) at God's intimate personal favor,[11] something made especially clear by its more frequent use as a reference to God's election of individuals (Abraham: Gen. 18:19; Moses: Ex. 33:12, 17; Deut. 34:10); in the case of the prophet Jeremiah, the temporal indication ("before I formed you in the womb I knew you") makes it quite clear that this relationship comes from God alone, and the parallel verb (". . . I consecrated you") shows that God links the choice of Jeremiah with a commission. According to Amos 3:2, Israel misunderstood God's election and nearness in the sense of the self-assurance of the favored one, instead

9. To this extent, one might say of the tradents' intention that Amos 3:2 "might serve as the motto not only for the book of Amos itself, but for the entirety of Israelite prophecy up to Deutero-Isaiah" (Marti, in loc.).

10. In this, Amos 3:2 is a precursor of the Deuteronomic expression regarding "Israel's election from among all the nations" (Deut. 7:6f.; 10:15; cf. 14:2), which in its own turn influenced the late Old Testament period. In Deuteronomy, too, the exclusivity of election is emphasized for the sake of intensifying Israel's own obligation to be a "holy people"; cf. H. Wildberger, "*bḥr* erwählen," *THAT* 1.280ff.; H. Seebass, "*bāchar,*" *TDOT,* vol. 2 (Grand Rapids: Eerdmans, 1975), 82–87 (with bibliography).

11. T. C. Vriezen, *Die Erwählung Israels nach dem Alten Testament,* ATANT 24 (Zurich: Zwingli, 1953), 36f., correctly emphasizes this.

of comprehending the commission to be a model for the world of nations. "I have known you" (*yd'*, v. 2)—"they do not know (*yd'*) how to do right" (v. 10): so the respective disposition of Yahweh's and Israel's "knowing." Thus has Israel wasted its uniqueness among the nations, and is now called to account by God against the standard of its experience with God ("therefore"). The kind of performance review originally implied by the verb *pqd* leads, as in Hosea (cf. Hos. 1:4), to an exclusively negative result, the consequence of which is thus the "punishment" of "offenses"[12] explicated by vv. 9ff.

Coercion to
Proclaim Destruction (3:3–8)

Prophetic proclamation of the sort Amos issues is always contested. The tradents make this clear by placing even before the actual rendering of the individual sayings themselves Amos' self-justification before his adversaries in the form of a longer disputation saying. Although Amos was unpopular, what he experienced did not just happen to him alone, but was the fate of prophets in general. Like numerous prophets after him, Amos did not want this divine oracle he had to proclaim; it was forced upon him.

Verses 3–6, 8 constitute a long chain of didactic questions[13] probably originally intended to persuade readers through conclusive arguments.[14] Essential to their understanding is that they seek to evoke not merely one particular insight, but rather (at least) three. The formal indication of this is that the customary form of the question (indicator) in vv. 3–5 (*hă*) is heightened with v. 6 (*'im*, "or") into a double question and then finally, in v. 8, into a rhetorical question (*mî*, "who?"). The various parallel verse sections are formed with even greater variation, something a translation has difficulty imitating: first, alternating pairs in vv. 3–5 (*biltî 'im* with verb, "unless . . . ," vv. 3, 4b; *wĕ-x 'ên* with noun, "and was x not there?" vv. 4a, 5a),[15] and then with the intensifying infinitive absolute

---

12. In contradistinction to the harsh term *peša'*, "transgression," which Amos uses for individual cases (cf. the discussion of 1:3 above), the tradents chose the term *'āwôn* following Hosea's terminology as a more comprehensive term for guilt.

13. The association of natural phenomena with human behavior shows that the background derives from wisdom teaching; cf. H. W. Wolff, *Amos' geistige Heimat*, 5ff., 11 (see also ET, *Amos the Prophet*).

14. This view is supported by the multiple contextual relationships and by the multistage conceptual process. At the oral stage, vv. 4–5, 6b (Renaud) and v. 8 (W. H. Schmidt, *Deuteronomistische Redaktion*, 184; L. Markert, *Scheltwort*, 88f.; Wolff, in loc.) might have constituted separate discourse units, whereas v. 3 provided the bridge from vv. 4ff. to v. 2, and v. 6a the bridge between the two units, as Renaud's perceptive analysis has demonstrated (loc. cit., 358f.).

15. This observation shows that v. 3 hardly represents—as has occasionally been assumed (e.g., Marti, in loc., and H. Gese, "Kleine Beiträge zum Verständnis des Amosbuches," *VT* 12 [1962]: 425)—a literary addendum to the unit.

("really," v. 5b). Finally, when by contrast v. 6 and v. 8 each emphatically formulate their two parallel questions analogously, they are abandoning this artistic form at the culmination for the sake of penetrating, unequivocal clarity.

[3:3–5] Verses 3–5 are already formulated with an eye on substantive intensification, and, anticipating the overall form on a smaller scale, provide multiple insights. Whereas v. 3 initially seems to refer only quite generally to the nexus of cause and effect, introducing thus the argumentation schema used consistently in what follows, v. 4 already offers something quite different than an arbitrary example of such logic, and anticipates rather the lion metaphor of v. 8 (and v. 12). The actual wording of the question ("does a lion roar . . . ?") prompts the reader to think involuntarily of the fear of losing one's life in a situation of extreme danger. No one encountering the lion can escape; its roar is an unmistakable sign for the prey that falls into its clutches. Read from the perspective of the section's culmination in v. 8, this metaphor without fail becomes transparent for Israel's own position before God, whose "lion's roar" is sounded because Israel is indeed his "prey."[16] The ominous undertones in v. 4 are amplified in v. 5, which in its own turn anticipates v. 6. The example of the birdcatcher introduces the metaphor of the trap, thus turning the reader's attention from the result (v. 4: the lion before its prey) to the process of falling into mortal danger: Not even a bird, which is otherwise out of human reach, can escape an invisible trap.[17] The verb "catch" (result = perfect in v. 4b; process = imperfect in v. 5b) connects these two dark animal metaphors with one another, conveying to the reader the idea of inescapable death; the amplification of the verb with the infinitive absolute in v. 5b ("when it has really caught nothing") cuts off any thought of possible escape.

[3:6] Verse 6, and with it the second part of the double question, leaves behind the metaphors from the animal world. Verse 6a does, however, pro-

---

16. Given this transparency in v. 4, one might also ask whether v. 3, with its "two" who "walk together," is not also referring—at least in a concealed fashion—to Yahweh and Israel; the LXX made this implication explicit by alluding to v. 2 ("without having known one another"). The MT also connects the verbs of v. 2 and v. 3 by means of a wordplay (the root *y'd* next to *yd'*). It seems less probable that an allusion is being made to Yahweh and the prophets in anticipation of v. 8 (Wolff, Renaud).

17. The Old Testament almost always uses the two terms for the trap or snare of birdcatchers parallel (*môqēš*, v. 5a, and *paḥ*, v. 5b). Reflections on some special meaning attaching to *môqēš* here (Vogt, "'Ihr Tisch werde zur Falle' (Ps 69,23)," *Bib* 43 [1962]: 80f.; Rudolph, in loc.: "bait"; Marti, in loc.; Driver, "Linguistic and Textual Problems: Minor Prophets I," *JTS* 39 [1938]: 262; Wolff, in loc.: "wooden missile") are not really necessary. Concerning the process of birdcatching, which can be reconstructed from Egyptian illustrations, cf. G. Dalman, *Arbeit und Sitte*, 6.336–39; O. Keel, *The Symbolism of the Biblical World*, trans. T. J. Hallett (New York: Seabury Press, 1978), 89–95, with illustrations 110–120.

vide the conceptual bridge not only generally to the experiential level of interpersonal relationships, but specifically to the experiential sphere of the city, about which v. 6b also speaks. This shows clearly that the pericope comprising vv. 3–8 does not fortuitously precede vv. 9ff., which concretely name "the city" of v. 6 as Samaria. The situation of acute, life-threatening danger connects vv. 4–5 with v. 6a. The new element over against those verses is the idea of warning. What occurs instinctively in the animal kingdom—the sensing of danger—must in human circumstances and especially in the secured area of the city be provided by a special institution. The watchman's trumpet, serving as a signal for the threat of war, is in connection with v. 8 a transparent reference to the function of the prophet, influenced perhaps by Hos. 8:1 (see below).[18] The following sections speak more specifically about the danger of war (vv. 11, 15; 4:3). As v. 6b makes clear, however, no one tone focuses on the special circumstances of war such that, as the first goal of the train of thought here, it might draw the reader's attention to the ultimate origin of all this danger in the larger sense, namely, Yahweh. Because Yahweh stands behind the lion, because he is both the birdcatcher and the attacking enemy, one should and indeed must take fright "in the city," and—something far more important even than this—should and indeed must sound the trumpet. Anything else would merely constitute random treating of symptoms without ever perceiving the actual cause of the disaster. It is not the prophet's intention in v. 6 to propagate some universally valid doctrine concerning God as the cause of all things[19]; his intention is to shake human beings into recognizing how threatened they really are by a God whom they previously have understood only as a guarantor of salvation and life.

[3:8] *This* is the God Amos encountered. Just as after him Jeremiah (Jer. 20:9: "if I say . . . I will not speak any more in his name . . . ") and Paul (1 Cor. 9:16: "for an obligation is laid on me . . . "), Amos does not find himself being asked whether he is to be God's instrument or whether God's words are pleasing to him; he must deliver them. The visionary accounts in Amos 7–9 show how this realization came to Amos. Verse 8, however—presumably once an individual oral saying—says in this context far more than merely that

---

18. Cf. the broad treatment of this notion in Ezekiel (3:16–21; 33), who in his own function as watchman must warn every individual Israelite of the threatening mortal danger, danger which in a deeper sense is yet identical with the one who is actually issuing the warning call. Ezekiel makes explicit what in Amos 3 is only implicit: Although the prophet as watchman is responsible for his warning reaching everyone, he is not responsible for the success of that warning.

19. Concerning this problem, cf. the discussion of the verse in F. Lindström, *God and the Origin of Evil: A Contextual Analysis of Alleged Monistic Evidence in the Old Testament*, trans. F. H. Cryer; CB.OT 21 (Lund: Gleerup, 1983), 199ff.

Amos' commission came about just as unwillingly as does a person's fear before the roar of a lion. This is a commission to deliver a message of destruction.[20] The God who speaks to Amos and whose words Amos cannot keep silent *is* like the lion roaring over its prey (v. 4); to that extent, no disaster occurs in the city without him (v. 6). Where he is about to pounce on his prey, there is only *one* prophetic function: "Set the trumpet to your lips!" (Hos. 8:1). Whether or not his message is heeded, the prophet's task of drawing attention to the birdcatcher's trap and of reporting the attacking enemy is thus of vital importance. Amos *has* heard the roaring of the lion (cf. 1:2); he *must* startle his people.

[3:7] During the period after the destruction of Samaria and also Jerusalem, later redactors tried to convert Amos' self-justification here into a timelessly valid doctrinal statement; but its prosaic formulation falls out of the poetic conceptual nexus, and as a thetic statement (Heb. imperfect instead of perfect, v. 6) it disrupts the argument chain of cause-effect connections in the questions of vv. 3–6, 8. It speaks the language of Deuteronomistic theology,[21] and its position between v. 6 and v. 8 is important. With Amos, it affirms the statement of v. 6b, namely, that Yahweh is the ultimate and only danger for Israel, connects this notion with Yahweh's own message to Amos from v. 8, and generalizes the connection between the two statements: Yahweh never visits upon Israel merely sudden and thus necessarily incomprehensible disaster; before his acts of destruction, Yahweh regularly sends the prophets as his closest intimates ("servants" as often in the Deuteronomistic history; cf. 2 Kings 17:13, 23; 21:10; 24:2), those who like Micaiah son of Imlah (1 Kings 22:19ff.) and Jeremiah (Jer. 23:18, 22) have access to Yahweh's "heavenly council" and thus come to know his innermost intentions and "counsel" (both rendered in Hebrew by *sôd*). The essential task of these prophets is thus to warn the people of God of the coming disaster, that is, to move them to repentance and to a change of disposition, which alone can prompt God to withdraw the coming disaster. The danger threatening Israel in its sin on the one hand, and the will to save and preserve Israel on the other, are two sides of one and the same God. For Israel, this means that it is not yet lost when it incurs guilt toward God and its fellow human beings, but rather only when it fails to heed its prophets (cf. 9:10) or prevents God's emissaries of warning

---

20. A different view is taken by W. Werner, *Studien zur alttestamentlichen Vorstellung vom Plan Jahwes*, BZAW 173 (Berlin/New York: W. de Gruyter, 1988), 172ff., who understands v. 8 as a universal truth: "When Yahweh speaks, every person becomes a prophet" (173).

21. Cf. W. H. Schmidt, *Deuteronomistische Redaktion*, 183ff., and Wolff, in loc.

from speaking (cf. 2:12).[22] Since God always sends prophets before he brings on disaster, Israel cannot be excused when it resists their message. After the destruction of Jerusalem, the primary intention of this verse is to point this out.

Oppression in the Capital City
Amos 3:9–4:3

3:9 Proclaim over the palaces in Ashdod,
 and over the palaces in the land of Egypt,
 and say, "Assemble yourselves on the mountains of Samaria,
 and see what great tumults are within it,
 and the oppressed[1] in its midst."
10 They do not know how to do right, says Yahweh,[2]
 those who store up violence and oppression in their palaces.
11 Therefore thus says *the Lord*[3] Yahweh:
 An adversary shall 'surround'[4] the land,
 and strip you of your defense;
 and your palaces shall be plundered.

12 Thus says Yahweh:
 As the shepherd rescues from the mouth of the lion
 two legs, or a piece of an ear,
 so shall the people of Israel who live in Samaria be rescued,
 at the support of a couch and 'headrest'[5] of a bed.
13 *Hear and warn the house of Jacob,*

---

22. Concerning this Deuteronomistic view of the prophets, cf. the extensive presentation of O. H. Steck, *Israel und das gewaltsame Geschick der Propheten,* WMANT 23 (Neukirchen-Vluyn: Neukirchener Verlag, 1967), esp. 60ff. Its roots are found in the theology of Hosea; cf. commentaries to Hos. 6:5 as well as Amos 7:10–17 (as an example of an early stage of its history of influence).

1. Or abstract plural (as in the parallel sentence) "the oppressions."

2. Originally, this divine oracle did not begin until the solemn emissary formula in v. 11. Later redactors were quick either to derive a transmitted saying of Amos expressly from Yahweh by means of the formula "says Yahweh," or thereby to expand a divine oracle within the text; cf. the individual discussion in Wolff's excursus on this formula, 143f.

3. Whereas v. 12 in the MT attests the older abbreviated form of the emissary formula, the addendum "the Lord" is absent in the case of v. 11 in the Peshitta, and in the case of 4:2 in the LXX and Peshitta.

4. See *BHS*.

5. Cf. the commentary.

says the Lord Yahweh, the God of hosts:
14 *On the day I punish Israel for its transgressions,*
  I will punish the altars of Bethel,
  and the horns of the altar shall be torn off
  and fall to the ground.
15 I will tear down the winter house as well as the summer house;
  and the houses of ivory shall perish,
  and many houses shall come to an end, says Yahweh.

4:1 Hear[6] this word, you cows of Bashan who are on Mount Samaria,
  who oppress the poor, who crush the needy,
  who say to their lords, "Bring that we may drink!"
 2 *The Lord*[3] Yahweh has sworn by his holiness:
  Days are surely coming upon you,
  when they shall take you away with thorns,[5]
  even the last of you with harpoons.[5]
 3 Through breaches in the wall[7] you shall leave, each one straight
     ahead;
  and you shall be flung out[8] to Hermon,[8] says Yahweh.

Bibliography: S. Mittmann, "Amos 3:12–15 und das Bett der Samarier," *ZDPV* 92 (1976): 149–67;
G. Fleischer, *Menschenverkäufer*, 80–93 (regarding 4:1–3); 201–23 (regarding 3:9–11); 246–63
(regarding 3:12–15).

Whereas 3:1f. tightly summarized the divine oracle, and 3:3–8 restricted it
qualitatively to the oracle of disaster, 3:9–4:3 now explicates it through examples. Here Amos' tradents employ a collection of three oracles against Samaria
(3:9–11, 12–15; 4:1–3). Although each contains a reproof of sin and an
announcement of destruction against the capital, they are to be clearly distinguished form-critically from one another. Whereas 3:9–11 summons an international review board to evaluate the injustice, v. 12 betrays its origin in a
controversy between the prophet and his listeners, while 4:1–3 is directed
specifically to a group of women. At least the latter two subunits derive from
individual oral proclamations delivered by Amos,[9] something already evident

6. Concerning the alternation between masculine and feminine forms in 4:1–3, cf. *G-K*[28], sections 144a and 135o, as well as the commentary.
7. Accusative of direction (*G-K*[28], section 118h).
8. Cf. LXX (and other versions; see *BHS*). Attempts at interpreting the unusual vocalization
of the MT are presented by Barthélemy, *Critique textuelle*, 655f.
9. In 3:9–11, the accumulation of abstract terms—unusual for the book of Amos—is immediately noticeable, so that this unit might also have been conceived as a superscription-like introduction to the Samaria-oracles (Fleischer).

in the fact that they accuse specific groups of persons: 3:12, the owners of houses with ivory furnishings, and 4:1, women of high rank. The context, however, forbids the reader from adopting this restricted perspective. The individual sayings all stand under the auspices of 3:1–8 (and 4:6–13), which are directed at the people of God as a whole.

The question of verse demarcation cannot be decided unequivocally here. Amos 4:1–3 apparently constituted for the tradents the conclusion to the oracles against Samaria,[10] since (1) the reproof against the women "who oppress the poor" (4:1) constitutes a framing inclusion to the identical charge in 3:9; (2) the announced punishment of exile (4:3) heightens the preceding announcements of disaster in 3:11, 15; and (3) the following cult criticism in 4:4f. finds its correspondence only in chapter 5, and cannot be separated from its liturgy-like continuation in 4:6–13. On the other hand, the late addendum of an admonitory saying in 3:13f., with its double emphasis on the verb "punish" in v. 14, created a framing inclusion to 3:2, now causing 4:1 to sound like a new beginning, something also prompted by the chapter division (which actually derives only from the Middle Ages). Originally, however, the summons "hear this word . . . " in 4:1 did not, like 3:1 and 5:1, introduce larger collections, but rather only the subunit 4:1–3.[11]

Tumult in Samaria
(3:9–11)

[3:9] With the language of herald instruction,[12] the prophet slips into the role of a king who sends messengers into foreign countries, more exactly, into their capitals, characterized by the "palaces," that is, the splendid multistory edifices of those of high rank, built with hewn stones (cf. 1:4, 7, etc.).[13] The foreign inhabitants are to form their own opinion by assembling (not in Samaria itself; so LXX: "on Mount Samaria" in accommodation to

10. So already Wellhausen, in loc., whose insight, however, was disregarded by many later exegetes.

11. Compared with 3:1 and 5:1, 4:1 especially lacks the relative clause explicating the speaker and discourse direction, as well as the *nota accusativi;* and the vocative identifies the limited group; cf. the considerations of K. Koch, *Amos,* part 2, 107f.

12. Concerning form and topos considerations, cf. F. Crüsemann, *Studien zur Formgeschichte von Hymnus und Danklied in Israel,* WMANT 32 (Neukirchen-Vluyn: Neukirchener Verlag, 1969), 50ff.

13. The excavations of K. Kenyon in Samaria have shown that the walled city consisted almost exclusively of administrative buildings, while the population dwelled on the slope of the city hill (K. Kenyon, *Royal Cities in the Old Testament* [London: Barrie & Jenkins, 1971], 82).

4:1; 6:1, but rather) on the mountains around Samaria, separated from the mount of the royal city itself only by what is in part a rather narrow plain. This fictitious scene is concerned with the evidence for Samaria's sin, which the international sense of justice is quite able to perceive (cf. 1:3ff.). That specifically Ashdod (LXX: "Assyria," as the more familiar parallel to the high power Egypt) and Egypt are summoned as the two witnesses probably derives from their own status as countries with especially splendid palaces, perhaps also ironically from their familiarity with oppression (so Rudolph), but in any case from their competence in judgment (Ashdod as the representative of a neighboring nation, Egypt as the representative of a high power?).

[3:10] What they will see is "confusion," "tumults" of the sort Prov. 15:16 contrasts with the fear of God (Prov. 16:8 uses "injustice" in the corresponding position). All this stems from the fact that in Samaria, people have lost the elementary sense for what is "right" (cf. the contrast: "they do not know . . . " and "you only have I known," v. 2, in each case *yd'*). Amos uses the terminology of wisdom in emphasizing the obvious nature of transgressions against justice, transgressions of which the reader is aware even without any familiarity with specifically biblical legal traditions. Those who suffer are the poor and the dependent, those who suffer violence in a double sense: The term *ḥāmās*, "brutality," refers originally to the "violent act that destroys life"—anyone who hears the cry for help *ḥāmās* of someone whose life is threatened is absolutely obligated to provide help[14]—and *šōd*, "oppression," actually refers to the devastation of land, in Amos probably to "the violence perpetrated against possessions and property."[15] Amos' association of these two concepts exerted considerable influence on his successors (cf. Jer. 6:7; 20:8; Hab. 1:3; 2:17; Ezek. 45:9; Isa. 60:18, et passim).

[3:11] Yahweh, however, will put an end to these activities through the attack of an enemy, to whom the riches gained through such violence will pass. Amos does not yet speak concretely about the Assyrians, who shortly after his appearance began to build up their own world empire. Far more important than the identity of the enemy is that Israel will be robbed of its power as a state and will become an occupied country; even more important, the palaces—the key word in this pericope (vv. 9a, 10b, 11b)—will as the point of departure for all this sin also be the locus of chastisement.

14. In addition to dictionary information, cf. esp. R. Knierim, "Studien zur israelitischen Rechts- und Kulturgeschichte I: *cht'* und *chms*" (Ph.D. diss., Heidelberg, 1957), 125ff., citation from 145; I. L. Seeligmann, "Zur Terminologie für das Gerichtsverfahren im Wortschatz des biblischen Hebräisch," in *Hebräische Wortforschung: Festschrift W. Baumgartner*, VTSup 16 (Leiden: E. J. Brill, 1967), 251ff., esp. 257ff. The Priestly source explains the coming of the Flood with this term (Gen. 6:11–13).

15. Seeligmann, ibid., 257.

Discussion of the Possibility
of Rescue (3:12–15)

Amos 3:12–15 includes two sayings that consider possibilities for preserving the guilty from destruction. The two arrive at completely different conclusions, a result of the fact that the more recent saying (vv. 13f.) is trying to transfer Amos' older saying (vv. 12, 15) into a fundamentally changed historical situation after a lapse of about two centuries: the time after the fall of Jerusalem (cf. the introduction). It has been inserted into the earlier saying, which now brackets it; this position makes it clear that despite the temporal distance, it seeks to be comprehended completely from the perspective of Amos' prophetic authority.

[3:12] Amos' older saying, commissioned by Yahweh, had completely denied its addressees any possibility of escaping the announced disaster. It begins with the emissary formula and a carefully constructed metaphor in which the comparison and interpretation are of equal length.[16] The rather unexpected introduction of the thematic word "rescue" and the following explicative comparison show that a dispute between Amos and his adversaries is being summarized in which the latter had rejected Amos' divine oracle by referring, for example, to Israel's election (v. 2) and to Yahweh's "saving" intervention in the crises of war during Israel's early period. Their firm conviction is that God is essentially his people's helper and assistant, not their annihilator. Amos, commissioned by God, counters this salvific certainty with sarcasm by drawing on the example of the shepherd's law; according to the latter, in the case of the loss of a sheep to a predator, a shepherd was to prove the attentiveness with which he executed his own task as an overseer by presenting a body part of the dead animal (Ex. 22:9–12 [10–13E]; cf. Gen. 31:39). Otherwise he must make compensation to the owner of the flock. The "rescue" of a small body part in this context naturally represents nothing more than proof that nothing could have prevented this death. Read in connection with vv. 3–8, the metaphor simultaneously forces the readers of this prophetic saying to realize that the God on whose automatic help they count is himself now the ravaging lion bringing death.

One cannot fail to notice, however, that precisely in v. 12 the prophet is not speaking, as he does in the visions, about the destruction of the people of God as a whole (so the context; cf. the "people of Israel" in v. 1 and v. 12). Here, those whom he considers irrevocably lost are first of all primarily the wealthy inhabitants of the capital, those who owe their own luxurious lives to the oppression of the poor (v. 10; 4:1), or who enjoy that luxury without worry and in indifference toward the fate of the poor (6:6). In his individual sayings, Amos

---

16. This is overlooked by authors who associate the concluding vocative with v. 13 (Gressmann, Weiser, Amsler), something also impossible based on considerations of content (see the discussion of v. 13).

was thus quite able to distinguish clearly between the guilty and those who suffer. The beds in v. 12b, like the number of houses in v. 15 and the women's drinking in 4:1, stand *pars pro toto* for the intoxicating revelry described more specifically in 6:1–7. Later scribes of this text already did not understand the terminology referring to the individual parts of the furnishings, and committed errors in the text's transmission[17]; more recently, however, S. Mittmann has drawn on archaeological material (contemporary Assyrian and Egyptian beds) in contributing considerably to clarifying the terminology. Following the conjecture *bĕdabbešet,* "camel's hump," one going back to B. Duhm, he suggests understanding the "support" and "headrest (in the form of a hump)" as references to the sitting areas on the two narrow sides of a bed, the first of which as a (rounded) headboard was part of the bed itself, and the second a removable pillow.[18] As Mittmann shows, most of these beds stood on lion legs or were decorated with lion countenances or other lion representations. Amos presumably constructed his so utterly different lion imagery for God in opposition to such apotropaic lion representations, which symbolized protection and security.

[3:15] The luxury of the upper classes will come to an end when God, through an enemy, destroys Samaria. The key word "house" is used four times in v. 15. In regard to v. 15a, scholars have often been unable to decide whether "winter house" and "summer house" are parts of a single edifice (heatable ground floor, airy upper story) or are referring to different buildings altogether. All linguistic and substantive probability militates in favor of the latter understanding; King Ahab already had a winter palace in the warm valley of Jezreel (1 Kings 21:1) in addition to his palace in Samaria (1 Kings 21:18), and a building inscription composed three decades after Amos by King Barrākib of Sam'al in northern Syria tells us it was considered undignified for the king of a small state not to possess both a summer and a winter palace.[19] Verse 15 presupposes that the wealthy in Samaria were inclined to follow the king's lead in this regard. The situation regarding interior decorating was similar. Great quantities of ivory coverings, intarsia, and plating, as the most expensive luxuries (cf. 6:4), have been found on furnishings in the royal quarters of Samaria during ex-

17. The MT is perhaps thinking anachronistically of damask, attested only since the Islamic period (cf. Arabic *dimaqs,* "silk"), while the LXX and other versions mistakenly identify it as the city Damascus.

18. Loc. cit., 149–67. Illustration no. 2 is especially of interest with regard to Amos 3:12; on this old Iranian illustration (of the tenth century?), a married couple sits opposite one another on the narrow sides of a bed, separated by a small table (on the bed!) with food and drink, and surrounded by musicians. A decade before Mittmann, H. Gese ("Kleine Beiträge zum Verständnis des Amosbuches," *VT* 12 [1962]: 427–32) came to a substantively similar conclusion; he read *'amešet* and derived this word as a loanword from Akkadian *amar(t)u/amaštu,* "head (of a bed)"; but cf. Mittmann's criticism, loc. cit., 152ff.

19. Cf. *KAI* I, text 216, lines 16–20, and the commentary in *KAI* II, 233f.

cavations.[20] With regard to (literally) "the many houses," one might compare the same expression in Isa. 5:8f., which explains how the proliferation of houses and property possessions among the rich in the capital presupposes the disenfranchisement of small farmers and merchants.

[3:13] The intention of vv. 13f. is quite different, which despite the emissary formula at the beginning of v. 12 are identified with an incomparably more solemn formula[21] as an oracle of Yahweh. Here readers are roused by the urgency of the final hour in the face of imminent catastrophe. An unnamed group of people is summoned to "warn" the "house of Jacob." Both expressions exclude the usual interpretation, namely, that the imperatives are directed, as in v. 9, to those inhabiting the palaces of Ashdod and Egypt. As more recent investigations have shown, the verb *'wd* hiphil (with the preposition *b*) does not mean "testify," as was usually the reading in earlier translations, but rather "enjoin, inculcate," "admonish," or "warn (in a threatening fashion)."[22] This is a verb that in the overwhelming majority of occurrences is specific to Deuteronomistic theology, and later, deriving from the latter, also to the theology of the Chronicler.[23] There, "warning" is usually the manner in which Yahweh—primarily through his prophets—tries to bring his sinful people to its senses in the face of imminent punishment, that is, tries to prompt them to turn from their "evil ways"; in their own turn, the latter result from disobedience to the will of Yahweh as passed

20. A representative selection can be found, e.g., in A. Parrot, *Samaria: The Capital of the Kingdom of Israel,* trans. S. H. Hooke; Studies in Biblical Archeology 7 (London: SCM, 1958), 63–72; K. Kenyon, *Royal Cities of the Old Testament* (London: Barrie & Jenkins, 1971), 71ff., esp. 83–89; H. Weippert, "Elfenbein," *BRL²,* 67–72.

21. The predication "Yahweh (the) God of hosts" occurs with unusual frequency in the book of Amos (eight of eighteen occurrences in the entire Old Testament), and usually also, as in 3:13, together with framing formulae such as "thus says Yahweh" and "says Yahweh"; cf. with regard to details the excursus in H. W. Wolff, 287f. This presumably reflects the reading of the book of Amos aloud in worship services during the postexilic period, and anticipates the solemn conclusion of the first doxology of judgment in 4:13bβ, with which it shares the polemic against Bethel (cf. v. 14).

22. The etymology of the verb, however, is disputed; cf. on the one hand I. L. Seeligmann, "Zur Terminologie für das Gerichtsverfahren im Wortschatz des biblischen Hebräisch," in *Hebräische Wortforschung: Festschrift W. Baumgartner,* VTSup 16 (Leiden: E. J. Brill, 1967), 251–78; 265f.; and on the other hand O. H. Steck, *Israel und das gewaltsame Geschick der Propheten,* WMANT 23 (Neukirchen-Vluyn: Neukirchener-Verlag, 1967), 69f., n. 2; and finally T. Veijola, "Zur Ableitung und Bedeutung von hē'îd I im Hebräischen," *UF* 8 (1976): 343–51 (with bibliography); C. van Leeuwen, " *'ēd* Zeuge," *THAT* 2.209–21, 216f.; H. Simian-Yofre, " *'wd,*" *ThWAT,* vol. 5 (Stuttgart: W. Kohlhammer, 1986), 1107–28, 1123–25.

23. Cf. merely Deut. 8:19; 32:46; 1 Sam. 8:9; 2 Kings 17:13, 15; Jer. 11:7, as well as Neh. 9:26, 29, 30, 34; 2 Chron. 24:19.

down to them and as continually "inculcated" or "enjoined" anew. This usage presumably derives from the worship service specifically of the Deuteronomic-Deuteronomistic epoch, for which the Levites' or prophets' sermons of admonition or repentance are attested in festival psalms.[24] In two of these psalms, this sermon commissioned by God is introduced as follows: "Hear, O my people, and I will speak, O Israel, I will admonish/warn (*'wd* hiphil) you" (Ps. 50:7; 81:9), before in what follows the author speaks of the people's disobedience. Amos 3:13 is apparently following this particular worship usage in which "hearing" and "warning" are already firmly associated; the psalms, however, distribute "hearing" and "warning" among the people and God, whereas in Amos 3:13, by contrast, they are hoped for by the same people. This can only mean that every individual member of the people of God whose eyes are opened to Israel's guilt through Amos' words and through the experience of the destruction of both the Northern and Southern Kingdoms, is called upon to assume the prophet's office of watchman (v. 6a) in summoning their own contemporaries to repentance. The theme of the overall context is, as a matter of fact, the impossibility of rescue! Why these survivors are called the "house of Jacob" is shown later by Amos 9:8–10: This refers to the new congregation after the exile; continually attentive to the word of God Amos has delivered, it has turned its back on the temptations of political power associated with statehood.[25] To that extent, the readers of the book of Amos must themselves first become the "house of Jacob."

[3:14] To this end, however, they must learn from the fate of Bethel. The threat with which the preachers of vv. 13f. inculcate their warning in an extremely involved construction (Marti) is related substantively to Amos' final vision (Amos 9:1). Linguistically, it is related through the twice-used verb "punish" to the tradents' thematic statement in 3:2; stylistically (concluding clause with a change of subject), it is related to the announcements of disaster in v. 11b and v. 15b. The oracles going back to Amos himself mention Bethel by name only together with Gilgal (4:4; 5:5). Later tradents associate Bethel with the most grievous sin conceivable ("Israel's transgressions" as in 2:6–8) insofar as it was there that the prophets were forbidden to speak (7:10–17) and—worse yet—the "sin of Jeroboam" took place, namely, the exchange of Yahweh for the image of the calf (cf. the excursus to Hos. 8:4–6). This is why the actualization

---

24. Concerning the details involved in dating and in determining the speakers, cf. J. Jeremias, *Kultprophetie,* 125–27.

25. Cf. the discussion of 9:8–10 below, and the more extensive discussion in J. Jeremias, "Jakob im Amosbuch," in *Hosea und Amos,* 257ff. (concerning 3:13: ibid., 268–70).

of the divine "punishment" of which 3:2 speaks begins in Bethel.[26] The altar destroyed and desecrated by King Josiah (2 Kings 23:4, 15) could never again become a place of asylum and of protection with Yahweh; like the earthquake (1:1), it is certain proof of the truth of the words of God delivered by Amos and thus also of the announcement of disaster to the later generation if it is not roused to repentance. The fifth vision, predicting the end of all contact between Israel and God with the destruction of the temple, is partially realized in the destruction of Bethel and Jerusalem; it will come to complete realization if the "house of Jacob" does not heed the warning of the prophetic message once and for all.

Against the Aristocratic Women
(4:1–3)

Amos 4:1–3 is an internally rounded off oracle of judgment in elevated prose reflecting oral discourse with much more immediacy than most of the other sayings of Amos that have come down to us. With its harsh pronouncement of judgment, it rounds off the composition in Amos 3:9–4:3, and in addition relates the reproaches of oppression (3:9–11) to the excessive luxury (3:12, 15) in the preceding sayings.

[4:1] Amos scolds the aristocratic women of the capital with an expression ("cows of Bashan") into which some scholars, by way of Ugaritic *btn*, "serpent" (or by way of Ps. 68:16f. [15f.E]), have unjustifiably read an element of mythological profundity;[27] it refers, however, to how well the women are nourished. The high plateau of Bashan (500–600 meters elevation) east of the Sea of Galilee (modern en-Nuqreh in Syria, though it probably includes the Golan Heights[28]) is an extremely fertile pastureland because of its basalt soil and plentiful rainfall, and was famous for its "fatlings" (Ezek. 39:18; Deut. 32:14) and its mighty bulls (Ps. 22:13 [12E]). Amos is not, however, concerned with the external appearance of corpulence nor with external ostentation as an expression of vanity and arrogance (so Isaiah with regard to

26. The expression "on the day I punish . . . " occurs only within the context of the exile (Ex. 32:34; Jer. 27:22; cf. Jer. 32:5).

27. This also yet applies to the careful suggestion of K. Koch (*Amos,* part 2, 23; idem, *The Prophets,* vol. 1, *The Assyrian Age,* trans. M. Kohl [Philadelphia: Fortress, 1983], 46), that this may be a reference to a cultic self-designation of the women themselves, since they worshiped the "calf of Samaria" (Hos. 8:5f.). Koch is transferring Hosea's ideas into the book of Amos. Fleischer (loc. cit., 86–88) has adequately addressed Barstad's cultic interpretation (*Religious Polemics,* 37ff.), which goes even further and is alien to the text. H. Weippert, "Amos—seine Bilder," 10f., offers a clear and sober interpretation of the imagery.

28. Cf. M. Noth, *The Old Testament World,* trans. Victor I. Gruhn (Philadelphia: Fortress, 1966), 63.

the women of Jerusalem, Isa. 3:16f., 24), but rather with egoistic indulgence
in life characterized by the perpetual need for extravagant revelry ("drinking"
wine, like the beds in 3:12b, stands *pars pro toto* for such revelry, which
6:4–6 then describes more precisely); this cost a great deal of silver, which in
its own turn had to be obtained by oppressing the dependent poor. The rare
term "lord, master" is possibly being used ironically as a reference to their
husbands (so Rudolph), or refers (through the masculine suffixes) to the mas-
ters of those who are dependent (so Fleischer). In any event, the women determine the proportions of such revelry. The Hebrew verb *'šq,* "oppress," can
refer both to the exploitation of someone's inability to pay as well as to
extortion, while *rṣṣ,* "flay; figuratively: ill-treat," refers originally to the
breaking of a reed or staff. Especially the latter verb makes it clear that Amos
is concerned not with individual instances of injustice, but rather with the
devastation of the existence of entire families.

[4:2] Only this explains the severity of the divine punishment. Within the
entirety of preexilic prophecy, the form of the divine oath to oneself[29] occurs
outside Amos (also in 6:8; cf. 8:7) only in Isaiah (5:9; 22:14; cf. 14:24); it
emphasizes—in a fashion similar to the oracles against the nations (" . . . I
will not revoke," 1:3, 2:6, et passim) and the visionary accounts ("I can no
longer pass them [i.e., Israel] by," 7:8; 8:2)—the impossibility of any withdrawal of judgment. Like 4:2, Amos 6:8 also associates this with the revelry
of the aristocratic Samaritans and with the announced exile. H. W. Wolff, in
loc., has pointed out that in Deuteronomistic literature exactly the reverse is
the case, namely, God amplifies the promise of the land with the oath (Deut.
6:10, 18, 23, et passim; cf. Gen. 24:7; Ex. 13:5, et passim); Wolff does quite
justifiably express his suspicion, however, that the latter usage is actually
later than Amos.[30] The contrast, however, does render discernible the almost
unbearable severity of the announcement of punishment: This announcement
of imminent exile revokes the promise to the fathers! The form of the divine
oath in the announcement of exile (together with the masculine form of address, "you") makes it clear to the reader that, along with the well-to-do
women at whom Amos' oral saying was directed, all the wealthy citizens in
Samaria (6:7), indeed all Israel (5:27; cf. 8:2) have gambled away once and
for all their existence as the people of God. Verse 2b first emphasizes the brutality of the deportation in the imagery of v. 1 ("cows of Bashan"). The
women can yet be glad if they, like livestock, are only prodded from behind

---

29. So Gen. 22:16; Isa. 45:23; Jer. 22:5; 49:13; otherwise "by himself, by his own life" (Amos
6:8; Jer. 51:14), "by his holiness" (Amos 4:2; Ps. 89:36 [35E]), "by his right hand" (Isa. 62:8), "by
my great name" (Jer. 44:26).

30. In this regard cf. the extensive discussion in L. Perlitt, *Bundestheologie im Alten Testament,* WMANT 36 (Neukirchen-Vluyn: Neukirchener Verlag, 1969), 62ff.

with the point of an ox-goad[31]; whoever among them is too slow will become acquainted with the "fish-thorns," that is, will be deported by means of fishing equipment (so the usual understanding) or—more likely—driven with harpoons (so Wolff, Rudolph).

[**4:3**] Verse 3 leaves this metaphor and transfers the situation to that of a conquered city through whose breaches (in the walls) the captive women, isolated from one another, now leave, "cast away" as are otherwise only the dead (8:3), a despised mass of humanity. The goal of the deportation is indicated only quite generally by the direction "to Hermon," the highest mountain in Israel today (at 2,800 meters) and visible from afar;[32] the direction is northwest, to the territory of the Arameans (5:27) or to Mesopotamia.

The Refusal to Return
Amos 4:4–13

4:4 Come to Bethel—and transgress;[1]
to Gilgal—and multiply transgression;[2]
bring your meat sacrifices in the morning,
your tithes every three days;
5 bring (cause to go up in smoke) a thank offering of leavened bread,[2]
and proclaim freewill offerings, as loudly as possible;[2]
for so you love to do, O people of Israel! says *the Lord*[3] Yahweh.

6 *I gave you cleanness of teeth in all your cities,*
and lack of bread in all your places,
yet you did not return to me, says Yahweh.

---

31. Literally: (artificial) thorns (Marti, Rudolph; cf. *G-K²⁸*, 87o). Attempts have also occasionally been made to derive the term *ṣēn* from Akkadian *ṣinnatu* (S. J. Schwantes, "Note on Amos 4:2b," *ZAW* 79 [1967]: 82f.; Wolff, in loc.), such that the ladies are "dragged away with ropes"; the parallelism, however, militates more in favor of the understanding "thorn," "prickle" (Prov. 22:5), and in Akkadian the nose-twine or -rope is usually called *ṣerretu* (cf. *HAL*, s.v., and S. M. Paul, "Fishing Imagery in Amos 4:2," *JBL* 97 [1978]: 184f.).

32. Numerous ancient exegetes suggest "the mountains of Armenia" instead; cf. Barthélemy, *Critique textuelle*, 654f.

1. In a sequence of two syndetic imperatives in Hebrew, the second frequently acquires consecutive or even final meaning; cf. 5:4 and *G-K²⁸*, 110f.

2. Sequential asyndetic imperatives as well as (at the beginning of v. 5) an infinitive absolute with the same function express haste, harshness, and relentlessness; cf., e.g., A. Weiser, *Profetie*, 162.

3. Cf. the discussion of 1:8.

7 *And I also withheld the rain from you*
   when there were still three months to the harvest;
   I would send rain on one city,[4] and send no rain on another city;
   one field would be rained upon,
   and the field on which it did not rain withered;[5]

8 *so two or three towns wandered to one town to drink water,*
   and were not satisfied;
   yet you did not return to me, says Yahweh.

9 *I struck you with blight and mildew;*
   I caused your gardens and your vineyards 'to wither';[6]
   the locust devoured your fig trees and your olive trees;
   yet you did not return to me, says Yahweh.

10 *I sent among you a pestilence as against Egypt,[7]*
    I killed your young men with the sword;
    your horses became the spoils of war;
    and I made the stench of your camp go up into your nostrils;
    yet you did not return to me, says Yahweh.

11 *I overthrew some of you, as when God overthrew Sodom and*
       Gomorrah,
    and you were like a brand snatched from the fire;
    yet you did not return to me, says Yahweh.

12 *Therefore thus I will do (the same) to you, O Israel;*
    because I will do this to you,
    prepare to meet your God, O Israel!

13 *For lo, the one who forms the mountains,[8] creates the wind,*
    reveals his plan to mortals;[9]
    makes the morning light into darkness,[10]

---

4. The perfect in v. 7aα lists factual circumstances in a summary fashion, while the iteratives in v. 7aβb and 8a provide the more exact details or the results; cf. *G-K*[28], 112h. The same applies to v. 9.

5. Third person feminine as neuter (Wolff, Rudolph); cf. *G-K*[28], 144c.

6. MT: "(I struck . . .) greatly" or "(I struck) the lot (of your gardens . . .)" is probably a scribal error ("blight" does not really fit gardens and vineyards) for *hehĕrabtî* (Wellhausen) or *ḥerabtî* (van Hoonacker), "I caused to dry up, whither."

7. Literally, "after the manner of Egypt," probably a proverbial expression; cf. on the one hand Jer. 10:24, 26, and on the other Deut. 28:27, 60.

8. The LXX offers a variant attested by no other version, but which sooner faciliates our understanding of the text: "who forms the thunder."

9. The hapax legomenon *śēḥ* is presumably a secondary form of the more common *śîḥ* (Robinson, Rudolph). Perhaps God's own plans are to be distinguished terminologically from those of human beings (Wolff).

10. Some Heb. mss. and LXX read "who makes the morning light and darkness," influenced perhaps by 5:8.

> *and treads on the heights of the earth—*
> *Yahweh, the God of hosts, is his name!*

Bibliography: W. Brueggemann, "Amos IV 4–13 and Israel's Covenant Worship," *VT* 15 (1965): 1–15; J. Jeremias, "Die Mitte des Amosbuches (Am 4,4–13; 5,1–17)," in *Hosea und Amos,* 198–213.

In contrast to the usual situation in the book of Amos, the larger unit comprising 4:4–13 is appended seamlessly, that is, without any transitional formula, to the collection of Samaria-oracles (3:9–4:3) which were emphatically rounded off internally by 4:2f. On the other hand, Amos 4:4–13 is clearly distinguished from the preceding material both formally (initial imperatives) and thematically (cult criticism of the sort not otherwise encountered until chap. 5). The closest analogies to this situation—8:(3)4ff. and 9:7ff.—suggest that 4:4–13 represents the extension of an earlier literary context (3:1–4:3). This extension is of enormous importance in understanding the book in its final stage.

Amos 4:4–13 itself is composed of two separate parts that should be clearly distinguished form-critically: an ironically formulated summons to undertake a pilgrimage in vv. 4f., deriving probably directly from Amos himself, and a six-strophe penitential liturgy coming most likely from the exilic period or from the early-postexilic period. In the present text, however, these two parts constitute an indissoluble literary unit, since the penitential liturgy commences by referring adversatively ("I for my part . . . ") to the saying of Amos ("for so *you* love to do"); that is, it picks up emphatically on that saying. Amos 4:4f. was conceivably and probably an originally independent rhetorical unit, while 4:6ff. was not, neither formally nor substantively, since some reference to grievous sin is required prior to v. 6 for reasons of content.

Pilgrimage as an Enhancement
of Transgression (4:4–5)

With Amos 4:4–5, a completely new theme commences in the book of Amos, one continued in chapter 5: transgression within worship. (This is why 4:4f. could have been part of chap. 5 in the earlier book of Amos, considering that the text contains only an accusation, but no announcement of punishment or positive demands.) In connection with this new theme, it is no longer individual groups in the capital that are being addressed, as in 3:9–4:3; rather, the entire people of God is now addressed as "O people of Israel" (v. 5b), as in the thematic statement of 3:1f.

[4:4] In 4:4–5, the prophet slips into the role of a priest who with the *terminus technicus bō'û* ("come to . . . ," "enter into . . . ") issues a summons in the name of God to a pilgrimage (cf. Pss. 95:6; 96:8; 100:2, 4; Isa. 1:12, et passim). The usual form of such summons continues with the priest declaring the goal and purpose of this pilgrimage to be praise of God and homage before him; he then explicates the summons to the pilgrimage with other imperatives portraying the actual course of the worship services in a general sense, and finally justifies the entire summons with a reference to Yahweh's will.[11] Amos alters with bitter sarcasm all three formal elements following upon this summons to pilgrimage, the first most severely of all. "Transgression," the harshest word in the Old Testament (and a comparatively rare one) for offenses against human beings (cf. the discussion of 1:3 above) is the actual goal of worship. The choice of this particular term from the legal sphere makes it clear that Amos is not calling the worship service itself or any of its individual acts "transgressions," but rather the assuaging of one's conscience brought about by the pilgrimage, which enables a person to act even more deliberately out of self-interest in daily life. This is the case regardless of which of the two famous and venerable sanctuaries in the southern part of the Northern Kingdom constitutes the goal of this pilgrimage: Bethel with the central sanctuary (Tell Beitîn, eighteen kilometers north of Jerusalem) and locus of the Jacob-tradition (Gen. 28:10ff.; 35), or Gilgal in the Jordan depression (near Khirbet el-Mefjer, two kilometers north of Jericho, a site associated with the conquest of the land) (Josh. 3f.).

Amos alters the second formal element by adding to the cultic acts the second-person plural suffix: "your sacrifices," "your tithes." Worship has become an end in itself and is celebrated for the sake of self-assuagement; it does not reach Yahweh, and no longer creates any fellowship with him. These individual cultic terms stand representatively for the pilgrimage as a whole, and are not drawing attention to individual acts that may, for example, be particularly repugnant to the prophet. It is striking enough that the Judean Amos says not a word about the calf image in Bethel, which is an abomination to the slightly younger Israelite Hosea. As the most familiar type of sacrifice during this period, "offerings of meat" were extremely popular because one could consume portions of the meat at the celebratory meal (cf. Hos. 8:13; 4:13); worship commences with these sacrifices on the morning of the day after arrival. Obligatory tithes characterized the following, "third" day, which presumably constituted the culmination if one may take Ex. 19:11, 15 as a standard. In connection with Bethel, Gen. 28:22 already traces the tithe back to Jacob; according to the earlier legal statute in Deut. 14:22, it consisted of produce from the field, though in the following period it also included wine and oil (Deut. 12:17; 14:23), which were then consumed at the festive meal.[12]

---

11. Cf. J. Begrich, "Die priesterliche Tora (1936)," in *Gesammelte Studien zum Alten Testament*, ed. Walther Zimmerli, TB 21 (Munich: Kaiser, 1964), 232ff., esp. 247.

12. As in the case of the meat offering, so also in that of the tithe, a portion was probably given to the priest; cf. Deut. 18:4 and in this regard also O. Eissfeldt, *Erstlinge und Zehnten im Alten Testament*, BWAT 22 (1917): 40f.; 50f.; W. H. Schmidt, "Zehnten," *RGG³*, 6.1878. Concerning the history of the tithe, cf. F. Crüsemann, "Der Zehnte in der israelitischen Königszeit," *WD*, N.S. 18 (1985): 21–47.

[4:5] Amos' contemporary Hosea consistently associates the "smoke/incense offering" with worship at the high places, which was adulterated by elements of the Baal religion (Hos. 2:15 [13E]; 4:13; 11:2); by contrast, Amos uses the term neutrally in connection with the thanksgiving offering,[13] which was a response to God's acts of deliverance or of preservation from disaster on behalf of individuals or groups. It was offered outside regular sacrificial services or following them, as were also the private freewill offerings. The latter, too, were probably presented as the similar fulfillment of a thanksgiving obligation[14]; because they were not binding, they were often claimed ostentatiously as "good works."

The saying ends as it began, namely, with a cutting edge in its alteration of the third form element as well. In all this, no one asks what actually pleases Yahweh, nor what he actually "loves"—he "loves" justice and righteousness (Pss. 11:7; 33:5; 37:28; Isa. 61:8), and "hates" festival worship without these (Amos 5:21); these participants merely follow their own will to self-assuagement. Such worship not only fails to create any sensibility for sin in daily life, but also—what a horrible reversal!—virtually prevents these people even from recognizing such transgression, and instead actually furthers the brutality already characterizing interpersonal relations in daily life.

Life-and-Death Encounter
with God (4:6–13)

Israel's willfulness, with which Amos' text concluded, encounters in v. 6 the emphatically underscored acts of God ("I for my part"). In prophetic writings (occurrences listed in Wolff, p. 213, n. 11) and in the imprecatory series in Leviticus 26 (six occurrences), this formula usually attaches the element of punishment to an accusation. Amos 4:6ff. quite noticeably presupposes that this punishment has in the meantime already taken place, specifically in the form of a withdrawal of blessing of precisely the sort the worship services (vv. 4f.) are supposed to secure. Verses 6–11, formulated in elevated prose, view in retrospect Yahweh's five acts of disaster, acts which although certainly punishing the worship transgressions of vv. 4f., simultaneously were to serve pedagogical purposes; these acts always met, however, with the same obstinacy on Israel's part (identical refrain: "yet you did not return to me, says Yahweh" at the end of vv. 6, 8, 9, 10, 11). The five strophes are constructed largely in parallel

---

13. Only Lev. 7:13a also says that it is offered "from leavened bread," while later passages (such as Lev. 7:12) prescribe unleavened bread and meat offerings. Concerning the translation and interpretation, cf. H.-J. Hermisson, *Sprache und Ritus im altisraelitischen Kult*, WMANT 19 (Neukirchen-Vluyn: Neukirchener Verlag, 1965), 33f.

14. Cf. the frequent parallel with the vow offering, and further also J. Conrad, *"ndb," ThWAT*, vol. 5 (Stuttgart: W. Kohlhammer, 1986), 237ff., esp. 239f.

fashion (God's action in the first-person singular perfect, followed by a particle with suffix of the second-person plural and an accusative object or an adverbial expression), but are of unequal length. Traces of growth stages (esp. in vv. 7f. and v. 10), which are also related to the obvious change of temporal determination (cf. note 4 above), have often been examined, but are of no great substantive significance, and previous attempts at reconstructing an original poetic form have been unpersuasive. The number five and the organization in pairs alluded to (vv. 6, 7f.: "I for my part"; vv. 9, 10: perfect—perfect—imperfect or imperfect consecutive; v. 11 as the culmination) may indicate that the visionary accounts (and the oracles against the nations) served as the model for this composition. It is not until v. 12—a difficult verse to understand—that attention is directed to the future: a warning summons to Israel to prepare for an encounter with God in the face of threatening measures on his part, followed by a short hymn (v. 13) finding its correspondence in 5:8f. and 9:5f.

What is the meaning of this composition? First of all, even a quick initial reading makes it clear that these past blows by God designed to bring Israel to its senses are not describing historically ascertainable individual events, but rather typical plagues[15]; one need only compare the trio of plagues so familiar from the books of Jeremiah and Ezekiel: famine, sword, pestilence. The closest, and occasionally identical, parallels are found (not in Isa. 9:7ff. [8ff.E], but rather) in the great imprecatory chapters at the conclusion to the Holiness Code and to the Deuteronomic law (Lev. 26; Deut. 28), except that there, in contrast to Amos 4, they function as a threat for the future, or more precisely: for the possibility of disobedience to the legal corpus variously explicated beforehand, whose gravity and significance is inculcated to the listener or reader through such imprecatory threats.[16] One other text besides Amos 4 portrays the customary plague series of Amos 4 as having already occurred (famine—thirst/drought—failed harvests—locusts—pestilence—sword), and does so in a comparable sequence (defeat—thirst/drought—famine—pestilence—failed harvests—locusts—affliction by the enemy, whereby the coincidence in wording is especially noticeable in the elements of drought—pestilence—failed harvest): it is Solomon's prayer in 1 Kings 8:33ff., though it is not the perfect that is used as the tense here, but rather the second future. This text is the key to understanding Amos 4:6–13 as a whole.

15. H. Graf Reventlow, *Amt*, 78ff., was the first to recognize this clearly; cf. R. Fey, *Amos und Jesaja*, 95f.; L. Markert, *Scheltwort*, 122.

16. Cf. the list of verbatim parallels specifically with Lev. 26 in Reventlow, ibid., 86f., and esp. in H. W. Wolff, 213. Wolff points out there that the earlier comminatory form of the curses might yet be preserved in vv. 7aβb, 8, 9aγ (perfect consecutive or imperfect; cf. note 4 above). I myself consider it probable that Lev. 26 served as a literary model for the authors of Amos 4; cf. the essay mentioned at the beginning of this chapter.

First, only here is every individual plague, as in Amos 4, associated with the theme of "return" (Wolff); in Lev. 26:40ff., this is the case only in a wholesale fashion in retrospect of all the plagues. Hence, as in Amos 4, all the plagues here have an explicitly pedagogical function in the divine plan. Second, and of far more significance: 1 Kings 8 imbeds this return—one fervently desired because of these plagues—into a liturgical progression with which Amos 4:6ff. apparently already assumes its readers are familiar. Every strophe in 1 Kings 8:33ff. (vv. 33f., 35f., 37–40; cf. the more extensive and linguistically somewhat later strophe vv. 46ff.) presents a virtually identical sequence of events: Israel incurs guilt—Yahweh enjoins a punishment/plague—Israel repents—Israel praises Yahweh—petition for compassion with a confession of sin—acceptance of this prayer—forgiveness and end to the plague. Regarding the case when Israel incurs such guilt prompting God's punishing acts, Solomon is thus not petitioning God directly for forgiveness, but rather for forgiveness only on the basis of (a) repentance (b) praise of Yahweh's name, and (c) a plea and petition for compassion (v. 33). It is difficult to say just how these three acts differ in specifics, since in the parallel strophe (v. 35) the sequence is plea—praise of Yahweh's name—repentance (turn from sin). Yet they must apparently be distinguished, even if v. 38 in the third strophe speaks only summarily of prayer (pleas) and compassion, and v. 47 only of repentance and pleading with a confession of sin without mentioning praise of Yahweh. In any case, Amos 4 is obviously familiar with the juxtaposition of these various penitential acts, since it does after all distinguish clearly between repentance or returning (vv. 6–11) and praise of Yahweh's name (v. 13). Does this mean that the difficult v. 12 ("prepare . . . ") is related form-critically to the pleading in 1 Kings 8:33, 35, 38? This is in any case supported by the fact that the summons to preparation (*kwn* niphal) in the Old Testament is customary only in connection either with war (Josh. 8:4; Ezek. 38:7) or with worship at the sanctuary (see discussion below). As far as the "pleading" in 1 Kings 8 is concerned, however, it is characteristic that only in v. 33 does it take place "in this house," that is, at the Jerusalem temple, which is what one ought to expect in Solomon's prayer at the dedication of the temple. By contrast, in v. 35 this pleading is conducted more precisely "toward this place," and in v. 38 "toward this house"; the later strophe vv. 46ff. explains more closely just what this means: This is a prayer from the land into which Israel was deported (v. 47), "toward their land, which you gave to their ancestors, the city that you have chosen, and the house that I have built for your name" (v. 48). In short: Solomon prays in the name of and for the generation of the exile, as attested externally as well by the long acknowledged Deuteronomistic language.[17]

17. Cf. esp. M. Noth, *Könige*, BK 9/1 (Neukirchen-Vluyn: Neukirchener Verlag, 1968), 175, 186ff., and E. Würthwein, *Die Bücher der Könige*, ATD 11/1, 2d ed. (Göttingen: Vandenhoeck & Ruprecht, 1985), 95f., 98.

In all probability, this also applies to Amos 4:6ff. First, the imprecatory rituals in Leviticus 26 and Deuteronomy 28, in the form presupposed by Amos 4, already derive from the exilic/postexilic period and are essentially post-prophetic.[18] Second, the final strophe of the poetic refrain composition in Amos 4:6ff., namely, v. 11—the only one with no parallel in the imprecatory rituals or in 1 Kings 8—uses a fixed expression ("as when God overthrew Sodom and Gomorrah") not attested until after the exile (Deut. 29:22 [23E]; Isa. 13:19; Jer. 49:18; 50:40), and which apparently presupposes the experience of Jerusalem's destruction. The train of thought in Amos 4:6–13 thus apparently takes its orientation from a *penitential ritual of the exilic community.*

The perspective in Amos 4, however, is clearly a different one than in 1 Kings 8. Whereas 1 Kings 8 is preparing a liturgical model for distress of the most varied sort, one through which Israel (by means of the threefold sequence: return—plea—praise) can prompt Yahweh to end the distress, Amos 4 is engaging in historical theology close to that of Deuteronomistic theology. It addresses an Israel that until now has continually resisted, in every instance of distress, the turn to which 1 Kings 8 seeks to move its own readers; indeed, it even resisted when Yahweh visited upon it punishment not anticipated in any series of plagues: "overthrow" (v. 11). Because even this most extreme act of God did not attain its pedagogical goal, the coming encounter with God (v. 12) is portrayed as the one, final chance for Israel's survival. In preparation for this final chance, the exilic community is presented with the book of Amos itself, with its harsh reproofs and demonstrations of culpability culminating in the demonstration of faulty worship in Bethel (and Gilgal). Verses 12f., with "pleading" and "praise of Yahweh's name," want to counter this with true worship.

[4:6–10] First, however, the community must, as a reaction to Amos' accusations, become aware of its own previous resistance to penitence; such resistance will unavoidably result in God visiting ever new punishments upon Israel. It must realize that with great patience Yahweh has repeatedly delayed his most extreme measure for punishing the people of God, namely, the catastrophe of the exile (v. 11), for the sake of trying to bring Israel to its senses through more provisional punishments. The sequence of famine—drought—failed harvest—locusts—pestilence—sword is not intended to be understood historically (the frequent search for evidence in historical witnesses is at the very outset already off the mark); neither are the experiences of merely one particular generation meant, and certainly not any experiences that might correspond exactly to this sequence of plagues. The sequence is, however, doubtless intended to reflect increasing severity. On the one hand, the first and second strophes (famine and drought/thirst, vv. 6–8), related by their analogous be-

---

18. Cf. the argumentation in J. Jeremias, *Kultprophetie,* 164ff., esp. 170f., following Baentsch, Noth, Kilian, and Feucht.

ginnings, yet consider exceptions to the lack of rain in the period so critical for the harvest[19]; the third (v. 9) moves from more frequently experienced harvest damage (*šiddāpôn,* "blight," caused by the hot wind from the eastern desert; *yērāqôn,* "mildew," refers to the whitening of dry grain as a result of worms[20]) to the dreaded plague of locusts (cf. esp. Joel 1:4), and from grain as daily food, to vegetables and fruits from the gardens, to the luxury of figs, oil, and wine. On the other hand, the fourth strophe (v. 10), by mentioning pestilence, presents a disease that snatches up not only livestock (cf. Ex. 9), but also human beings themselves, and proceeds from a historical comparison ("as against Egypt") to the immediate experience of history ("sword"; "the stench of putrefaction," cf. Joel 2:20).

[4:11] This intensification is most tangible, of course, in v. 11, which leaves the customary language of the tradition of curses and speaks instead of being "overthrown," the totality of which is underscored by the comparison with the fate of Sodom and Gomorrah. This does not refer, as is occasionally assumed (e.g., Wolff), to the fall of Samaria, and even less to an earthquake, for which this verb is never used absolutely (though this represents a frequent interpretation, most recently Rudolph);[21] the reference is rather much more likely to the destruction of Jerusalem and its temple in 586 B.C.E., as already suggested by the previously mentioned exilic and later occurrences of the fixed expression "as when God overthrew Sodom and Gomorrah." An intensification of *this* experience is utterly inconceivable in Old Testament thinking. This implies that the addressees must understand themselves as a "brand snatched from the fire" (cf. the identical metaphor for the high priest Joshua at the end of the exile, Zech. 3:2); in the original text, the verb "snatch" is identical with the term "rescue" from 3:12, presumably a conscious allusion to the latter. The survivors of the catastrophe of 586 are by no means "rescued"; rather, they can and should understand their lives as an unmerited miracle involving certain consequences.

Yet not even this "overthrow" with the loss of temple, land, and king, nor even the exile, have been able to move Israel to "return to Yahweh," a concept

---

19. This refers to the spring rains (February/March); cf. the experiences reported by Dalman, *Arbeit und Sitte,* 1.130–33. Length, the circumstantial quality of some formulations, and conceptual inconsistency (e.g., the mention of fields between that of cities) clearly indicate growth traces in vv. 7f. An analogous situation applies to v. 10aγ.

20. Cf. Dalman, *Arbeit und Sitte,* 2.334 and 1.326f., as well as, with regard to mildew, R. Gradwohl, *Die Farben im Alten Testament: Eine terminologische Studie,* BZAW 83 (Berlin: A. Töpelmann, 1967), 31f. These two grain diseases always occur together; the oldest witness is the imprecatory chapter Deuteronomy 28 at v. 22 (otherwise Hag. 2:17; 1 Kings 8:37; 2 Chron. 6:28).

21. The standard passage, Gen. 19:21–25, already speaks of "cities" as the object of such "overthrow," and the usual result of such "overthrow" is that one can no longer settle at the site so affected (Isa. 13:19; Jer. 49:18; 50:40, and Rudolph himself, in loc.). Only once—though now quite unequivocally—is the reference to the "overthrow of mountains" (Job 9:5).

which in the terminology of Amos 4 (*šûb 'ad*) is also a central theme of the admonitory sermon of Hosea's pupils (Hos. 14:2–4 [1–3E]), and above all of the Deuteronomistic revivalists during the exile (Deut. 4:30; 30:2; cf. 1 Sam. 7:3; 2 Kings 17:13; 23:25).[22] As vv. 12f. together with vv. 4f. (and 3:14) suggest, this expression in Amos 4 is referring in particular to the turn away from the antidivine cult in Bethel (and Gilgal) to the true worship of the Sinai tradition.

[4:12] For the survivors, however, this is not merely a question for possible consideration, but rather one of life and death. In sharp contrast to the litany-like, harshly accusatory indictment of vv. 6–11, with its plural address to individuals, v. 12 presents a cuttingly incisive oracle of judgment, introduced by the typical "therefore" and with its collective you-address to the assembled community, which is twice solemnly called "O Israel." The different experiences of distress of individuals (plural address, "you," in vv. 6–11) demands a reaction on the part of the community as a whole (v. 12); the later tradents share this understanding virtually unaltered with Amos himself. The oracle of judgment is, to be sure, characterized by a puzzling brevity, since ultimately the emphasis lies not here, but rather on the encounter with God it is intended to prepare. Its much-discussed "thus (I will do to you)" has drawn three fundamentally distinct interpretations (discounting textual corruption): Either the reference is to a symbolic act (such as the shattering of the earthenware jug in Jer. 19) accompanying the oracle itself, representing thus the antecedent of the speaker's "thus"; or the reference is to some misfortune that has already occurred and to which the speaker might point his finger.[23] The problem with this understanding is that the decisive element—the act itself—must be complemented. Or exegetes have referred the "thus" to what immediately follows, that is, to the judgment associated with the encounter with God, but must then reckon with a lacuna in the text or with textual corruption,[24] since v. 12b clearly distinguishes God's threatened act on the one hand, and the encounter with God on the other. Hence the most probable solution is the third possibility, namely, to refer the "thus" back to the preceding material, that is, to the experience of Jerusalem's destruction (v. 11), and to translate "thus (the same)" or "(similarly) thus." In that case, v. 12 would make it quite clear to the survivors of the

22. For them, such return or repentance is "the decisive and final word of Moses for the generation of the exiles" (H. W. Wolff, "The Kerygma of the Deuteronomic Historical Work" [trans. F. C. Prussner], in H. W. Wolff and W. Brueggemann, *The Vitality of Old Testament Traditions,* 2d ed. [Atlanta: John Knox, 1982], 97).

23. Concerning the first variation, cf., e.g., A. R. Johnson, *The Cultic Prophet and Israel's Psalmody* (Cardiff: University of Wales Press, 1979), 183f., n. 2; concerning the second variant, cf. Wolff, in loc., who imagines the liturgy being spoken at the sanctuary of Bethel destroyed by Josiah.

24. Rudolph, in loc., conjectures (following Budde, Sellin, and Morgenstern): "because you have done this to yourself, prepare . . . "; Koch, *Amos,* part 2, 27, follows.

Jerusalem catastrophe that yet another refusal to return would result in the death not only of individuals—as previously—but rather of the entire community.[25] This is the manner in which the later tradents appropriate Amos' harsh message about the "end of Israel" (8:2).

Verses 12b-13 describe how this death can yet be avoided. Verse 12b makes use of cultic terminology taken specifically from the Sinai tradition: The summons to "prepare" (*kwn* niphal, either as *verbum finitum* or as participle with *hyh*)—attested otherwise, as already mentioned, only in connection with war—is issued there to Moses (Ex. 34:2) and to Israel (Ex. 19:11, 15). In each instance, the goal is a meeting with God, which in Ex. 19:17 is also—and even in exactly the same way—described as "to encounter God" (literally: "[to go] toward God").[26] In Exodus 19, such preparation includes sanctification rites such as the washing of clothes as well as abstinence, since such preparation does, after all, anticipate God's holiness, whose proximity is deadly (vv. 10-15; cf. 20:18-21). This emphatic resonance with Exodus 19 must probably be interpreted to mean that Israel's imminent worship encounter with the unapproachable and dangerous God involves the same fundamental decision as in its first encounter with God at Sinai. Just as Israel's relationship with God was established at that earlier time, so also is that relationship at stake now because of Israel's refusal to return. Perhaps the specific dating of Israel's "preparedness" to the third day in Ex. 19:11, 15 is also resonating; this would then sharply contrast the third day of the present incriminating worship in Bethel (and Gilgal) (Amos 4:4). The third day as such is not important, but rather the counterpart whom the people worship: the deity of Bethel (cf. the exegesis below of 4:13b and 3:14; the Deuteronomistic theologians speak of "Jeroboam's sin") or of Sinai. Hence it is up to Israel whether its encounter with God—to use Amos' following words—results in God "passing through" with death (*'ābar bĕ*, 5:17) or in him "passing by" Israel in compassion (*'ābar lĕ*, 7:8; 8:2).

[4:13] Everything depends on Israel yet knowing or realizing anew just who its counterpart really is. The traditional hymn in v. 13, introduced by the prophetic call to attention ("for lo!"), has a double function in this context. First,

---

25. So esp. W. Berg, *Die sogenannten Hymnenfragmente im Amosbuch,* Europäische Hochschulschriften 23/45 (Bern: Herbert Lang; Frankfurt: Peter Lang, 1974), 242ff.; similarly K. Eberlein, *Gott der Schöpfer—Israels Gott: Eine exegetische-hermeneutische Studie zur theologischen Funktion alttestamentlicher Schöpfungsaussagen,* Beiträge zur Erforschung des Alten Testaments und des antiken Judentums 5 (Frankfurt am Main/New York: Peter Lang, 1986), 229ff. The same would result by assuming that the background of the threat is actually the oath-formula "may the gods do this and this (Heb. 'thus and thus') to me if I do not . . ." (1 Kings 19:2 et passim). The "thus and thus" then refers to something ultimate, or death. The same applies to the possibility that the "thus" is referring to the following chap. 5; there, too, the predominant theme is death.

26. Esp. Brueggemann, loc. cit., 2–6, draws attention to these relationships, though he is too quick to interpret them liturgically ("covenant renewal").

it represents that particular act which in 1 Kings 8:33ff. constitutes "praising Yahweh's name" and there was inextricably connected with repentance, confession of sin, and pleading for compassion.[27] It is that act which F. Horst called exomologesis, "functioning simultaneously as confession and as doxology (acclamation) in view of the deity who unveils (punitive) power,"[28] now usually called "judgment-doxology." With it, Israel publicly acknowledges the destruction of Jerusalem and the exile as God's just judgment, which the prophet Amos announced in advance. The second function transcends this first, formal one, and involves issues of content. This hymn quite noticeably says nothing about sin and forgiveness. Instead, on the threshold between life and death (v. 12) it shows Israel who this Yahweh is whom it must face. Here it is decisive for understanding the individual statements that in v. 13 (as in 5:8[f.] and 9:5f.) the hymnic predicates used are interpreted anew in this context.

Excursus:
The Doxologies in the Book of Amos

Praise of the creator who rules sovereignly over both human beings and nature occurs twice more in the book of Amos, each time abruptly interrupting the context of prophetic discourse, and each time in strict participial construction and concluding with the refrain "Yahweh is his name" (5:8[9] and 9:5f.). Whereas earlier scholarship (up to World War I) largely considered these to be the marginal remarks of pious readers or redactors,[29] scholars in the following period gradually realized that, given both the formal and the substantive similarities, the three hymnic fragments must be interpreted together and in all likelihood once constituted a single hymn. Various attempts have been made to reconstruct the original hymn, often with reference to the closest parallel in Job 9:5–10; none of the suggested reconstructions, however, has been able to assert itself. Beyond this, F. Crüsemann has tried to demonstrate behind the doxologies of the book of Amos an independent preexilic hymnic type not attested in the Psalter.[30] To be sure, the Old Testament parallels to the Amos-doxologies (texts from Deutero-Isaiah as well as late texts from Jeremiah and Job) are without exception later. The evidence suggests that the Amos-doxologies date at earliest from the exilic period (Berg, Crenshaw; later:

---

27. Based on these relationships, the term *ydh* hiphil, "praise," can occasionally assume the meaning "confess guilt"; cf. esp. Ps. 32:5.

28. F. Horst, "Die Doxologien im Amosbuch (1929)," *Gottes Recht: Studien zum Recht im Alten Testament,* ed. Hans Walter Wolff, TB 12 (Munich: Kaiser, 1961), 155–66; 164. Cf. the following excursus.

29. Cf. the thorough outline of the history of scholarship in W. Berg, loc. cit. (n. 25), 53ff., esp. 213ff., as well as the more concise presentation of J. L. Crenshaw, *Hymnic Affirmation of Divine Justice: The Doxologies of Amos and Related Texts in the Old Testament,* SBLDS 24 (Missoula, Mont.: Scholars, 1975), 5ff., esp. 25ff.

30. *Studien zur Formgeschichte von Hymnus und Danklied in Israel,* WMANT 32 (Neukirchen-Vluyn: Neukirchener Verlag, 1969), 83ff., esp. 95ff.

Foresti, Mathys; see below), that is, they originated at earliest approximately contemporaneous with Amos 4:6–12, of which 4:13 is an inextricable part. Crüsemann, however, is credited with working out the close relationships obtaining between the divine predicates in the doxologies and ancient oriental hymns, and especially the religiopolemical function of the refrain "Yahweh is his name."

More rarely has the question been addressed concerning just how the appropriated hymnic statements are to be interpreted within the context of the book of Amos, although F. Horst, as already mentioned, did reveal their new function as a "judgment-doxology" as early as 1929 by disclosing the relationship between the hymns and sacral law through reference to penitential inscriptions from Asia Minor, to Alexandrian law, and especially to Joshua 7 and Job 5 and 9.[31] What is both noteworthy and as yet unexplained is why such judgment doxologies used hymns with creation themes, albeit hymns containing by no means the usual creation statements. Since the same situation obtains in the book of Job (Job 9:5–10; cf. 5:8–16), this cannot be accidental. In my opinion, there are especially two—seemingly opposite—themes in these hymns that made them seem so appropriate for their new function in the books of Amos and Job[32]: first, the stability of heaven (Amos 9:6), the stars (5:8), and the earth and mountains (4:13), showing that Yahweh is at the helm of this world, despite his apparent rejection of Israel in the destruction of Jerusalem; and second, emphasis on the fact that it is this same Yahweh who is able to "overthrow" (4:11). That is, it is he who "turns deep darkness to morning," just as in a reverse fashion he "darkens the day into night" (5:8), or "in his anger overthrows" even the mountains, the most stable things imaginable within human experience (Job 9:5), and shakes the earth (Amos 9:5; Job 9:6). In short, this Yahweh is the one who is able at any time to reverse completely what to human beings seems to be the natural order of things, and the one before whom nothing rebellious can endure, but who can just as easily illuminate the darkness. Accordingly, he is the one before whom a guilty and chastised Israel must humble itself if it is to move toward a new future instead of toward destruction.[33] Thus must these hymnic statements be cautiously understood on two levels, that is, their original statements within the tradition must be distinguished from their new understanding in the doxology of judgment within the book of Amos itself.[34] Inserted interpretations (such as

---

31. Cf. note 28 above. Among the authors who followed this line of thinking, one should mention esp. G. von Rad, ("Gerichtsdoxologie," *Schalom: Studien zu Glaube und Geschichte Israels: Festschrift A. Jepsen,* ed. K.-H. Bernhardt; Arbeiten zur Theologie 1/46 [Stuttgart: Calwer, 1971], 28–37; repr. in *Gesammelte Studien,* vol. 2, TB 48 [Munich: Kaiser, 1973], 245–54), H. W. Wolff, and J. L. Crenshaw (loc. cit.). Earlier scholars (e.g., Morgenstern, Weiser) thought these might represent congregational confessions presented after the worship reading of sections from the book of Amos.

32. A similar view has been taken recently by S. Gillingham, " 'Der die Morgenröte zur Finsternis macht': Gott und Schöpfung im Amosbuch," *EvT* 53 (1993): 109–23; 114f.

33. The double sense of these statements — statements that simultaneously seek to issue an urgent warning before destruction as well as to entice Israel to a new beginning — has recently been correctly emphasized by H.-P. Mathys, *Dichter und Beter: Theologen aus spätalttestamentlicher Zeit,* OBO 132 (Freiburg, Switzerland: Universitätsverlag; Göttingen: Vandenhoeck & Ruprecht, 1994), 109f., in discussion with F. Foresti, "Funzione semantica dei brani participiali di Amos: 4,13; 5,8s; 9,5s," *Bib* 62 (1981): 169–84, who in a one-sided fashion finds in these doxologies protoapocalyptic proclamations of worldwide chastisement.

34. K. Koch has followed this methodological premise most closely; cf. the following note.

the second line of the verse in Amos 4:13) make this distinction clear. The sequence of divine predicates is similarly structured in several reiterations (cf. the third line in v. 13 with the second and third lines in 5:8; and the fourth and fifth lines in 5:8 with the third and fourth lines in 9:6) such that the intention of these statements is disclosed ever more clearly. Ultimately, it must be described from the perspective of the end (namely, of 9:5ff.). It is especially the cosmic dimension characterizing all the doxologies that becomes fully comprehensible only from this perspective.

Finally, the question of redaction history has also been addressed recently: What does the positioning of the hymns yield for understanding the book of Amos as a whole? While K. Koch has persuasively interpreted the final doxology in 9:5f. as the former conclusion to the book,[35] in the essay mentioned at the beginning I have tried to show that the pericopes comprising 4:4–13 and 5:1–17 constitute the middle of the (younger) book of Amos through their doxologies, as well as the key to its understanding after the exile. I also refer the reader to the introduction to this commentary. One should note especially in this regard that the doxologies in 4:13 and 5:8(f.) follow imperatives (4:12; 5:4–6), whereas the final one in 9:5f. — by contrast — follows the announcement of the destruction of the temple (9:1–4). During the exile, they are thus praising both Yahweh's just judgment (9:5f.) as well as his renewed willingness to grant a new beginning to "the brand snatched from the fire" (4:11).

The observation has still not yet been fully explored which led Wolff, following Sellin, to his disputed thesis that the book of Amos was edited anew during the age of Josiah. Wolff noted that the first two hymnic pieces stand in immediate proximity to passages mentioning Bethel (4:4f. and 4:13 frame 4:4–13; 5:8 enters in immediate proximity to 5:4–6), and that the third follows the fifth vision, which although not mentioning Bethel by name is nonetheless doubtless referring to it with the sanctuary destroyed by Yahweh (see below).[36] The signal function the name "Bethel" possessed for the exilic/postexilic penitential ritual can be seen, for example, in Hos. 10:15. Hosea mentions the city of Beth-arbel, which was completely destroyed and whose inhabitants were horribly massacred; a theologian from the exilic period then adds: "Bethel has done the same to you because of your great wickedness." Bethel represents the primal sin of the chastised people of God; the Deuteronomistic history stereotypically calls this "the sin of Jeroboam,"[37] because at the division of the kingdom Jeroboam I established Bethel (and Dan) as competitors to Jerusalem as the imperial sanctuary. After the fall of the

---

35. K. Koch, "Die Rolle der hymnischen Abschnitte in der Komposition des Amos-Buches," *ZAW* 86 (1974): 504–37. His understanding of the closely positioned hymns in 4:13 and 5:8 as the conclusion to partial collections (similarly earlier H. Guthe, "Der Prophet Amos," in *Die Heilige Schrift des Alten Testaments,* vol. 2, ed. E. Kautzsch and A. Bertholet, 4th ed. [Tübingen, 1923], 37) is less persuasive. On the other hand, Koch is credited with having drawn the related hymn at the beginning of the book (Amos 1:2; following suggestions presented by Wolff) into the discussion.

36. Wolff, 111f. et passim; cf. idem, "Das Ende des Heiligtums in Bethel," *Archäologie und Altes Testament: Festschrift K. Galling,* ed. A. Kuschke and E. Kutsch (Tübingen: Mohr [Siebeck], 1970), 287–98.

37. Cf. the study with this name, *Die Sünde Jerobeams: Studien zur Darstellung Jerobeams und der Geschichte des Nordreichs in der deuteronomistischen Geschichtsschreibung,* by J. Debus, FRLANT 93 (Göttingen: Vandenhoeck & Ruprecht, 1967), esp. 93ff.

Northern Kingdom, it stood for idolatrous, syncretistic cultic activity (2 Kings 17:7ff.), and simultaneously for the failure to communicate with God resulting from worship in the sanctuaries at the high places. The doxologies counter this with praise of the true God who destroys the high places (4:13b) and establishes his own cosmic sanctuary over against them (9:6). Only from him can deliverance be expected.

It is especially the first and third lines in Amos 4:13 that become comprehensible from the perspective of the appropriated hymnic tradition: As the creator[38] of mountains and wind, Yahweh is responsible both for the enduring, predictable side of this world (Pss. 30:8 [7E]; 46:3 [2E]; 65:7f. [6f.E], et passim) as well as for its changing, unexpected occurrences (Pss. 48:8 [7E]; 139:7, et passim); as the one who changes the morning light into darkness through the gathering of clouds,[39] he can also alter history in an instant, a sentence which although primarily threatening is at the same time to be understood—as 5:8 shows—as enticing. Between these two statements stands a sentence which, as has long been recognized, cannot have belonged to the earlier creation hymn. Moreover, it is also ambiguous. Either God uncovers human plans—in which case the reference is probably to the refusal to return in vv. 6–11—or (in this context and in view of the verb "reveal" seeming much more likely), he does not leave human beings in the dark concerning his own plans.[40] In this case, however, the sentence would move into close substantive proximity with Amos 3:7: Israel is unpardonable; because it has prophets it does, after all, already know about God's coming acts. Finally, the last line in the verse ("who treads on the heights of the earth") has a long history in the hymnic tradition extending back far into the pre-Israelite age; here it extols the victorious power and superiority of God.[41] In the context of Amos 4, this line, like its closest substantive parallel Micah 1:3, is quite probably to be understood in the sense of the destruction of the cultic high places at Yahweh's theophany, and is to be referred to Bethel (vv. 4f.).[42] The creator of mountains (v. 13a) destroys the high

38. The first verb (*yṣr*) refers originally to the activity of the potter, while the second (*br'*) is reserved for God alone. Wolff, in loc., points out that the two verbs together occur otherwise only in Deutero-Isaiah (Isa. 43:1, 7; 45:7, 18), which supports the dating presented above.

39. Rudolph, in loc., following Wellhausen and others, translates against the usual syntax (in a double accusative, the indication of goal is usually second; *G-K*[28], 117ii): "who makes the darkness into the morning light," and does so because otherwise "the completely bright day lies between" (171); this shows, however, that he has not paid attention to the distinction between tradition and redaction.

40. Concerning the argumentation behind this view, cf. in addition to Wolff, in loc., esp. Koch, loc. cit. (note 35), 513–15; Mathys, loc. cit. (note 33), 111f.

41. Cf., e.g., R. Hillmann, "Wasser und Berg: Kosmische Verbindungslinien zwischen dem kanaanäischen Wettergott und Jahwe" (Ph.D. diss., Halle, 1965), 185–94; J. L. Crenshaw, " '*wĕdōrēk 'al-bāmotê 'āreṣ,*' " *CBQ* 34 (1972): 39–53.

42. So also, e.g., Wolff, in loc.; Crüsemann, loc. cit. (note 30), 102f., note 5; Koch, loc. cit. (note 35), 508–13; Crenshaw, loc. cit. (note 41), 43.

places of human beings (v. 13b), thereby rendering impossible any confusion between a Baal-like Yahweh (the God worshiped in Bethel, vv. 4f.) and the God of Sinai. Wherever in the book of Amos the solemn name "Yahweh, (the) God of hosts" resounds (altogether nine times), a name which in 4:13 expands the older refrain "Yahweh is his name" (5:8; 9:6), this particular contrast is resonating. Nothing more stands in the way of Israel's "return."

2. The Prophetic Oracle (Amos 5–6)

Death and Life
Amos 5:1–17

5:1 Hear this word that I take up over you in lamentation,
O house of Israel:

2 Fallen, no more to rise,
is maiden Israel;
forsaken on her land,
with no one to raise her up.

3 For thus says *the Lord*[1] Yahweh:
The city that marched out a thousand
shall have a hundred left,
and that which marched out a hundred
shall have ten left.
To the house of Israel.[2]

4 For thus says Yahweh to the house of Israel:
Seek me and live;[3]

5 but do not seek Bethel,
and do not enter into Gilgal
or cross over to Beer-sheba;
for Gilgal shall surely go into exile,
and Bethel become a place of disaster.

6 *Seek Yahweh and live,*
or he will permeate[4] *the house of Joseph like fire*
and it will devour, with no one to quench it.
To the house of Bethel.[2]

---

1. See *BHS,* and cf. the discussion of Amos 1:8.

2. The two poetically superfluous dative constructions concluding v. 3 and v. 6 are probably to be interpreted as subscript commentaries; cf. W. H. Schmidt, "Suchet den Herrn, so werdet ihr leben," in *Ex Orbe Religionum: Festschrift G. Widengren,* Studies in the History of Religions 21–22; vol. 1 (Leiden: Brill, 1972), 133n1. Concerning the intention, cf. the discussion of v. 6 below.

3. Cf. the analogous construction of a consecutive or final imperative in 4:4 and, in this regard, *G-K*[28], 110f.

4. The interpretative possibilities of the verb *ṣlḥ* in Amos 5:6 are enumerated in *HAL,* 961; E. Puech, "Sur la racine `ṣlḥ' en hébreu et en araméen," *Sem* 21 (1971): 5–19, and M. Saebø, "*ṣlḥ* gelingen," *THAT* 2.551–56. The context requires a meaning corresponding substantively to the more customary formulation in Jer. 4:4 and 21:12.

7 You that turn justice to wormwood,
   and bring righteousness to the ground!

8 (*But it is*) *he who made the Pleiades and Orion,*
   and turns deep darkness into the morning,
   and darkens the day into night,
   who calls for the waters of the sea,
   and pours them out on the surface of the earth,
   Yahweh is his name,
9 *who brings "collapse" against the strong,*[5]
   and "causes"[6] *destruction to come upon the fortress.*

10 They hate the one who reproves in the gate,
   and they abhor the one who speaks more loudly.
11 Therefore because you collect rent from the poor[7]
   and take from them levies of grain,
   you have built houses of hewn stone,
   but you shall not live in them;
   you have planted pleasant vineyards,
   but you shall not drink their wine.
12 For I know how many are your transgressions,
   and how great are your sins—
   you who afflict the righteous, who take a bribe,
   and push aside the needy in the gate.
13 *Therefore the prudent will keep silent in such a time;*
   for it is an evil time.

14 Seek good and not evil,
   that you may live,
   so that Yahweh, *the God of hosts,* will (really) be with you,
   just as you assert.

---

5. In Amos 5:9, *blg* is related possibly to Arabic *blġ*, which in the Af. [verb form] means "to occasion, cause" (J. J. Glück, "Three Notes on the Book of Amos," in *Studies on the Books of Hosea and Amos,* in *Die Ou Testamentiese Werkgemeenskap in Suid-Afrika, 7th and 8th Congresses* (1964/65) [Potchefstroom: Rege-Pers Beperk, 1965], 115f.). The LXX probably read *šeber* instead of *šōd* ("devastation") as the object, which probably came into the MT from v. 9b, and vocalizes *'ōz* ("the fortress") instead of *'āz* ("the strong"), both of which perhaps represent attempts to smooth out the awkward MT (Barthélemy, *Critique textuelle,* 662f.).

6. All versions read the hiphil of *bw'* (instead of the qal of the MT: "destruction comes").

7. Generally speaking, this hapax legomenon either is derived, following Torczyner's lead ("Presidential Address," *JPOS* 16 [1936]: 6f.), from Akkadian *šabāsu* (with metathesis of the first radicals), or ascribed to dittography (*būs* and *būṣ*) of the more common verb for "trample." The *parallelismus membrorum* militates for the former solution.

15 Hate evil and love good,
   and establish justice in the gate;
   it may be that Yahweh, *the God of hosts,*
   will be gracious to the remnant of Joseph.

16 Therefore thus says Yahweh,
   the God of hosts, the Lord:
   In all the squares there shall be wailing;
   and in all the streets they shall say, "Alas! alas!"
   They shall call the farmers to mourning,
   and those skilled in lamentation, 'to wailing';[8]
17 in all the vineyards (there shall be) wailing,
   for I will pass through the midst of you,
   says Yahweh.

Bibliography: N. J. Tromp, "Amos V 1–17: Towards a Stylistic and Rhetorical Analysis," *OTS* XXIII (1984): 56–84; J. Jeremias, "Tod und Leben in Am 5,1–17," in *Hosea und Amos,* 214–30; G. Fleischer, *Menschenverkäufer,* 94ff. (esp. concerning vv. 7, 10–12).

In Amos 5:1, the reader reaches the most important section in the middle part of the book of Amos. Chapters 3–4, introduced programmatically as a divine oracle, are now juxtaposed in chaps. 5–6 with the analogously introduced first-person oracle of the prophet himself. This is intended, however, not only as a reaction to chaps. 3–4, but in its own turn refers at a decisive point to new divine oracles; in 5:1–17, this is the case in v. 3, vv. 4f., and vv. 16f. Chapters 5–6 are divided into three parts: A quite artistically constructed ring composition (5:1–17) is followed by two units with consciously constructed parallel details, each variously introduced by an "alas, woe" (5:18–27 and 6),[9] the primary catchphrase of the lament for the dead, which the superscription in 5:1 already introduces as the theme of the prophetic oracle.

Amos 5 represents the middle of the book of Amos not only in a purely external sense (i.e., according to chapter numbers), but also substantively.

1. Within the structure of the earlier book of Amos, chap. 5 constituted the innermost core of the composition. Just as the oracles against the nations (Amos 1–2) and the visionary accounts (Amos 7:1–9:6) — variously related and linked

8. Either the MT has been subjected to word exchange, or this represents the conscious insertion of the stylistic device of hypallage (cf. W. Bühlmann and K. Scherer, *Stilfiguren der Bibel: ein kleines Nachschlagewerk,* Biblische Beiträge 10 [Fribourg, Switzerland: Verlag Schweizerisches Katholisches Bibelwerk, 1973]); so Barthélemy, *Critique textuelle,* 664f.

9. This transparent structure already obviates any need for arbitrarily adding an additional "alas, woe" in 5:7 (or 5:9: Koch), as do the majority of modern commentaries without any support from the textual tradition.

with one another—provided an external framework around the collection of sayings in chaps. 3–6, so also, within this collection itself, did the two larger units concentrating on the transgressions of the capital Samaria (Amos 3:9–4:3 and Amos 6) enclose the central chap. 5.

2. As regards content, this chapter speaks far more generally and fundamentally about Israel's relationship with God than do its surroundings; death and life constitute its predominant key words, worship and justice its predominant themes. Although it has hardly been considered and is by no means of merely secondary significance, the central theme of "justice and righteousness" in the book of Amos is restricted to chaps. 5–6.

3. Above all, however, Amos 5:1–17 is structured in a formally artistic fashion like no other unit within the book of Amos. Because up till the most recent present this artistic structuring has not been adequately understood, critical scholarship has repeatedly altered the traditional text without reason. Even though few authors have gone as far, for example, as A. Weiser and W. Rudolph, whose commentaries completely reorganize entire verse groups, still the overwhelming majority of exegetes assume the presence of serious transmission errors leading to inconsistent fissures in the text (e.g., v. 7 is clearly connected with v. 10, the "therefore" in v. 16 finds its substantive presupposition in vv. 10–12, etc.). Since the end of the 1970s, however, exegetes have recognized that 5:1–17 constitutes a consistently structured, so-called "concentric figure" or "ring composition" juxtaposing an external framework with the theme "death" (vv. 1–3, 16–17), an inner framework with the theme "life" (vv. 4–6, 14–15), a middle section with the theme "breach of justice" (vv. 7, 10–13), and a hymnic core (vv. 8–9).[10] A different form and topos correspond to each theme, something most clearly discernible with the theme of "life," which is characterized completely by the imperative, more specifically by the summons "seek" (vv. 4, 5, 6, 14). Expressed schematically, Amos 5:1–17 is thus organized into sections A (vv. 1–3), B (vv. 4–6), C (v. 7), D (vv. 8f.), C' (vv. 10–13), B' (vv. 14f.), A' (vv. 16f.). These individual parts are not intended to be, nor should they be, interpreted in isolation from one another. Rather, the reader is to traverse a conceptual progression both commencing and ending with the pitiless lament for the death of Israel (A/A'), because this people of God obstructed the implementation of justice (C/C'); this seemingly inflexible logic, however,

---

10. Primary credit goes to J. de Waard, "The Chiastic Structure of Amos V 1–17," *VT* 27 (1977): 170–77. In addition to the bibliography cited at the beginning, cf. also G. Crocetti, "'Cercate me e vivrete,'" in *Quaerere Deum: Atti della XXV settimana biblica*, ed. A. Bonora (Brescia: Paideia, 1980), (85–105) 92–94; A. V. Hunter, *Seek the Lord! A Study of the Meaning and Function of the Exhortations in Amos, Hosea, Isaiah, Micah, and Zephaniah* (Baltimore: St. Mary's Seminary and University, 1982), 102–4; R. Martin-Achard, 38f.; G. Fleischer, *Menschenverkäufer*, 94f., and others.

is now unexpectedly interrupted by the insertion—between the lament and its justification—of a twofold summons to seek God, accompanied by the promise of life. This can only mean that one might, by following that summons, sunder the connection between sin and death (B/B'). Finally, in the middle—which always bears the main emphasis in ring compositions—this progression issues in praise of the God who both kills and bestows life (D). As I have tried to demonstrate in the essay mentioned at the beginning, the basic outline of this consciously artistic structure already goes back to the first tradents of Amos, while the core of the doxology (v. 8) and its interpretation in v. 9 (as well as vv. 5aβ, 6, 13) were not added until the exilic/postexilic period. The basis of the composition are three originally separate sayings of Amos, each of which refers back to a divine oracle: vv. 2f.; vv. 4f.; vv. 7, 10, 12, 16f. (as a fourth saying possibly also v. 11).

Lament for the Living
(5:1–3 [A])

[5:1] The superscription in v. 1 is structured as a contrast to 3:1. The construction corresponds exactly to that of 3:1, rendering the four deviations then all the more visible: (1) The speaking subject is no longer God, but rather the prophet. (2) The tense has changed: Yahweh *has* spoken; in consequence, the prophet now *begins* to speak. (3) The group addressed in the vocative is now no longer the "people of Israel," that is, the people of God, but rather the "house of Israel," that is, the constituted commonwealth[11]; this expression sets the tone for the entirety of chaps. 5–6 (5:1, 3, 4, 25; 6:1, 14), whereas the designation "people of Israel" (3:1, 12; 4:5) is now consistently avoided. Above all, however, (4) the content of the following discourse, with its superscription-like characterization as a "lamentation," is executed in a drastic fashion. Because the people of God has utterly failed over against its Lord, the prophet summons the members of the state to their own funeral. It is uncertain whether the superscription of 5:1 (in a stage of oral delivery that can no longer be reconstructed) ever served specifically the funeral lament in v. 2 and its justification in v. 3; in the present text, the conscious parallel positioning of 3:1 and 5:1 shows that it applies to chaps. 5–6 as a whole. This corresponds to the fact that the ring composition in 5:1–17 ends in vv. 16f. with the theme of funeral lament, and that in 5:18ff. and chap. 6 two larger units now follow characterized by the central expression of the funeral lament ("alas, woe"). The theme of death governs chaps. 5–6 from beginning to end; only occasionally does the contrasting theme of life come into focus.

---

11. Cf. the excursus "'Israel' in the Book of Amos," in Wolff, 164, and the extensive discussion in D. J. Block, "Israel's House," *JETS* 28 (1985): 257–75.

[5:2] The prophet's discourse begins with a classic lament for the dead, already recognizable by its characteristic rhythm (bicolon structure of 3 + 2 accented syllables) and by the predominating perfects, reflecting the actuality and finality of the fate of death.[12] On the surface, it is the lament for a young girl who died all too young and in the blossom of her years. As a "maiden" (*bĕtûlâ*), she is as yet unmarried, though she may already be promised to a man, and thus engaged (Deut. 22:23f.). The decisive element is that she dies before fulfilling her life and without descendants, and cannot be saved by any medicines (v. 2b). The identification of the maiden with "Israel" and the reference to "falling" (a reference with a hidden meaning, since one usually falls by the sword) and being forsaken on "her ground" or "land" force the listener/reader into an unaccustomed reaction. The audience must transfer to a collective a genre that originally laments an individual dead person, and—even more difficult—must view as a corpse a collective that at the time this prophetic oracle is issued seems yet very much alive. The first stage of transfer does have certain models in Israel's surroundings insofar as cities, especially capitals, can be viewed as young women married to the city's divine patron[13]; by contrast, a transfer of this notion to a state, and in a funeral lament, no less, is not attested prior to Amos and can only be attributed to this prophet's own boldness.[14] By already treating his listeners as dead persons, Amos wants to rouse them into recognizing the hopelessness of their situation.

[5:3] Like every other prophetic oracle, however, this one is grounded in a divine oracle (v. 3) as well. Verse 2 already anticipates the conclusion from the divine oracle. A prophet is more than a funnel into which God pours preformulated divine oracles; otherwise a prophet like Jeremiah could not, in Jeremiah 1, refer to his own youth as a sign of unsuitability. The divine oracle now speaks—as v. 2 already did by way of allusion—about military catastrophe (cf. earlier, e.g., 3:11 and 4:2f., and later, e.g., 5:27 and 6:7f., 14). A group of a "thousand" or "hundred" refers to military units of this number. The prepositioning of v. 2, however, makes it quite clear that the tenth returning home from battle bears absolutely no hope; rather, like the piece of an ear from the animal ripped to shreds by the lion in 3:12, this tenth is evidence of catastrophic defeat; our own concept of "decimation" (originally: every tenth person is killed) is surpassed tenfold. (The subscript to the verse is to be viewed with v. 6.)

---

12. Cf. still H. Jahnow, *Das hebräische Leichenlied im Rahmen der Völkerdichtung*, BZAW 36 (Giessen: Töpelmann, 1923), esp. 90ff.

13. Cf. A. Fitzgerald, "BTWLT and BT as Titles for Capital Cities," *CBQ* 37 (1975): 167–83; 172ff.

14. Cf. C. Hardmeier, "Texttheorie und biblische Exegese," *BEvT* 79 (1978): 280ff.; 353ff.; Bjørndalen, *Allegorische Rede*, 161ff.

Forfeited Promise of Life
(5:4–6 [B])

Surprisingly, the lament of vv. 2f. is followed immediately by God's own summons to "seek" him, accompanied by a promise of life. Is the death of the "maiden Israel" avoidable after all? A distinction must be made here. The divine oracle in vv. 4f., which in its formal completeness presumably once might have constituted an independent rhetorical unit (Wolff), formulates its summons and promise with striking brevity (v. 4b: two words), while all emphasis is on the broadly explicated warning against faulty searching for God in v. 5, itself basically an accusation. The (later) prophetic words in (v. 6 and) vv. 14f. consciously offer a commentary on and update the brief divine oracle, and are the first to address explicitly the conditions under which Israel—or at least a remnant— "might" survive; the artistic form of the ring composition enhances this tendency by immediately juxtaposing the funeral lament and promise of life.

[5:4] The brief divine oracle in v. 4 ("seek me and live") thus undergoes various interpretations in vv. 5, 6, 14f., interpretations it obviously also needs given its brevity. Since as an admonitory saying accompanied by promise it has no analogy in the book of Amos, and because on the other hand this promise of life under fulfillment of certain conditions is familiar both from the wisdom tradition (Prov. 4:4; 9:6; 15:27; 21:21, et passim) and from the priestly tradition (Lev. 18:5; Ezek. 18:9ff.; 20:11f., et passim), this is most likely a citation from tradition[15] whose truth the prophet maintains, while his contemporaries' interpretation is vehemently disputed (v. 5). This is commensurate with the fact that the introduction to the divine oracle, "for (*kî*) thus says Yahweh," is consciously formulated analogous to v. 3, and that in this context v. 4, like v. 3, grounds or justifies the lament for the dead of v. 2[16]: By "seeking" Yahweh not at all, or at least only falsely, Israel has forfeited its own life.

To be sure, the condition for this promise of life, namely, the "seeking" of God (*drš*) has probably consciously been chosen because of its ambiguity. With its different meanings,[17] this term is better suited than any other for revealing the cleft between Amos and his contemporaries. In many instances, it does indeed refer to the seeking out of a sanctuary to encounter God's nearness and blessing and to call upon him in prayer. As v. 5 shows, this is apparently the

---

15. G. Warmuth, "Das Mahnwort," *BET* 1 (1976): 28f., esp. drew attention to the citation character of v. 4b. In tradition, however, such promise did mean the attainment of full life, of life in the fullest sense, whereas in the context of Amos 5 the reference is primarily to surviving catastrophe.

16. Rudolph's concessive understanding of *kî* ("to be sure, Yahweh has spoken thus") is extremely improbable given the parallel to v. 3.

17. Cf. esp. W. H. Schmidt, loc. cit. (note 2), 128ff.; S. Wagner, "*dārash*," *TDOT*, vol. 3 (Grand Rapids: Eerdmans 1978), 298–304.

only way Amos' contemporaries understood the term; pilgrimages and worship services were accordingly conducted in ever greater numbers (cf. 4:4f.; 5:21ff.). For Amos, such "seeking" leads to ruin. Far more frequently, however, this term refers to the seeking out of a prophet in a situation of distress (sickness, drought, enemy attack); through his authority for prayer and for the issuing of valid divine oracles, those in distress hoped to bring an end to the distress or at least to learn God's will in the present situation (cf. esp. Isa. 30:1f. and Hos. 10:12).[18] As we know from the first two visions (7:1–6), Amos did also intervene spontaneously for Israel in this fashion, though he soon (7:7f.; 8:1f.) had to learn the limits of God's patience with his guilty people. Nonetheless, in view of the impending destruction of the people of God and in view of the impossibility of yet pleasing God through cultic acts (cf. 4:4f.; 5:21ff.), the prophet and the prophetic word remain Israel's only possible point of contact with God, contact that is now a condition for its very survival. We do not learn more than this from v. 4b. Rather than from v. 4b, it is only from the more recent vv. 14f. that we first learn just how concretely Amos saw this possibility.[19] In any case, it was not until the later, specifically postexilic period that the concept of "seeking God" acquired the general sense of holding to God and to his will instead of to other powers. Later readers—probably already the author of v. 6—encountered Amos' words here with this particular meaning resonating in their ears.

[5:5] One is able to say much more unequivocally just what constituted such faulty "seeking of God" for Amos. For him, pilgrimage to the imperial sanctuary in Bethel, the site of the Jacob tradition, and to the venerable sanctuary of Gilgal in the Jordan depression, in which it was especially the tradition of the conquest that was preserved and kept alive (see the discussion of 4:4 above), would lead to the same destruction to which these very sanctuaries themselves would succumb (cf. 9:1ff.). The Hebrew text expresses this in wordplays on the names of the cultic sites that are difficult to imitate in translation (J. Wellhausen's translation attempt is well known: " . . . for Gilgal will go to the gallows [Ger. "Gilgal wird zum Galgen gehn"], and Bethel shall become the devil's [Ger. *Teufel*]"); the root *gālâ*, "go into exile," is taken from Gilgal, while the divine designation El in Bethel is bowdlerized into *'āwen*, "disaster" (as is the case in several instances in Hosea). Amos 5:5 does not ground this judgment; such grounding is found in (the originally immediately

18. Cf. C. Westermann, "Die Begriffe für Fragen und Suchen im Alten Testament," *KuD* 6 (1960): 2–30 repr. in *Forschung am alten Testament: Gesammelte Studien,* TB Neudrucke und Berichte aus dem 20. Jahrhundert, 24, 55 Altes Testament; vol. 2 (Munich: Kaiser, 1974), 162–90; 177ff.; J. Jeremias, *Kultprophetie,* 140–47; (G. Gerlemann and) E. Ruprecht, "*drš* fragen nach," *THAT* 1.462–65.

19. The most skeptical view is taken by A. Weiser, *Profetie,* 190ff., who understands 5:4 as being intended ironically.

following) v. 7, as well as in 4:5f. and again in the following unit 5:21ff.: The people of God have separated worship from daily life, and now engage in cultic activity at the pilgrimage sanctuaries for the sake of self-assuagement. In contradistinction to 4:4, Beer-sheba—situated deep in the south—is added, primarily as the locus of the Isaac tradition (cf. the discussion of 7:9, 16), though conspicuously only in v. 5a, and not in the words of judgment in v. 5b. The warning "do not cross over to Beer-sheba," however—on the surface an allusion to the border crossing into Judah—is picked up again at the conclusion to the pericope, where the original text used the same verb (*'ābar*) to announce Yahweh's deadly "passing through" and to associate it with pilgrimage to Beer-sheba (v. 17b). Here we can see how an earlier oral saying (yet lacking any reference to Beer-sheba) is expanded for a more complex written text. Concerning the meaning of this expansion, see the discussion of 8:14 below.

[5:6] Whereas v. 5 expands the number of condemned sanctuaries, v. 6 in a reverse fashion restricts these and concentrates on the main hotbed of sin, Bethel ("to/concerning the house of Bethel" in the sense of "because of the sin of Bethel"), as 3:14 also did in a similar fashion (cf. Hos. 10:15) as well as, implicitly, the continuation of 4:4f. in 4:6ff., especially in 4:12f. As in these exilic/postexilic texts, so also in 5:6 the catchword Bethel is referring to the faulty worship of God in Canaanite worship, or, in the language of the Deuteronomistic history: "the sin of Jeroboam." The commentary character of v. 6 is evident and has long been recognized. Verse 6 picks up on the positive aspects of the preceding divine discourse, transfers it into prophetic discourse (one would have to paraphrase: "Indeed, do what he has commanded . . . "), and structures it into an ultimative warning by appropriating the conceptuality of the oracles against the nations and depicting Yahweh (in his wrath) as a menacingly devouring fire (cf. in the earlier text Yahweh's deadly presence, v. 17b). For the Northern Kingdom (the more familiar term "house of Joseph" is cast under the influence of the unusual expression "remnant of Joseph" in v. 15), there is no defense against this danger (appropriation of the construction in v. 2b: "with no one to raise her up"). The only parallel within the book of Amos to this ultimative warning with its emphasis on the last chance is found in Amos 4:12; and just as the latter warning issues into the doxology of 4:13, so also in chap. 5 does it issue into the doxology of v. 8, separated only by the reproof of breach of justice from the earlier text, inserted for the sake of preserving the logic of the ring composition. (Within the exilic/postexilic penitential ritual, v. 7 occupies the role of 4:6–11, namely, that of emphasizing Israel's unwillingness to repent and return.)

Breach of Justice
(5:7 [C])

In the earlier text, it is not yet v. 5 with its warning against faulty seeking of
God, but rather only v. 7 (along with vv. 10–12)—with its demonstration of culpability—that reveals the real reason prompting the lamentation for Israel. Its isolated position between v. 6 and vv. 8f., a position comprehensible only from the
perspective of the ring composition, has caused problems for both earlier and more
recent exegetes. The LXX translated the verse with extremely artificial singularity and, like vv. 8f., associated it with God; the majority of more recent exegetes
(since G. A. Smith, 1896) have conjectured an expression of woe in analogy to v.
18 and 6:1, though without any real support from the textual tradition. Rather, the
participial style common in the book of Amos (cf. 3:12; 6:13, et passim) is picked
up again in v. 12b and frames the structural unit C (v. 7)—C' (vv. 10–12). For the
first time in the book of Amos, guilt or sin is conceptualized rather than presented
through individual examples (cf., e.g., 2:6–8). Israel has wasted its greatest gift. It
was especially M. Buber and, later, K. Koch[20] who demonstrated that "justice and
righteousness" in the book of Amos are not indications of the goal toward which
the people of God would have to move; that is, they do not represent guiding ideals
for behavior. Rather, these are entities already given by God, as it were internally
established qualities which Israel itself cannot create; it can, however, certainly
corrupt them by changing (the Hebrew says "overturn" in order to emphasize the
violent character of the deed) their savory sweetness into the inedible bitterness of
wormwood (which grows especially in the wilderness; 6:12 adds: turn into poison). Or it can "push them to the ground," thus robbing them of their efficacy, that
is, of their ability to protect the weak (v. 12). Here "justice" refers to the impartial
application of the law "in the gate" (cf. vv. 10, 12, 15), and "righteousness" to the
corresponding behavior in daily life allowing the other person—and the weak in
particular—to be treated justly (for particulars, cf. the discussion of v. 24 below).
Verses 10–12, which in the earlier book of Amos directly followed v. 7, show how
such breaches of justice are committed.

Doxology (5:8–9 [D])

[5:8] In the hymn of v. 8, the actions of Yahweh (singular participle)
are abruptly juxtaposed with those of Israel (plural participle). The content of the two verses also positions them antithetically: Whereas Israel

20. M. Buber, *The Prophetic Faith* (New York: Harper & Row, 1960), 100–102; K. Koch,
"Die Entstehung der sozialen Kritik bei den Profeten," in *Probleme biblischer Theologie:
Festschrift G. von Rad,* ed. H. W. Wolff (Munich: Kaiser, 1971), 236–57; 249ff. H. W. Wolff,
Amos' geistige Heimat, 40ff. (see also ET, *Amos the Prophet*), has shown that this conceptual pair
as such derives from the wisdom tradition.

"turns" justice into its opposite, Yahweh "turns" the darkness (the term used here often refers to the dangerous proximity of the realm of the dead) to light and light to darkness. Differently than in the appropriated hymnic tradition (cf. the excursus on the doxologies), in this context such "turning" refers to more than merely the creator's maintenance of the cosmos: Yahweh, who so sovereignly governs day and night, can "overturn" Israel's fate in an instant. Strikingly, Yahweh's positive act (changing darkness to morning) stands first; here the text wants primarily to encourage those who are in despair (in exile or amid severe circumstances after the exile) to "seek Yahweh" anew (v. 6), and only secondarily does it threaten destruction as v. 6b did previously.

[**5:9**] It was presumably these brighter tones that prompted a later poet in v. 9—even after the emphatic conclusion to the traditional hymn with "Yahweh his name" (v. 8; cf. 4:13; 9:6)—to emphasize the destructive power of God's actions, influenced perhaps by 4:11, which compared the destruction of Jerusalem with the "overthrow" of Sodom and Gomorrah. During the late period of the Old Testament, such anticipation of destruction coming precisely against the "strong" implies a warning against arrogant self-confidence.

[**(5:8)**] Yet even the earlier hymn probably did not—as tradition presumably did—employ the notion of Yahweh collecting water and pouring it out over the earth as a reference to the fructifying, vivifying acts of God, but rather much more likely as a recollection of destructive storms or (with the rabbinic tradition [*b. Ber.* 59a]) of the Flood (Koch). Elsewhere, the most frequent object by far associated with Yawheh's "pouring out" is his wrath.[21] The most uncertain interpretation is that of the first, isolated statement in v. 8a, which praises Yahweh's activity as creator in heaven rather than on earth (mountains and wind in 4:13). Either the "Pleiades and Orion" (which also occur as a pair in Job 9:9 and 38:31) are to be associated with the change of seasons such that the "turning" of darkness to light would be anticipated by the alternation of heat and cold,[22] or the sentence is to be understood as religious polemic against the temptations of the Babylonian astral cult (cf. 5:26).

---

21. This predication has presumably been appropriated from the parallel in 9:6, since it uses participles with the article as otherwise only 9:5f. does (Crüsemann, *Studien zur Formgeschichte von Hymnus und Danklied in Israel,* WMANT 32 [Neukirchen-Vluyn: Neukirchener Verlag, 1969], 100). By contrast, many exegetes assume that 9:5f. only gradually grew to its present length. However that may be, in the present text 5:8 constitutes a kind of prelude to the more unequivocal statement in 9:6, in which the allusion to the Flood is quite tangible. (This is why the Masoretes vocalized the final verb as narrative.)

22. So Rudolph, following Fohrer (in the latter's commentary to Job), and esp. K. Koch, "Die Rolle der hymnischen Abschnitte in der Komposition des Amos-Buches," *ZAW* 86 (1974): 517–20, who considers the two constellations primarily as weather initiators.

However that may be, in the final stage Amos 5:1–17 constitutes a parallel composition to 4:4–13, as Wolff already recognized. During the exile, the warning passed down from Amos against pilgrimages to Bethel and Gilgal (4:4f.; 5:5) became an accusation associated with the fundamental perversion of true worship specifically in Bethel: The acknowledgement that Israel was previously incapable of turning away from "Bethel"—despite the fall of both Samaria and Jerusalem (4:6–11; 5:4f.)—leads in both instances to an ultimative warning (4:12; 5:6) issuing in a doxology (4:13; 5:8[f.]) with which the survivors of the catastrophe of exile should (1) acknowledge that God's past judgment actually constituted just punishment, and (2) seize the last chance for reorienting their lives. In both instances, Yahweh's singularity ("Yahweh his name") comes to expression in his act of "overturning" (4:11 [13]; 5:8).

Breach of Justice and Oppression
(5:10–13 [C′])

[5:10, 12] The perversion of justice about which v. 7 had spoken in a fundamental, metaphorical fashion, is depicted in vv. 10 and 12 through concrete examples taken from the administration of justice in the city gate. The space in the arcade of the city gate with its chambers or, in certain instances, the open space between the outer and inner gate, usually represented the only free area in the densely populated cities of the ancient Orient. This administration of justice without any professional officials—such are attested only in the Southern Kingdom in the capital of Jerusalem, presumably in connection with revisionary procedures—is based essentially on the integrity of the judge appointed from the circle of elders (v. 10a) and, to an equal extent, on the reliability (in the original text literally "the completeness") of the statements by witnesses (v. 10b), which generally provided the background evidence on which the judge's decision was based. It is precisely these sensitive parts of the application of law that the wealthy and powerful exploit to their own advantage (v. 12b). Both by paying bribes and by exerting their personal influence, they steer decisions in their own interests; in so doing, they necessarily become enemies to those who should receive justice from the court (in Hebrew, "innocent" is the accompanying adjective to the concept of "righteousness") but who, because they lack such power and influence, are turned away (2:7 uses the same verb to refer to the rejection of a person's legal concerns).[23] The reader senses the indignation in the prophet's words as he moves from portraying injustice (v. 10) to addressing the guilty (cf. 6:3); he describes their mode of bend-

---

23. Concerning this usage, cf. G. Liedke, *Gestalt und Bezeichnung alttestamentlicher Rechtssätze*, WMANT 39 (Neukirchen-Vluyn: Neukirchener Verlag, 1971), esp. 93.

ing justice with the harshest designation for sin in the Old Testament, namely, "transgression" (v. 12a; cf. 1:3ff.; 2:6, et passim). His emotion becomes fully comprehensible only when one considers that the "justice in the gate" of the Old Testament regulated much more comprehensive civil claims than does our own system of justice, and to that extent the justice a given individual did or did not receive there far more frequently affected that person's overall existence, including, for example, the person's "honor" (that is, his position and respect in the community). Hence an intact society that yet permits corrupt administration of justice is for Amos an impossibility of far different proportions than for modernity.

[**5:11**] Section C', however, is intent on presenting a more comprehensive demonstration of guilt than C (v. 7). Hence between v. 10 and v. 12, commensurate with the conceptual rhythm of the ring composition, a saying focused on social thematic has been inserted; this saying presumably once constituted an independent rhetorical unit, since (1) it is introduced in this context rather circumstantially ("therefore because . . . "); (2) it concludes with its own oracle of disaster, in contrast to vv. 7, 10, 12; and (3) it has no part in the linguistic links between vv. 7, 10, 12, and vv. 14f. (see below). Rather than introducing a new theme, v. 11, positioned as it is between the verses addressing the bending of justice, intends to make it quite clear that such perversion of justice causes the entire social order to collapse, since the actions of the powerful are no longer subject to any functioning control. This is demonstrated by the example of public dues, which apparently burdened the poor with excessive levies of natural produce that threatened their very existence.[24] The merciless wealthy, those who profit from such injustice, lived in palace-like houses built of hewn stones instead of clay bricks or field stone, and owned precious vineyards. The prophet threatens them with an imprecatory form common in the ancient Orient (the so-called curse of futility), one that associates a meaningful activity with a meaningless outcome[25]; such people are heading for destruction.

[**5:13**] For the rest, however, vv. 10–12 lack any announcement of divine judgment, since they are related to the lamentation in vv. 2f. and 16f.

---

24. Cf. the thorough argumentation for this interpretation in Fleischer, loc. cit., 164ff. Private leases of the sort suggested by most exegetes are not attested in Palestine until after the beginning of the Hellenistic period.

25. Cf., e.g., Hos. 4:10; Micah 6:14f.; concerning the parallels from the ancient Orient, cf. W. Schottroff, *Der altisraelitische Fluchspruch,* WMANT 30 (Neukirchen-Vluyn: Neukirchener Verlag, 1969), 67f., 153ff., and recently T. Podella, "Notzeit-Mythologem und Nichtigkeitsfluch," in *Religionsgeschichtliche Beziehungen zwischen Kleinasien, Nordsyrien, und dem Alten Testament,* ed. B. Janowski, K. Koch, and G. Wilhelm, OBO 129 (Fribourg, Switzerland: Universitätsverlag; Göttingen: Vandenhoeck & Ruprecht, 1993), 427–54; 428–38. The imprecatory form makes it clear that in oral discourse, v. 11 addressed a limited group of persons; in the context of 5:1–17, their behavior exemplifies that of all Israelites. Cf. also the revocation of the curse at the end of the book in 9:14f.

After the exile and from the circle of the wisdom tradition, a later reader used this gap to draw attention to the "evil time"[26] under which he understood his own generation in light of Amos' words, and to warn against inappropriate speech, that is, presumably against any intrusive objections to God's chastising acts (cf. the friends in the book of Job). Amos himself was not silent, trying rather to shake his contemporaries to their senses.

Conditional Promise of Life
(5:14–15 [B'])

The earlier text culminates conceptually in the admonitory saying in vv. 14f. The conceptual progression has moved from the sentence of death (A) to the demonstration of wasted life (B), and thence to the accusation of having destroyed the community through breach of justice (C). Before arriving once more at the sentence of death (A'), the possibility of life is mentioned one more time, albeit in an extremely restricted fashion. One can easily see that vv. 14f. (like v. 6) provide an interpretation of the divine oracle of v. 4b; compare merely the more urgent final clause "that you may live" with the traditional "and live" of v. 4b. A more important observation is that even the wording of vv. 14f. makes references to the discussion of Israel's sin in vv. 7–13* (i.e., vv. 7, 10–12); v. 15a appropriates the verb "hate" from v. 10, the indication of place "in the gate" from v. 10 and v. 12, and the term "justice" from v. 7. Hence one can understand vv. 14f. only after having read vv. 7–13*; they are definitely not to be appended directly to vv. 4–6 (so Rudolph and others). Verses 14f. are not concerned with the possibility of life in any general sense, but rather with the possibility of life in the face of God's sentence of death (A) based on Israel's own breach of justice (C). Expressed differently: verses 14f. were never an independent saying (as vv. 4f. presumably were); they are not older than the ring composition itself, but rather constitute its hinge insofar as they relate Amos' message of disaster to his promise of life, and thus inquire concerning the totality of Amos' proclamation.

This creates a seemingly contradictory situation for vv. 14f. On the one hand, God's sentence of death over Israel is firm; the conceptual progression moves toward vv. 16f. On the other hand, this death is not fated, but rather can in principle be avoided. Indeed, for Amos and his tradents, this requires merely something quite self-evident, or even something immediately at hand; one need only transfer the summons to "seek God" from v. 4b to the "seeking of good." Anyone familiar with the Old Testament knows immediately that this concept of "the good" is not concealing some philosophical system of virtue. It is equally impossible to understand this concept as a summary of all the regula-

---

26. In Micah 2:3, as well, the "evil time" represents circumstances after the exile.

tions of the commandments. The situation here is rather that described by G. von Rad in 1960[27]: "This is not the language of a man who wants to regulate life by law. In Amos's view, what Jahweh desires from Israel is something very clear and simple." In this, Amos and his tradents by no means stand alone among the prophets. The contemporaries Hosea (8:3), Isaiah (5:20), and especially Micah (3:2) spoke quite similarly about "the good"; a full century later, Jeremiah uses slightly different terminology in speaking about the same thing: "Doing justice and righteousness" for him is identical with "knowledge of Yahweh" (Jer. 23:15f., et passim), and the anonymous prophet in Micah 6:8 reminds "every person" individually that "you have been told what is good. . . ."

The particular emphases of Amos' own words are discernible from three features. First, vv. 14f. derive from a situation of dialogue and are arguing polemically against a salvific faith that from the promise of God's protective presence in the cult derives a justification for libertinism of action. Such faith is attested specifically with regard to Jerusalem (cf. Micah 3:11: "Yahweh is with us! No harm shall come upon us," or Jeremiah's temple sermon, Jer. 7), and the formulation of v. 14b, recalling the Zion psalms,[28] sooner suggests that the categories used in describing this dispute were drawn from the Jerusalem worship service.

[5:15] Second, the summons to do good in v. 15 is described concretely such that, on the one hand, the revulsion against evil[29] stands first and is consciously expressed by the same verb that in v. 10 refers to the revulsion the guilty experience before the upright decision of the judge; on the other hand, however, the contrasting concept of the "love of good" lends this summons an emotional component. Third—and above all—the "establishment of justice in the gate," by referring back to vv. 7–13*, introduces an indispensable concrete component of "the good": the application of law free of outside influence. For Amos and his tradents, absolutely everything depends on this. Without it, Israel cannot be God's people; and without it, Israel's survival is impossible.

But is this survival possible even with it, given the now irreversible devastation among the people of God? This notion is expressed at the end, but only with the most extreme caution and reserve. Rescue is yet possible, but at most

27. G. von Rad, *Old Testament Theology,* vol. 2, trans. D. M. G. Stalker (New York/Evanston: Harper & Row, 1965), 186.

28. Cf. esp. the plural in "Yahweh with you" with the refrain in Ps. 46 ("Yahweh of hosts is with us"). The Zion psalms can also be evoked later by the metrically superfluous, solemn divine predication "Yahweh, the God of hosts" (vv. 14b, 15b, 16a), whose intention is to recall for postexilic readers the content of the doxologies (4:13; 5:8; 9:5f.). Concerning their polemical meaning (against the cult of Bethel, v. 6), cf. the exegesis of 4:13.

29. With this term, the tradents are picking up formally on Amos' own warning against faulty seeking of God through pilgrimages (variously: "do not seek . . . ")! The content of "evil" was explicated in vv. 7, 10–12. For 5:21–24, too, these two aspects (worship and justice) belong inextricably together.

only for "the remnant of Joseph." "Joseph" refers either (as does "Ephraim" in Hos. 4ff.) to the torso state of the Northern Kingdom left on the mount after the Assyrian provinces of Dor, Megiddo, and Gilead were separated in 733 B.C.E.—almost three decades after Amos—or to the surviving inhabitants after the fall of Samaria itself in 722. In any case, the designation "Joseph," which no other prophet from the eighth century uses, consciously avoids the name "Israel." We can no longer determine whether the term "remnant" is simultaneously suggesting that only a limited number of inhabitants will be able to change their behavior. Yet even this changed "remnant" will only "perhaps" be preserved. Amos was called to announce to a guilty Israel God's "punishment" (3:2) and his deadly proximity (5:17); his tradents do not dare portray to their own generation God's salvation in any bright colors, a generation that already had experienced this judgment at least partially; they do, however, leave space for God's own freedom to restrict his chastising actions and to allow compassion to reign in some as yet unforeseeable way. This "perhaps" has undergone a significant history of influence within the Old Testament; compare especially Zeph. 2:3; Joel 2:14; and Jonah 3:9. Rabbi Ami reportedly wept every time he read scriptural passages with the divine "perhaps" (*b. Ḥag.* 4b). In context, however, its intention is not just restricting; it simultaneously seeks to touch on God's concern even for those worthy of death if they have the strength to change. This concern surpasses his loyalty to his own chastising word.

God's Deadly Proximity
(5:16–17 [A'])

The only thing certain for both Amos himself and his tradents is that which has been immediately commissioned, namely, the lamentation, standing over chaps. 5–6 in the manner of a superscription (cf. v. 1). It is all-comprehensive in the strictest sense, excludes no one, and applies both inside and outside—everywhere in the city, and everywhere in the fields. The working farmers must be fetched to support the lamenting women, whose number no longer suffices for the dead. Attention passes finally to the vineyards as the site of greatest joy, since the harvest of wine and oil was the greatest occasion for Israel's festival of joy as such; even they are transformed into places of mourning. After all these enumerations of places of lament, and all the enumerations of those affected by grief, the brief justification—comprising only two words and once more confirmed in a concluding fashion as the words of Yahweh—comes as a crushing blow. It is not God's absence that leads to Israel's death, but rather: "I will pass through the midst of you." With this uniquely formulated concluding sentence, the composition returns to the collective perspective of the beginning ("maiden Israel," 5:2; cf. by contrast the plural imperatives "seek . . . " in vv. 4, 6, 14). This statement evokes two associations. The first is of a traditio-historical nature, recalling the departure event at the exodus as it is evoked anew in every Passover celebration; there Israel celebrates the fact that it was spared while Yahweh "passed through" Egypt and slew the firstborn. Now it is Israel itself that is threatened, and not merely its firstborn. The other association concerns Amos' third and fourth visions, where the end of God's patience and willingness to forgive are described with the same verb, though with a different preposition such that Yahweh now can "no longer pass them (i.e., Israel) by" (*'ābar lě:* 7:8; 8:2). Amos 5:17 describes the alternative: the deadly act of "passing through the midst of " (*'ābar bě*). If Yahweh acts thus, Israel is lost; its "end has come" (8:2). In this situation, the divine "perhaps" of 5:15 is Israel's only hope.

The First Woe (The Day of Yahweh)
Amos 5:18–27

5:18 Alas for those who desire the day of Yahweh!
Why do you want the day of Yahweh?
It is darkness, not light;
19 as if someone fled from a lion,
and was met by a bear;
or went into the house and rested a hand against the wall,
and was bitten by a snake.
20 Is not the day of Yahweh darkness, not light,
and gloom[1] with no brightness in it?

21 I hate, I despise[2] your festivals
and I take no delight in your solemn assemblies.
22 *Unless you were to bring me burnt offerings!*[3]
I will not accept your grain offerings;
and your offering meals of fatted animals
I will not look upon.
23 Take away from me the noise of your songs;
I will not listen to the melody of your harps.

1. All versions vocalize the Hebrew consonants as a substantive; only the MT vocalizes as an adjective ("dark").

2. As is often the case with verbs of feeling and thinking, the perfect has present meaning; cf. Joüon, section 112a; Brockelmann, *Syntax,* section 41c.

3. The frequently expressed assumption that v. 22aα is to be understood as an accusation whose second part was mistakenly omitted, falters on the fact that only v. 22aα interrupts the "I" of Yahweh, and only the "burnt offerings" in v. 22aα stand without the suffix "your."

24 But let justice roll down like waters,
    and righteousness like an ever-flowing stream.
25 Did you bring me sacrifices *and grain offerings the forty years* in
    the wilderness, O house of Israel?
26 *And did you[4] take up Sakkuth[5] your king, and Kaiwan,[5] your
    images,
    your star-god, which you made for yourselves?*
27 Therefore I will take you into exile beyond Damascus,
    says Yahweh, *whose name is the God of hosts.*

Bibliography: C. van Leeuwen, "The Prophecy of the Yōm YHWH in Amos V, 18–20," *OTS* 19 (1974): 113–34; W. Würthwein, "Kultpolemik oder Kultbescheid?" in *Tradition und Situation: Studien zur alttestamentlichen Prophetie: Festschrift A. Weiser* (Göttingen: Vandenhoeck & Ruprecht, 1963), 115–31, reprinted in idem, *Wort und Existenz* (Göttingen: Vandenhoeck & Ruprecht, 1970), 144–60; A. B. Ernst, "Weisheitliche Kultkritik," *BThSt* 23 (1994): 99–126.

Amos 5:18–27 is composed of two originally independent rhetorical units: an oracle of woe concerning the hope of Amos' contemporaries in Yahweh's ultimate fulfillment of salvation on the "day of Yahweh," an oracle still clearly exhibiting the character of dialogue or disputation (vv. 18–20: prophetic discourse), and an oracle of cult criticism progressing from an admonition to practice justice and righteousness to a concluding announcement of judgment (vv. 21–24, 27: divine discourse). These two oral units, however, are intended to be read together as a unified written text. This is clear not only from the fact that v. 21 follows vv. 18–20 seamlessly and without any transition, but also and especially from the fact that the structure of vv. 18–27 as a whole (through the addition of v. 25) exactly parallels chap. 6. Both compositions are structured in four progressive parts: First, in each instance, a conceptually self-enclosed cry of woe against excessive self-confidence stands at the beginning in the form of prophetic discourse (5:18–20; 6:1–7). There then follows divine discourse in which Yahweh's revulsion and antipathy toward Israel's behavior and life are expressed with the most penetrating incisiveness and in part identical wording ("I hate," 5:21; 6:8). Next, a question follows as the most striking element and the one most in need of interpreta-

4. Many modern exegetes (e.g., Weiser, Rudolph) understand the verb in v. 26 as perfect consecutive, i.e., as future, in the sense of an announcement of disaster. Militating against this is not only the understanding of all the versions, but also that of the final addendum to the text itself (" . . . which you made for yourselves"). A. S. van der Woude, "Bemerkungen zu einigen umstrittenen Stellen im Zwölfprophetenbuch," in *De la Torah au Messie: Festschrift H. Cazelles,* ed. M. Carrez, J. Doré, and P. Grelot; AOAT 212 (Paris: Desclée, 1981), 486f., discusses significant substantive counterarguments. Concerning the two possibilities for translation, cf. *G–K²⁸,* 112x and 112rr.

5. The Masoretes distorted the Assyrian-Babylonian divine names with the vowels of *šiqqûṣ,* "abomination."

tion (5:25; 6:12). Finally, the divine sentence of chastisement announces exile and persecution by a hostile nation (5:27; 6:14). Despite differences regarding details, this parallel structure between 5:18–27 and chap. 6 is so obvious that the two textual complexes must be interpreted in analogy to one another, like two strophes of the same poem.

The Day of Yahweh
(5:18–20)

[5:18] Both larger units begin with an "alas, woe," which in the original text evoked a tone incomparably more severe than that evoked by our own terms of lament, "woe" and "alas." *Hôy* is the central catchword of the funeral lamentation as announced in 5:1 in the manner of a superscription and then also carried out immediately before the present pericope (v. 16: *hô-hô*); a mere few decades earlier, the cry of the lamenting women, " *'Abbā' hālak, hôy hôy,*" "the father has gone away, woe, woe," could yet be heard in the streets of Jerusalem. To that extent, the same applies to this "woe, alas" as was said about the lament for the dead in 5:2: Presumably the first person to do so,[6] Amos uses a familiar genre in a daring and completely new way not only by transferring its individual manner of expression (i.e., the lament over an individual dead person) to a collective, but also and especially by addressing the living persons standing before him as persons who are already dead. As elsewhere as well (3:12; 5:7; 6:13), he uses the participle to characterize the culpable parties (as the continuation shows, in the vocative), except that here (as well as in the following piece, vv. 21ff.) he denounces not their injustice, but rather their insufficient or even completely absent consciousness of sin.

The concept of the "day of Yahweh" colors the entire history of prophecy after Amos, and particularly that of the postexilic period; the most famous passages include Isaiah 2 and 13, Zephaniah 1, and above all the book of Joel, whose central theme it constitutes. A whole series of features emerges ever more clearly that are constitutive for Yahweh's hostile acts—either against Israel or against its enemies. In Amos 5, the oldest occurrence, no such fixed conceptual notion is yet perceivable. Rather, this text reflects a passionate dispute between Amos and his audience concerning the character of the "day of Yahweh." (Cf. the utterly atypical argumentative questions in the oracle of woe in

---

6. Both E. Gerstenberger, "The Woe-Oracles of the Prophets," *JBL* 81 (1962): 249–63, and H. W. Wolff, 242ff. (concerning 5:7), as well as Wolff earlier in *Amos' geistige Heimat,* 12ff. (see also ET, *Amos the Prophet*), suspected that tribal wisdom already formulated oracles of woe with participles. This thesis has received a largely critical reaction, and has been disputed with weighty arguments esp. by C. Hardmeier, "Texttheorie und biblische Exegese: Zur rhetorischen Funktion der Trauermetaphorik in der Prophetie," *BEvT* 79 (1978): (esp.) 256ff.

vv. 18b, 20, in which the prophet is not, however, concerned with weighing various points of view, but with life and death, as shown by the "woe, alas.") Amos did not coin this term, but rather vehemently contradicts the understanding of its content in the opinion of his audience. The context reveals unequivocally only that for Amos' contemporaries, the "day of Yahweh" was something to be desired, apparently the fulfillment of salvation in respite before all enemies and in a final, ultimate revelation of God.[7] Although Amos does not deny that the "day of Yahweh" fundamentally may indeed bear such features, he does deny such for his own contemporaries (cf. the emphatic "you" in the question of v. 18b). For him, the "day of Yahweh" seems essentially to demonstrate its ultimate character in its conclusive revelation of the relationship between Yahweh and Israel. This relationship, however, is such that this encounter between Israel and its God can only end in death, analogous to God's deadly "passing through" in the immediately preceding verse.

[5:19] The two interwoven similes from the life sphere of a shepherd in v. 19 are supposed to document this; each begins with the fortunate rescue of someone from the most extreme mortal danger (escape, return home to the protection of one's own house) and ends in the unexpected, deadly actions of an animal. Together, they state that despite any previous experiences of deliverance—experiences with which Amos is just as familiar as are his self-confident listeners—only one thing is certain for Israel on the "day of Yahweh": sudden death, however it might occur. (Concerning the inescapability of death, compare 2:14–16 and 9:2–4.)

[5:20] This death is also the focus of the symbolic language, familiar especially from the psalms, framing the animal similes both as an anticipatory thesis (v. 18bβ) and as a conclusion from the simile itself (v. 20); it uses "light" for life (Ps. 36:10 [9E], et passim), and "darkness" for death (Isa. 9:1 [2E], et passim). This is the same language that on the first day of creation distinguishes the condition for life (the created "light") from the previous chaos ("darkness"), from which that "light" is expressly separated (Gen. 1:2–4). The concluding statement, " . . . with no brightness in it," extinguishes any nascent glimmer of hope.[8]

7. The former emerges indirectly from the simile in v. 19, the latter from the positioning of v. 18 after v. 17 (where God's proximity means death for Israel), and both together from the concept *nōgah,* "brightness" (v. 20b), which is negated at the conclusion and which in numerous passages (Ps. 18:13, 29 [12, 28E] par. 2 Sam. 22:13, 29; Hab. 3:4, 11; cf. Isa. 9:1 [2E]) depicts Yahweh coming to help his people; cf. F. Schnutenhaus, "Das Kommen und Erscheinen Gottes im Alten Testament," *ZAW* 76 (1964): 98f. These statements do not enable us to reconstruct any popular understanding of eschatological expectation (cf. esp. H. Gressmann, *Der Ursprung der israelitisch-jüdischen Eschatologie,* FRLANT 6 [Göttingen: Vandenhoeck & Ruprecht, 1905], 141ff.) or any form of eschatologie mediated through the cult (S. Mowinckel, *Psalmenstudien II: Das Thronbesteigungsfest Jahwäs und der Ursprung der Eschatologie* [Oslo: J. Dybwad, 1924], 229ff.).

8. As Weiser and Rudolph have shown, the darkness in this concluding statement is sustained in the Hebrew by the accumulation of O-sounds carrying forward the *hôy* of the lamentation.

The Rejection of Worship Activities
(5:21–27)

Amos 5:21–27 seamlessly follows 5:18–20, but then abruptly changes — without any introduction — from prophetic to divine discourse, something not formally discernible as such until the divine oracular formula at the end of v. 27. The logical relationship between the two parts corresponds to that between v. 2 and v. 3: Just as there the prophetic lamentation for Israel needs the divine oracle as its grounding, so also is the prophetic thesis in 5:18ff. — namely, that the "day of Yahweh" means death for Israel — grounded in the divine rejection of Israel's worship. Lacking any possibility of contact with God, Israel is already the living dead.

It is not just since the Enlightenment that interpreters have struggled and argued intensively concerning the understanding of the pericope 5:21–27, which contains Amos' most severe criticism of the cult. This was already the case during the Old Testament period itself, as shown by the three interpretations that have accrued to the text in v. 22aα, v. 25, and v. 26, interpretations that are utterly different, though composed consistently in prose. In modernity, the understanding of the pericope by liberal theology has exerted the greatest influence. It found in 5:21ff. the core of Amos' message, and cast this into a succinct formulation asserting that Amos demanded justice instead of worship, that is, a supplanting of cultic religion by correct behavior on the part of human beings freed from the obligations of external ceremonies.[9] All subsequent exegetes either explicitly or implicitly deal with this understanding.

[5:21–23] Any exegesis must take as its point of departure a double basis. First, the rejection of worship activities begins with a bang: The harshest and most emotionally-laden verbs come first, and do so in contrasting perfects, whereas after v. 21b modal or iterative verb forms predominate. Since God's rejection begins substantively with comprehensive items — the festivals (v. 21) — and only afterward mentions sacrifices (v. 22) and music (v. 23), this criticism clearly is not addressing substantive details of the cult; rather, festivals, sacrifices, and music represent *pars pro toto* the worship service as a whole, and together constitute a contrast to "justice and righteousness" (v. 24). To this extent, the understanding of liberal theology seems to be correct.

Second, as in 4:4f., Amos consciously picks up anew on *priestly* language and decisively recasts it; that is, he again slips into the clothing of an alien office. This is evident in the case of the substantives: The priest summoned Israel to "festivals" (primarily the three great pilgrimage festivals are so designated) and to "solemn assemblies" (the Hebrew term connotes primarily abstinence from work); it was naturally the priest who presented sacrifices — viewed in v.

---

9. It was P. Volz who saw most sharply in Amos 5 a separation occurring between prophetic and cultic religion (*ZST* 14 [1937]: 63–85). Cf. from contemporary scholarship the superscription in Rudolph's commentary: "Not the Cult, but rather Justice."

22 with respect to the two essential functions of the early period, as the gift (cereal offering) and as the establishment of fellowship;[10] and at least in Jerusalem, in addition to professional musicians and singing guilds (or, later, Levites), the priests were responsible for music during worship ("songs," i.e., vocalists, and "melodies" of musical instruments are common terms in the psalms; the "harp" or—another suggestion—the "lyre" or "lute" is one of the two oldest stringed instruments in the Old Testament).[11]

Of much greater significance, however, are the verbs and their function, appropriated almost without exception from the official sphere of the priest. This applies most clearly to the verb "accept" (*rṣh*) with God as its subject in v. 22. With this verb, the priest pronounced whether a sacrificial animal or act was or was not accepted, that is, whether the animal or act was or was not commensurate with the ritual regulations (Lev. 1:3f.; 7:18ff.; 9:5–7; 22:23, 27, et passim; cf. Jer. 14:12; Ps. 51:18 [16E]).[12] Quite the same applies in substance to Yahweh "taking delight in [savoring]" these sacrifices (cf. Gen. 8:21; Lev. 26:31; 1 Sam. 26:19), which to be sure is never used technically in ritual prescriptions and in Amos 5:21 is already being applied freely to worship activities as a whole. A different sphere of priestly judgment is evoked by the wordpair "(love—) hate" with Yahweh as the subject, deriving from the torah, that is, from instruction in daily life (cf. Pss. 11:5, 7; 33:5; 37:28; and esp. Isa. 61:8; perverted in Amos 4:5).[13] A third and final sphere of such activity is evoked by the verb "hear" or "not hear," with Yahweh as the subject; it was with this verb that the priests usually pronounced whether Yahweh had heard (answered) or rejected the prayers of individuals (cf. esp. Jer. 14:11f.).[14]

10. Cf. R. Rendtorff, *Studien zur Geschichte des Opfers im Alten Israel,* WMANT 24 (Neukirchen-Vluyn: Neukirchener Verlag, 1967), 191f. The restriction of the *minḥâ* to vegetable offerings takes place only later (Rendtorff, ibid., 192f.). Mention of the "fatted animals" at the meal offering (offering of well-being; only here in the Old Testament in the singular *šlm*) is probably already alluding to the theme of luxurious enjoyment in Amos 6:4–6; cf. in this regard also Hos. 8:13; Jer. 7:21.

11. Cf. Wolff, in loc.; most recently H.-P. Rüger, "Musikinstrumente," *BRL²*, 234–36, and H. Seidel, *Musik in Altisrael: Untersuchungen zur Musikgeschichte und Musikpraxis Altisraels anhand biblischer und ausserbiblischer Texte,* BEAT 12 (Frankfurt am Main/New York: Peter Lang, 1989) (each with bibliography).

12. Cf. the argumentation in Rendtorff, loc. cit., 253ff.; prior to that in *TLZ* 82 (1956): 339–42, and already E. Würthwein, "Amos 5:21–27 (1947)," in idem, *Wort und Existenz* (Göttingen: Vandenhoeck & Ruprecht, 1970), 55–67.

13. In context, this simultaneously picks up on Israel's own "hate": Because Israel hates not "evil" (v. 15), but rather a just decision (v. 10), Yahweh accordingly "hates" its festivals, i.e., any contact with Israel.

14. I have elsewhere (*Kultprophetie,* 159, following J. Begrich, "Das priesterliche Heilsorakel [1936]," *Gesammelte Studien zum Alten Testament,* TB 21, ed. Walther Zimmerli [Munich: Kaiser, 1964]s. 217ff.) tried to show that this is sooner referring to priestly than to prophetic functions (so E. Würthwein, "Kultpolemik oder Kultbescheid? Beobachtungen zu dem Thema 'Prophetie und Kult,'" in idem, *Wort und Existenz* [Göttingen: Vandenhoeck & Ruprecht, 1970], 144–60, 155ff.).

There are three fundamental differences, however, between the original use of this language by the priests and its new use by Amos: (1) The priests conveyed the sacrificial acknowledgment impersonally (in what is known as the *passivum divinum*), and passed on the torah in a detached, instructional fashion ("what Yahweh loves/hates"); Amos speaks his own judgment in the authoritative "I" of Yahweh. (2) The priests were charged with either accepting or rejecting in God's commission a single sacrificial animal, a single act, a single prayer; Amos' judgment in the name of God rejects Israel's worship as a whole. This potential did not inhere in priestly language as such.[15] (3) The priests issue summons to "festivals for Yahweh," to "sacrifices for Yahweh"; Amos' God sees only "your festivals," "your sacrifices" before him, that is, rites unable to reach or affect him (cf. "for so *you* love to do . . ." in 4:5). In Amos 5:21ff., then, it is not the significance of worship that is being weighed against the significance of the ethos such that worship activities, compared with that ethos, are devalued (as liberal theology imagines); rather, Israel in its sin is being told that its worship activities are no longer reaching God in the first place, and to that extent have become perverted into "service to oneself." For Amos, this is the case not because sacrifices are offered falsely (so the later, probably postexilic v. 22aα), and certainly not because foreign powers are venerated (so the later continuation in v. 26), but rather because without "justice and righteousness" (v. 24) there is no possibility for contact between Israel and God to begin with. Israel celebrates Yahweh as if its relationship with God were intact, utterly unaware that he is not even present at the celebration. To that extent, the "end of Israel" (8:2) already commences in the rejection of its worship. The inefficacy and meaninglessness of its worship is a manifest sign that Israel is only seemingly yet alive, and in reality is not only consecrated to death, but indeed is already dead, and as such is the object of the lamentation the prophet strikes up in vv. 1f., vv. 16f., and v. 18.

[5:24] In all this, however, what God expects from Israel[16]—and yet what the automated nature of worship now virtually obstructs—is not some great effort or accomplishment, but rather that which is the closest and most natural thing in the world for the people of God. As already pointed out in

---

15. This distinction becomes most evident in the use of non-priestly verbs: in v. 21 in the intensifying "I despise, reject," and in v. 23 in the transition to the imperfect (or infinitive absolute) "away from me . . . ," which is associated with what is probably intended as an intensifying transition to singular address. This intensification in its own turn, along with the singing of psalms, refers precisely to the most intimate sphere of worship.

16. The older understanding of v. 24 as an oracle of judgment (Keil, Sellin, Weiser), already problematical because of the jussive in v. 24a, and especially given the imagery in v. 24b, has been refuted often; cf., e.g., Rudolph, 211f., and J. Vollmer, *Geschichtliche Rückblicke*, 42f., n. 154.

reference to v. 7, "justice and righteousness" for both Amos and the other classical prophets are not some sort of behavioral goals, but rather primarily gifts from God which Israel can allow to flourish, can support, or can obstruct, indeed (5:7; 6:12) can "overthrow." Amos is in no way thinking of collective life ordered by individual regulations, but rather of the possibility of solving impartially conflicts that may arise in the community ("justice"), and of a basic disposition on the part of individuals that takes the good of the community as its behavioral orientation, with special attention given to the weak and the poor. In the Old Testament, "righteousness" is a relational concept; hence there are no gradations, that is, no partial or "approximate" righteousness. "Righteousness" is either actualized or is absent altogether. This is related to the fact that in the concept of "righteousness," deed and consequence coincide; "righteousness" refers thus equally to behavior for the good of the community as well as the good of that community which it brings about (cf., e.g., the righteous actions of the king in Ps. 72:2 with 72:3, which describes the almost naturally produced good fortune issuing from such righteousness). Ultimately, however, such good fortune is not produced by human beings; it is God's fortune. This is why in the psalm just cited (Ps. 72), the congregation petitions God so ardently at the enthronement festival for the bestowal of "your judicial authority" and "your righteousness" upon the king (v. 1), since these gifts of God are the precondition for all righteous actions and thus for all good fortune. Amos intends something comparable here: Israel has had so many experiences with God's "righteousness," that is, with his salvific good fortune—for example, in his deliverance from the far more powerful Amorites (2:9)—that it can hardly keep "righteousness" from flowing both freely and even perpetually (so the comparison with the brook that does not dry up even in the summer).

Did Amos yet believe it possible for Israel, who "brings righteousness to the ground" (v. 7), to change? There is even less chance of answering this question than in the case of 5:4. It is striking, however, that in the book of Amos the word pair "justice and righteousness" is restricted to chaps. 5–6, which, despite the dark undertones of lamentation and in contrast to all other chapters in the older book of Amos, yet exhibit a certain openness, either through words of admonition such as 5:4–6 and 14f., or through didactic questions such as 5:25 and 6:12, whose intention is to facilitate a certain degree of insight. If not the prophet Amos himself, then at least his tradents did not use the conceptual pair "justice and righteousness" primarily in their accusation (so 5:7), but rather more likely—in an admonitory or questioning fashion—to point out a possible path.

[5:25] After 722, the tradents specified these guidelines more precisely; with reference to the theology of Hosea, they used the didactic question in v. 25 to confront the present—characterized by sacrificial worship—with the wanderings in the wilderness as the time of ideal fellowship with God.[17] It is not their intention to instruct their contemporaries about history—the discussion of some "age of Moses without sacrifices" is looking past the text itself—but rather to guide them away from their trust in automated "righteousness" generated by the performance of as many sacrifices as possible (cf., e.g., Hos. 8:11–13; 10:1f.) and toward the salvific beginnings of genuine fellowship with God in the wilderness (e.g., Hos. 9:10; 2:16f. [14f.E]) as the model of "righteousness" that is genuinely lived. For Hosea and, following him, the disciples of Amos (as well as for the tradents of Jeremiah, see Jer; 2:2f.; 7:22f.), the period of the wanderings in the wilderness was to that extent the model of living, actualized "righteousness"; at that time, faith was not in danger of being overwhelmed by the cult of Baal—something that became quite obvious in Israel's sacrificial mentality[18]; Israel was dependent solely on Yahweh. Amos himself nowhere mentions Baalism as a threat; his tradents, however, clearly saw that his criticism of the cult was continued with equal astuteness by the prophet of the Northern Kingdom, Hosea.

[5:26] During the exilic or postexilic period, the appropriation of this Hoseanic condemnation of the cult of Baal prompted a further expansion of Amos' criticism of the cult. This continuation shifts the text's accusation to the level of worship of foreign gods in a way Amos himself never did. The allusion, by way of the names of the astral deity Sakkuth and of Kaiwan, is to the allure of the Assyrian-Babylonian astral cult—more precisely, the cult of Saturn—which arrived with the Assyrian army of occupation and with the resettlement of Babylonians to the former Northern Kingdom (2 Kings 17:19–31); later, the same temptation threatened the Judeans during the Babylonian exile (Isa. 40:26 et passim).[19] The verb "take up, lift" is referring probably to processions and emblematic standards.

17. The "forty years" in v. 25, otherwise attested only after the beginning of the exile and in connection with Deuteronomistic and Priestly theology (cf. the discussion of 2:10 above), probably represent an accrual within v. 25. Something analogous probably also applies to the mention of "grain offering" in the singular (common during the later period; plural in v. 22), which is striking next to the plural "(meat) sacrifices." The two terms together, referring presumably to meat and vegetable offerings, are probably intended to designate the sacrificial cult as a whole. Cf. note 10 above.

18. In both Hosea and in Amos 5:25, the "animal sacrifice" (zbḥ) is representative for this sacrificial mentality; cf. esp. Hos. 6:6; 8:13.

19. "Succoth-benoth" mentioned in 2 Kings 17:30 can hardly be separated from the Sakkuth mentioned in Amos 5:26; cf. W. H. Schmidt, *Deuteronomistische Redaktion,* 190. Furthermore, the circumstantial construction of the verse also shows that it came about in several growth stages; the appositions refer in part to one deity, and in part to two. The core is probably composed of terms from the Babylonian-Assyrian astral cult (E. A. Speiser, "Note on Amos 5:26," *BASOR* 108 [1947]: 5f.; Barstad, *Religious Polemics,* 123–25), even though only the deity Kaiwan is securely attested as an astral god (R. Borger, "Amos 5,26, Apostelgeschichte 7,43 und Šurpu II, 180," *ZAW* 100 [1988]: 70–80). Finally, the language of the prohibition of images affected the text, specifically in a form common especially in Ezekiel (7:20; 16:17).

[5:22a] Finally, the latest, postexilic interpretation in v. 22aα explains the rejection of Israel's worship with its false sacrifices; with the burnt offering, one dedicated completely to the deity, it counters these false sacrifices with the central sacrificial type of the postexilic temple, just as the concept of "presenting burnt offerings" also characterizes the late historical work especially of the Chronicler.

[5:27] This much, however, is indeed certain for Amos' tradents: An Israel that proves to be incapable of turning radically to its God-given "righteousness" must enter the kind of isolation from God represented by the exile. For the survivors of the battle, this is how the "death" of the "maiden Israel" (v. 2) looks in its concrete form. The territory of exile, however, is "unclean land" (7:17), that is, land lacking any possibility of worship and any possibility of a blessed end to life near one's God. What Amos described in anticipation "beyond Damascus" (i.e., beyond the experiences of the past wars with the Arameans) had long become a reality in the form of the Assyrian deportations by the time his tradents committed these words to writing; and the later community, the one that spoke the doxology of judgment over the book of Amos, also understood the fate of the Judean exile in Babylon from the perspective of the older words of Amos, as shown by the appropriation of 4:13bβ at the solemn conclusion of v. 27.

The influence exerted by Amos 5:21ff. was unusually broad even during its own period, something attested by the plethora of prophetic texts responding to Amos 5. The slightly younger contemporaries Hosea (6:6; 8:13) and—as the one closest to Amos himself—Isaiah (1:10–17), as well as Jeremiah a full century later (6:19–21; 14:11f.), and, finally, Malachi during the postexilic period (1:10; 2:13), all engaged in this bold transfer of priestly pronouncements concerning individual sacrifices, behavior, and prayers to the worship activities of their own period as a whole. Although E. Würthwein observed the connection between these texts most precisely, he erroneously tried to explain them as versions of the genre of "prophetic cultic decision" concerning worship; several modern exegetes have followed his lead here (e.g., Wolff, Soggin). I am firmly convinced, however, that such a genre never existed.[20] It is no accident that all the previously mentioned texts pass negative judgments concerning worship activities, while the hypothetical positive versions of this alleged genre would have ascertained only what was the obvious and self-evident presupposition of any worship service: that God is indeed ac-

---

20. I have tried to demonstrate this in detail in *Kultprophetie,* 157–62; similarly also Rudolph, 209 with n. 3. This conclusion does not alter my opinion that we owe to Würthwein what is probably the most profound interpretation of Amos' cult criticism.

cessible in such worship. There is a failure to recognize the unusual elements of this prophetic use of priestly language, especially the expansion of pronouncements over individual sacrifices, individual prayers, and so on, to the worship service as a whole. Rather, like few others, Amos' words here made an unforgettable impression on his contemporaries among the prophets and, beyond them, also on later readers.

Neither, however, was Amos any absolute innovator in the characterization of this language. He was preceded by words of the wise, juxtaposing worship activities and daily life in this way: "To do righteousness and justice is more acceptable to Yahweh than sacrifice" (Prov. 21:3; cf. v. 27 and 15:8). Such estimative comparatives are already attested with similar content in Egyptian wisdom from the pre-biblical period.[21] These instructional pieces, however, concern the behavior of the individual, and to that extent are worlds apart from Amos' judgment concerning worship activities.

The Second Woe (Samaria's Arrogance) Amos 6

6:1 Alas for those who are at ease in Zion,[1]
   and for those who feel secure on Mount Samaria,
   the notables of the first of the nations,
   to whom the house of Israel resorts![2]

---

21. "The Instruction for King Meri-ka-Re," line 129; cf. John A. Wilson, *Ancient Near Eastern Texts Relating to the Old Testament,* ed. James B. Pritchard (3d. ed.; Princeton: Princeton University, 1969), 417.

1. Amos himself addressed only the Northern Kingdom, since his commission (Amos 7:15) directed him to the Northern Kingdom; what follows is clearly directed against Samaria. In the Old Testament, however, "Zion" is otherwise never used as a general expression for the fortress of a capital (contra Fohrer, "Zion," *Theological Dictionary of the New Testament,* vol. 7 [Grand Rapids: Eerdmans, 1971], 295), but rather is always a term for the temple plaza in Jerusalem (or for Jerusalem as a whole). It may be that a later redactor wanted to ensure that Judean readers would refer these words to themselves, and accordingly altered an earlier term for Samaria's royal citadel (e.g., *māṣôr*) to "Zion"; cf. the more unequivocal analogous case ("Judah" instead of "Israel") in Hos. 12:3 (2E). It is more likely, however, that the written text from the very outset had Judeans in mind, and is describing the circumstances in Samaria from their perspective (trust in Zion). Marti, Snaith, and Wolff (the latter with extensive argumentation) consider the entire dative construction "for those who are at ease in Zion" to be a post-interpretation, though in so doing they destroy the parallelism.

2. Perfect consecutive with iterative meaning (van Gelderen, 157).

2 *Cross over to Calneh, and see;*
   from there go to Hamath the great;
   then go down to Gath of the Philistines.
   Are you better than these kingdoms?
   Or is 'your' territory greater than 'their' territory,[3]

3 O you that put far away the evil day,
   and bring near a reign[4] of violence,

4 who lie on beds of ivory,
   and lounge on their couches,
   and eat lambs from the flock,
   and calves from the stall;

5 who bray[5] to the sound of the harp,
   and to ever new instruments of music;[6]

6 who drink wine from bowls,
   and anoint (themselves) with the finest oils,
   but are not grieved over the ruin of Joseph!

7 Therefore they shall now be the first to go into exile,
   and the revelry of the loungers shall pass away.[7]

8 *The Lord*[8] *Yahweh has sworn by himself*
   Says Yahweh, the God of hosts:[9]
   I abhor[10] the pride of Jacob
   and hate his palaces;
   and I will deliver up the city and all that is in it.

9 *If ten people remain in one house, they shall die.*

---

3. MT: "Is their territory greater than yours?" is based presumably on a tendentious alteration of the suffixes (Rudolph, following Geiger and Wellhausen).

4. Literally: "the sitting on the throne" (Wellhausen); cf. 1:5, 8.

5. Concerning the semantic possibilities of this hapax legomenon, cf. *HAL,* 910.

6. Literally: "Like David, they have invented music instruments for themselves." This comparison with David, metrically superfluous and apparently unknown to the LXX, is presumably of later origin; the Chronicler's history is the first to mention "David's instruments" (cf. 1 Chron. 23:5; 2 Chron. 29:27, et passim), and the postexilic period is the first to attest the full (*plene*) orthography of his name (Fleischer, loc. cit., 233n45). It is possible that v. 5b in its entirety is an addendum, since its language is attested esp. in the late period (Fleischer, ibid.).

7. Translators often try to imitate the alliteration of the Hebrew here, e.g., Duhm: [approximately] "and the louts unlearn this loudness," or Wolff: "and suppressed is the spree of the sprawlers."

8. This addendum is yet absent in the LXX; see the discussion of 1:8.

9. This divine oracular formula—superfluous after the oath formula—is yet absent in the LXX and was probably added only for the sake of the divine predicate. Regarding its meaning, cf. the discussion of 4:13.

10. The unusual orthography (*t'b,* elsewhere "long for," instead of *t'b*) intends perhaps to keep this strong emotion at a distance from God (so Wolff, following Geiger).

10 *And if an uncle or another relative*[11] *shall take up the body to bring it out of the house, and shall say to someone in the innermost parts of the house, "Is anyone else with you?" the answer will come, "No." Then the relative shall say, "Hush! We must not mention the name of Yahweh."*

11 See, Yahweh commands,
and the great house shall be shattered to bits,
and the little house to pieces.

12 Do horses run on rocks?
Does one plow 'the sea'[12] with oxen?
But you have turned justice into poison
and the fruit of righteousness into wormwood—

13 you who rejoice in Lo-debar,
who say, "Have we not by our own strength
taken Karnaim for ourselves?"

14 Indeed, I am raising up against you a nation, O house of Israel,
says Yahweh, the God of hosts,[13]
and they shall oppress you from Lebo-hamath to the Brook of Arabah.

Bibliography: G. Fleischer, *Menschenverkäufer*, 224–45; S. D. Snyman, "Amos 6:1–7 as an Intensification of Amos 3:9–11," *In die Skriflig* 28 (1994): 213–22.

Chapter 6 rounds off the composition of Amos 3–6 in a twofold fashion. First, it now introduces a second woe which, as shown above, corresponds exactly to the first in 5:18–27 in a four-stage structure: (1) at the beginning a formally independent oracle of woe in prophetic discourse against the self-confidence of Samaria's inhabitants (vv. 1–7); (2) transition to divine discourse bringing to expression Yahweh's revulsion and "hatred" (v. 8 with vv. 9–11 as a consequence of this discourse); (3) abrupt introduction of a question to prompt the reader's insight (vv. 12f.); and (4) concluding announcement of

11. The MT is generally interpreted from the root *śrp*, "his burner"; given the fact that the burning of corpses was not customary in Israel, however, this is extremely improbable. This hapax legomenon is as yet unexplained. Rabbinic tradition (Maag, *Text*, 164f.; Barthélemy, *Critique textuelle*, 670f.) suggests a degree of kinship (an uncle on the mother's side) comparable to a *dôd* (an uncle on the father's side). It is possible, however, that each of the first three words has been transmitted erroneously.

12. As already recognized in the eighteenth century (J. D. Michaelis), the MT is based on the amalgamation of two independent words.

13. Neither does the LXX* yet attest this expanded divine oracular formula, which alters the customary meter; cf. v. 8.

disaster in renewed divine discourse (v. 14). Second, chapter 6 offers a collection of sayings directed specifically against the inhabitants of the capital, sayings corresponding substantively to the first thematic collection in 3:9–4:3, including considerable correspondence at the level of details;[14] the two collections bracket the central sections 4:4f. (6–13) and 5:1–27. The chapter is based on the extensive oracle of woe (vv. 1–7) and on at least one individual oral saying (vv. 13f.; perhaps also v. 12) and several smaller units that carry forward the older words of Amos already at hand (concerning v. 8, cf. 4:2 and 3:9–11; concerning v. 11, cf. 3:15; concerning v. 12, cf. 5:7); these smaller units underwent later explicative commentary in the prose verses 2:6b and 9f.

Revelry in Samaria
(6:1–7)

Like Amos 5:18ff., Amos 6 is characterized by a lamentation for the living (concerning the "woe, alas," cf. 5:18). In v. 1a and again after v. 3, this lamentation employs the participles so familiar to Amos (and his followers), which in v. 1b and v. 3b (cf. vv. 5b, 6b) are continued in freer forms (substantives or finite verb forms). Finally, it issues in an announcement of disaster ("therefore," v. 7); as is customary in the prophetic oracle of judgment, this announcement anticipates the stipulated fate of death of the lamented as having not yet occurred.

A precise exegesis of this lamentation must determine whether the revelry described in vv. 4–6 is of a private or institutional nature. Only when one understands that the latter is the case, does the text acquire its sharp profile. In particular, only then do the striking parallels to the characterization of worship activities in 5:21–23 (the eating of meat, the musical instruments, singing)[15] come into focus in their intended sense, as does also the analogous association of feelings of security, repression of all notions of misfortune, and worship celebrations in 5:18–20 and 5:21, as well as in 6:1, 3 and 6:4ff.

Excursus:
The Cultic Meal (mrzḥ)

This question depends on the understanding of the next-to-last word (marzēaḥ), occurring otherwise in the Old Testament only in Jer. 16:5, where the funeral repast takes place in the "marzēaḥ-house," a repast attested quite frequently outside Israel. The LXX

14. Here 6:1–7 picks up esp. on 3:9–11 (Snyman; but with v. 4 also on 3:12, with v. 6 on 4:1, etc.); the same applies to 6:8 (but cf. also 4:2), while 6:11 draws from 3:15.

15. Cf. E. Otto, "Die Stellung der Wehe-Worte in der Verkündigung des Propheten Habakuk," ZAW 89 (1977): 95.

is divided, translating technically in Jer. 16:5 as "cultic meal" (*thiasos*), then in Amos 6:7—perhaps because of a misunderstanding of the final word—"neighing of horses" (though Symmachus uses *hetaireia*, "companionship, camaraderie," in both passages; cf. Vulgate *factio* and *convivium*). Outside the Old Testament, the term *mrzḥ* refers to an institution attested "from Piraeus in the north to Elephantine and Petra in the south, and from Carthage and Marseille in the west to Palmyra in the east"[16]; it occurs on Ugaritic, Aramaic, Phoenician-Punic, Nabatean, and Palmyrene inscriptions encompassing a period of two millennia (from the fourteenth century B.C.E. in Ugarit to the sixth century C.E. on the mosaic map of Medeba, though the overwhelming majority of witnesses are considerably later than Amos). A great many individual differences are discernible. Basically, these were religious fellowships (Eissfeldt: "cultic associations") comparable to the Greek *thiasoi;* the cultic meal and especially the enjoyment of wine played a central role. Witnesses also attest, for example, the election of chairpersons, rental contracts, and gift documents for the assembly house as well as specific social obligations of the associations. These associations represented a significant economic factor and were usually composed of members of a city's upper classes since, after all, only the propertied could afford the luxury of feasts and the expenditures required by the association's duties. This is commensurate with the fact that the term *mrzḥ* could refer not only to the institution itself, but also to the cultic celebration and to the place of assembly.[17]

C. Clermont-Ganneau (*CRAI* [1898], 355) was the first to associate Amos 6:7 with the linguistic usage of a Phoenician and a Punic inscription; in 1921, H. Gressmann ("ἡ κοινωνία τῶν δαιμονίων," *ZNW* 20, 224–30) was already able to adduce nine extrabiblical witnesses, whose number then quickly grew during the following period. More recent German scholarship, however, was strongly influenced by the thesis of the scholar best acquainted with the texts, namely, O. Eissfeldt; he distinguished the two biblical occurrences from the extrabiblical ones by deriving the former from a different root: *rzḥ* II, "shout, cry out," instead of *rzḥ* I, "assemble."[18] This distinction, however, is rather artificial, particularly considering that the etymological derivation of *mrzḥ* is as yet unexplained; one can at most say with R. Meyer that the biblical term possesses a further meaning as "cultic fellowship."[19] The connection between Amos 6 and this institution presumably comes to expression most clearly in the fact that the wine is served in vessels

16. O. Eissfeldt, "Kultvereine in Ugarit," *Kleine Schriften,* vol. 5 (Tübingen: Mohr [Siebeck], 1973), 119. Concerning this material and its interpretation, cf., in addition to Eissfeldt's contributions (ibid., 118ff.), esp. D. B. Bryan, "Texts Relating to the *Marzeaḥ:* A Study of an Ancient Semitic Institution" (Ph.D. diss., Baltimore, 1973); H. M. Barstad, *Religious Polemics,* 127–42. Further bibliography in H. J. Fabry, "*marzeaḥ,*" *ThWAT,* vol. 5 (Stuttgart: W. Kohlhammer, 1984), 11–16.

17. As far as the oldest Ugaritic texts are concerned, scholars have disputed especially the relationship between the institution and the cult of the dead. This question, however, is of interest only for Jer. 16:5; it has no significance for Amos 6.

18. "Etymologische und archäologische Erklärungen alttestamentlicher Wörter," *OrAnt* 5 (1966): 165–76; repr. in *Kleine Schriften IV* (Tübingen: Mohr [Siebeck] , 1968), 285–96. He was followed by, e.g., Wolff and Rudolph.

19. "Gegensinn und Mehrdeutigkeit in der althebräischen Wort- und Begriffsbildung," *UF* 11 (1979): 604.

otherwise attested exclusively in cultic contexts as containers for the blood of sacrificial animals, for oil as part of the cereal or grain offerings, and possibly also for libations (*mizraq,* v. 6; *HAL* translates—appropriately for the other occurrences—"sprinkling basin").[20] The verb "anoint" (*mšḥ*) in v. 6 also occurs almost exclusively in cultic contexts.[21]

[6:1, 3] Whatever may indeed be presupposed for Amos in the way of extrabiblically attested organizational forms of the *marzēaḥ,* Amos himself is obviously referring to more than merely spontaneous private celebrations. On the other hand, however, no great emphasis is placed on the cultic character of these gatherings in Amos 6[22]; such comes to expression (besides in v. 6 as just mentioned) only indirectly in these celebrations' (vv. 4–6) striking similarity to the worship activities characterized in 5:21–23. What is decisive for Amos' criticism is that these celebratory meals foster that particular self-confidence about which v. 1 and v. 3 speak. Such self-confidence is based first on the site of this revelry. When the inhabitants of Jerusalem are later warned, on the basis of Amos' oracle, against "being at ease in Zion," the juxtaposition of Zion and "Mount Samaria" shows that the royal citadel in Samaria was granted a status comparable to that of Zion (the second line might even be translated "who trust in Mount Samaria"), even though it was not associated with any Yahweh temple (nor, since the revolution of Jehu, with any Baal temple). The celebratory meals possibly occupied this gap. Second, the aforementioned self-confidence is also based on the popular faith in election according to which Israel is the "first" among the nations, since the conviction "Yahweh is with us" (5:14) banishes any thought of defeat or misfortune (v. 3; cf. v. 13). Within such a conceptual horizon, the prophetic announcement of a "day of Yahweh" that is "dark," and that accordingly brings God's judgment rather than his salvation (5:18–20), can only sound absurd (cf. Isaiah's similar oracle of woe against the reveling Jerusalemites, who "do not regard the deeds of Yahweh," Isa. 5:11f.). This carefree attitude is based, third, on social status. Only the upper class (literally: those who are "notable," i.e., "distinguished") partake in these celebratory meals; at the same time, however, they are thus the point of orientation for the directionless crowd.[23] Finally, this sense of security is based on the

---

20. Cf. the precious fourth-century drinking goblet published by N. Avigad and J. Greenfield, which according to a Phoenician inscription was made "to the *marzeaḥ* of the sun god" ("A Bronze *phialē* with a Phoenician Dedicatory Inscription," *IEJ* 32 [1982]: 118–28).

21. Exceptions are Isa. 21:5 and Jer. 22:14.

22. One certainly cannot, as Barstad does (loc. cit., 141; cf. 129), read into this text a polemic against foreign religious customs based on the term *mrzḥ* alone, a polemic which for Barstad then additionally becomes the key to Amos' criticism of the cult.

23. Because of its strikingly general statement—literally: "to whom the house of Israel comes"— v. 1bβ has variously been considered to be faulty, though no really persuasive explanation of the error has yet been presented. Concerning the "house of Israel," cf. the discussion of 3:1 and 5:1.

undiscussed dominion over those who are dependent, dominion based on destructive "violence" (concerning this term, cf. the discussion of 3:10 and 4:1 above), about which v. 3b speaks parenthetically with an emotionally laden address (cf. the analogous transition to direct address in the oracle of woe in 5:18); that is, it is based on securing power and wealth by restricting the life sphere of the poor.

[6:4–6a] Inwardly secured in this way, the upper class celebrates. The couches on which they lounge (the verb is used otherwise not in connection with human beings, but rather with hanging clothes) are decorated with precious ivory (see the discussion of 3:12, 15 above). Only the best meat is eaten: select, tender lambs, calves tethered in the stall so as to gain more fat through immobility.[24] The substantive analogy to the sacrificial worship activities in 5:22 ("fatted animals") is consciously posited, allowing the intensification of demands for high quality to appear as an intensification of sin as well. Music accompanies these meals,[25] though the harp (or lyre or lute; cf. the discussion of 5:23), the traditional stringed instrument, no longer suffices; in a fashion again going beyond even worship activities, ever more extravagant instruments are used (zithers? cymbals? drums?) to accompany the loud singing. The primary reproach, however, seems to come only with v. 6, where the emphasis on drinking from "bowls" refers probably not to any excess in enjoying wine, but rather to a violation of the boundary between God and human beings, since "bowls," as mentioned, otherwise occur only in connection with sacrifices. Verse 6aβ constitutes an effective conclusion to the participial series insofar as the term translated "finest" (oils) recalls the "first" among the nations in v. 1: What a perversion of election! Instead of following the ancient custom of dedicating the best among one's possessions to the deity, such election tries to actualize itself through luxury. In both the Old Testament and in the Near Eastern sphere at large, oil is frequently mentioned along with wine as a sign of good living; the reference here is to bodily hygiene and to cosmetic uses.[26]

[6:7] With the expression "therefore," the oracle of woe shifts in conclusion to an announcement of disaster more specifically portraying the manner of death of the addressees, picking up substantively on 5:27. In the future, the privilege of the "first" among the nations will manifest itself not in the "first-class" nature of its luxuries, but rather in the "first experience" of imprisonment bringing to

---

24. A different view is taken by H. Weippert, "Amos—seine Bilder," 7–10, who understands v. 4b as referring to the young calf still bound to the mother animal.

25. Wolff, in loc., correctly recalls the large number of contemporary illustrations of banquets with music.

26. Cf. the *šmn rḥṣ* ("washed oil"?) variously mentioned on ostraca from Samaria, and representing the highest quality; concerning its use and production, cf. V. Sasson, "*šmn rḥṣ* in the Samaria Ostraca," *JSS* 26 (1981): 1–5, and esp. L. E. Stager, "The Finest Olive Oil in Samaria," *JSS* 28 (1983): 241–45.

an end the excessive revelry of its models ("loungers" picks up on v. 4). The cultic meal whose original intention—if we have understood the term *mrzḥ* correctly—was to establish contact with God, has estranged the distinguished Samaritans from God once and for all by rendering them utterly unfeeling toward the lives of the poor (vv. 1, 3). The alienation from God accompanying such festive revelry and celebrations, celebrations which were actually supposed to foster the most intense feeling of vitality, symbolizes rather that those who have confused luxury with religion are now utterly given over to the power of death ("woe, alas"). These revelers are the first whom God pushes away from himself. What the divine oracle in 5:27 said about Israel as a worshiping community, the prophet now focuses in 6:7 on those in the capital who bear the primary responsibility. It is helpful to bear in mind through all this that Amos was speaking these words amid a vigorous period of external peace and domestic prosperity.

[6:2] By the time Amos' tradents committed chapter 6 to writing, his words had become tangible for the readers themselves. If one wishes to avoid the embarrassing assertion that v. 2—which so obviously interrupts the style of the oracle of woe with a summons—is actually alluding to some economic troubles in Calneh and Hamath unknown to us (Rudolph, Soggin), then one can hardly separate the verse from the events of the year 738 B.C.E. At that time, the founder of the Assyrian world empire, Tiglath-pileser III, conquered his northern neighbor Urartu and then turned toward northern Syria; in addition to smaller kingdoms such as that in the northwest whose capital was Calneh (Assyrian: Kullani), he also conquered the important city Hamath (modern Hamah), restricting it to its core territory (the city itself was destroyed in 720); it is called "Hamath the great" because after 800 B.C.E. it had assimilated nineteen originally independent kingdoms.[27] Under the impact of this victory, the Northern Kingdom Israel (like the Arameans and other states) paid tribute to Tiglath-pileser.

Yet even given this historical situation, v. 2 is presupposing a yet unbroken feeling of security among the inhabitants of Samaria, a feeling it wants to jolt. It is unclear why Gath is mentioned (presumably modern Tell eṣ-Ṣâfī, west of Aseka); it is the only Philistine city not mentioned in Amos 1:6–8, and (different from Calneh and Hamath) was smaller than the Northern Kingdom. Was it conquered during the campaign of Tiglath-pileser against Philistia in 734 (its final subjugation did not come

27. Cf. A. Alt, "Die syrische Staatenwelt vor dem Einbruch der Assyrer," *Kleine Schriften,* vol. 3 (Munich: Beck, 1959), 214ff., and esp. J. D. Hawkins, "Kullani," *RLA,* 6.305f.; idem., "Hamath," *RLA* 4.67–70, each with bibliography.

about until 711)? In any event, it is probably mentioned for the sake of Judean readers, since it was situated near the Judean border and for a time had belonged to Judah.[28] Regarding the history of influence of the summons "cross over . . . ," see Jer. 2:10; concerning the history of influence of the questions, see 2 Kings 19:11–13.

[6:6b] By contrast, v. 6b, with its striking change of tense, presupposes at least the events of 733 B.C.E. (if not the fall of Samaria in 722/21); this is the case if our understanding of the name "Joseph," which is restricted to chaps. 5–6, is correct (see the discussion of 5:15 above). At that time, the Northern Kingdom Israel was robbed of its richest territories as a result of what is known as the Syrian-Ephramite war; these territories were then turned into the Assyrian provinces of Dor, Megiddo, and Gilead. Israel itself was reduced to its mountainous core territory. Not even this experience seems to have dampened the revelry of the Samaritans (literally: "they have not caused themselves any pain/illness over it"); here the final collapse of the torso state "Joseph" was indeed foreseeable. Isaiah 5:12 could have served as a formal model.

The Fall of the Capital
(6:8–11)

[6:8] Lacking any terminological link with vv. 1–7, yet with maximum emotional charge, the divine discourse commences anew in v. 8; through the inclusion of the twofold "says Yahweh, the God of hosts," this discourse does not come to its conclusion until v. 14, at least as far as later readers were concerned, though formally it initially determines the character only of v. 8 itself. In 5:21, Yahweh's "hatred" resulted merely in a "rejection" of Israel's worship; in 6:8, this "hatred"—the counterconcept to God's "love" in circumscribing his will—and his "abhorrence," which in later prophecy is usually directed against idols and their worship, results in Samaria being delivered over to its enemies. The emotional intensification is grounded substantively in the fact that in 5:21ff., God did not reject worship as such, but rather because it was detached from justice and righteousness, and indeed had usurped their position. Amos 6:8, however, picking up on 3:9–11, mentions the "palaces" of the notables as the site at which the real sin, "violence and oppression" (3:10; cf. 4:1; 6:3), is practiced; at these same palaces, celebration takes place in the form of the previously (vv. 4–6) described cultic meals, which for all practical purposes obstruct any recognition of one's own sin. At the same time, this sin is

---

28. Perhaps even during the time of Amos; cf. 2 Chron. 26:6 and in this regard P. Welten, *Geschichte und Geschichtsdarstellung in den Chronikbüchern,* WMANT 42 (Neukirchen-Vluyn: Neukirchener Verlag, 1973), 153–63.

conceptualized ("pride, arrogance") such that oppression, revelry, and political boasting (described in vv. 13f.) are all covered. Amos' tradents presumably appropriated this concept from Hosea's proclamation (cf. Hos. 5:5; 7:10; 12:8f. [7f.E]; 13:6). In Amos 6:8, it designates that particular, unshakable self-confidence that has no need for Yahweh because it does not anticipate any misfortune coming from him (cf. 6:1, 3); that is, it considers him to be a "beneficent God." As 8:7 will show later, this concept shimmers for the reader insofar as it refers at once both to election ("the nobility of Jacob") and to the perversion of election ("the pride of Jacob").[29]

God's "hatred" and "abhorrence" of the violence being perpetrated in Samaria's palaces are amplified even more by the introduction to the verse. The divine oath, a form not attested before Amos,[30] picks up on 4:2, where it similarly was used in connection with the sin of the privileged in Samaria and with their revelry accompanied by oppression. It announces unavoidable, absolutely irrevocable chastisement, just as does, in the oracles against the nations, the stereotypical expression "I will not revoke it (the punishment)" (1:3 et passim), and, in the visionary accounts, the expression "I can no longer pass them (i.e., Israel) by (and spare them)" (7:8; 8:2). Everything in Samaria is delivered over; the enemy is nothing in and of itself, it is merely God's instrument (v. 14). Because sin in Samaria has reached proportions precluding any prospect of change, it is no longer possible to differentiate between the guilty and the innocent.

[6:11] Hence, at the divine order not only do the palaces crumble (v. 8), but with them the other houses as well, both those made of hewn stone (cf. 5:11) as well as those made of more easily damaged fieldstone; they are either "shattered to bits" or "sundered," as the end rhyme in the original text expresses it. Perhaps v. 11 was once the conclusion to an independent saying; more likely, however, it was developed as an intensification from 3:15, where the same verb, "tear down," is used for the destruction of Samaria's houses. The introduction "see, behold" already anticipates the analogous conclusion in v. 14, which, like v. 8, also uses the first-person of Yahweh.

[6:9–10] In addition, with vv. 9f. the tradents created a bridge between the two divine discourses. In its narrative prose style, this bridge possesses the character of commentary explicating both the end of v. 8 and, in anticipation, v. 11. To illustrate the unavoidability of all the inhabitants of Samaria being annihilated, it posits in v. 9 the case that a single house might remain intact containing ten survivors, the quorum for a

---

29. Cf. J. Jeremias, "Jakob im Amosbuch," in *Hosea und Amos,* 257ff.

30. God can swear only by himself. The specific nuances in the expression "by himself, by his own life" become discernible from swearing rites in Mesopotamian contracts; cf. Wolff, in loc.

congregation.[31] In all probability, this example derives from a combination of v. 8b ("the city") and 5:3 ("the city . . . that marched out a hundred shall have ten left") for the sake of intensifying 5:3. This case, however, is excluded, and the case taking this even further is then discussed: A single person might survive in the innermost parts of the house; that person is then discovered by one of the men who take away corpses (if the beginning of v. 10 has been transmitted accurately, mention of the uncle suggests that all the person's closest as well as younger relatives are already dead). After the possibility that a second person might have survived in the house has been excluded, the dialogue between the two focuses on the term *hās,* "hush," which in worship services commands silence in the presence of God (Hab. 2:20; Zeph. 1:7; Zech. 2:17 [13E]; Neh. 8:11). Here, however, its intention is to obstruct God's deadly nearness, which would become a threat at the mere mention of God's name (e.g., in a lament; cf. 8:3 in what follows).[32] Thus does the last survivor of a city in ruin, through this very silence, testify to the judging God—and this after the reveling city itself previously had made continual and thoughtless use of this name (5:21ff.; 6:1ff.).

The Final Question
(6:12–14)

Amos 6:12–14 is composed of two originally independent units. The accusation in v. 13 now adds to the social and religious arrogance of 6:1–7 the theme of military hubris, and remains securely linked to the prediction of devastating defeat in v. 14. The question in v. 12, however, offers a reproach concerning the perversion of justice and righteousness, introducing thus a completely different idea into what is otherwise a substantively extremely self-enclosed chapter, one whose parallels with 5:7 extend even into wording. Although in its formal self-enclosure v. 12 might once have been an independent individual saying, in the present context it and v. 13 are syntactically inextricably bound together.[33]

[6:12] Of far more significance is the observation that elsewhere in Amos, the theme of justice and righteousness is by no means associated specifically with the

---

31. Cf. Amos 5:3 and esp. Gen. 18:32; Isa. 6:13; also Rudolph, in loc., and H. A. Brongers, "Die Zehnzahl in der Bibel und in ihrer Umwelt," in *Studia biblica et semitica: Festschrift T. C. Vriezen* (Wageningen: H. Veenman, 1966), 30–45, 32. Cf. the minyan still practiced today, i.e., the stipulation that at least ten men are required for a Jewish worship service.

32. Cf. W. Schottroff, *"Gedenken" im Alten Orient und im Alten Testament: Die Wurzel zākar im semitschen Sprachkreis,* 2d. ed., WMANT 15 (Neukirchen-Vluyn: Neukirchener Verlag, 1967). 250f. Against this background, the refrain in the doxologies—"Yahweh his name" (4:13; 5:8; 9:6)—acquires a jubilant tone for later readers.

33. The popular solution in scholarship, namely, to add an additional "woe, alas" in v. 13, is as unsupported and arbitrary as in the case of 5:7.

capital Samaria (Amos 5:7, 14f., 24; cf. the different terminology in 3:10), and certainly is not limited to it. This cannot be explained through harmonization by asserting that Samaria has transgressed to a greater extent; as explicated earlier in the discussion concerning 5:24, such comparative explications of righteousness are wholly inappropriate to the concept. Rather, Amos' disciples have in v. 12 consciously introduced a "foreign body" into a chapter (6) otherwise strictly limited to themes associated with Samaria. It interrupts the logic of vv. 8–11 (the inescapability of the death sentence for everyone) by appealing to its readers' understanding and, with the aid of absurd comparisons, by trying to open their eyes to the contradictory nature of their actions (regarding the first question, it is essential to understand that at the time of Amos, horses were used not as riding animals, but rather as draft animals for [military] wagons [chariots]). In so doing, the verse again presupposes (as in 5:7, 24; see the discussion) an understanding of "justice and righteousness" as gifts already given to Israel; it can "overturn" them, that is, pervert them (in addition to the bitter "wormwood" in 5:7, the image of deadly poison is now introduced), but must not "fulfill" them in the sense of behavioral goals or ideals. Such an appeal basically still reckons with the possibility—however reserved—of Israel coming to its senses and subsequently changing; moreover, within the chapter's structure it stands in exactly the same position in which 5:24 (the summons to allow "justice and righteousness" to flow freely) and 5:25 (the question from Hoseanic tradition whether God has demanded sacrifices instead) stand within the first woe (5:18–27), there, too, amid the logical tension between absolute condemnation ("I hate, I despise . . . ," 5:21) and a final appeal for understanding.

[6:13–14] This much, however, is certain: The self-confident in Samaria are and will remain lost because their well-being does not allow any doubt in their own "righteousness" to arise in the first place. In v. 13, their alienation from God is demonstrated in a new area, one which for the Old Testament people of God was especially delicate. This is shown, for example, by the narratives in the book of Judges, which emphasize repeatedly that God alone has preserved Israel from horrible defeats against stronger enemies, or by what is known as Isaiah's memorial with the well-known theme of "faith" (Isa. 7). The military in Samaria is emancipated, does not need God for its wars, and determines its own goals. Lo-debar (north of the Jabbok, not yet located with any certainty)[34] and Karnaim (modern Sheikh Sa'd, north of the Yarmuk, six kilometers south of Nawa)[35] were apparently taken from the Arameans only shortly

---

34. M. Metzger, "Lodebar und der *tell el-mghannije,*" *ZDPV* 76 (1960): 97–102, has tried to locate it near Mahanaim; Z. Kallai, *Historical Geography of the Bible: The Tribal Territories of Israel* ([Jerusalem] Leiden: E.J. Brill, 1986), 265, thinks it lies much farther north. S. Mittmann, *Beiträge zur Siedlungs- und Territorialgeschichte des nördlichen Ostjordanlandes,* ADPV (Wiesbaden: Harrassowitz, 1970), 242–46, offers a plausible solution mediating between the two.

35. D. Kellermann, " 'Aštārōt—'Ašterōt Qarnayim—Qarnayim: Historisch-geographische Erwägungen zu Orten im nördlichen Ostjordanland," *ZDPV* 97 (1981): 45ff.

before the appearance of Amos.[36] Karnaim was the most important city of the Bashan, and after the fall of Damascus in 732 B.C.E. became the capital of an Assyrian province; Lo-debar could then correspondingly represent Gilead. Perhaps, however, these two locales were chosen only because of the wordplay: "you who rejoice in a thing of nothingness (so the vocalization of the Massoretes and LXX), who say, 'Have we not by our own strength taken horns (as a symbol of strength) for ourselves?' "[37]

However that may be, the feeling of military superiority generated by such local successes will be reversed when God himself now (so-called *futurum instans*) intervenes in history and makes "a nation"—Amos does not yet speak of the Assyrians—into his instrument (cf. 3:11: "an adversary"). Just as God once "raised up" a deliverer when Israel was in distress (Judg. 3:9 et passim), so also now is raised up a power that will administer the deathblow to a guilty Israel. Is the verb "oppress" consciously referring to the experience in Egypt (Ex. 3:9 [Elohist]), as Hosea does later ("they shall return to Egypt," Hos. 8:13; 9:3)? For the Northern Kingdom Israel, v. 14b circumscribes virtually the widest possible geographical area. Lebo-hamath, which in several Old Testament passages refers to Israel's northernmost boundary (in the expansion of the Davidic kingdom), probably refers to a city (M. Noth) rather than to a territory ("the entrance of Hamath"); it has recently been identified especially with Lebweh, south of the headwaters of the Orontes.[38] The "Brook of Arabah," that is, of the southern Jordan depression, is located either west of the northern end of the Dead Sea in the *Wâdī Qelṭ* or east of this in the *Wâdī Kafrein*. In any case, the reference is to the greatest extent of the Northern Kingdom in a north-south direction.[39]

36. Cf. M. Haran, "The Rise and Decline of the Empire of Jeroboam ben Joash," *VT* 17 (1967): 278–83.

37. Z. Kallai, loc. cit., with n. 348. Cf. the analogous wordplays in 1:4.

38. Cf. O. Keel, M. Küchler, and C. Uehlinger, *Orte und Landschaften der Bibel*, vol. 1 (Göttingen: Vandenhoeck & Ruprecht; Zurich: Einsiedeln, 1984), 247, and B. Mazar, "Lebo-hamath and the Northern Border of Canaan," in idem, *The Early Biblical Period: Historical Studies*, ed. S. Ahituv and B. A. Levine (Jerusalem: Israel Exploration Society, 1986), 189–202, where the Egyptian and Assyrian sources for the location are also adduced. The territorial designation has also recently been defended by H. Donner, *Geschichte des Volkes Israel und seiner Nachbarn in Grundzügen*, Grundrisse zum alten Testament 4; vol. 2 (Göttingen: Vandenhoeck & Ruprecht, 1986), 283; cf. also O. Eissfeldt, "Der Zugang nach Hamath," *Kleine Schriften V* (Tübingen: Mohr [Siebeck], 1973), 205–11. Concerning the discussion between Noth and Elliger in the years 1935/36, cf. W. Zimmerli, *Ezekiel 2*, Hermeneia (Philadelphia: Fortress, 1983), 528–30.

39. This boundary description is strikingly similar to the salvific-prophetic oracle to Jeroboam II in 2 Kings 14:25. Was Amos consciously taking issue with this in his own oracle (so O. Eissfeldt, "Amos und Jona in volkstümlicher Überlieferung," *Kleine Schriften*, vol. 4 [Tübingen: Mohr (Siebeck), 1968], 140), or was 2 Kings 14:25, in a reverse fashion, taking issue with Amos' message (so F. Crüsemann, "Kritik an Amos im deuteronomistischen Geschichtswerk," in *Probleme biblischer Theologie: Festschrift G. von Rad*, ed. H. W. Wolff [Munich: Kaiser, 1971], 57ff.)?

Part III

THE VISIONS
(AMOS 7:1–9:6)

The First Four Visions
Amos 7:1–8; 8:1–2

7:1 This is what *the Lord*[1] Yahweh showed me: Behold, he was forming locusts at the time the latter growth began to sprout (*it was the latter growth after the king's mowings*). **2** When they had begun to eat[2] the grass of the land completely, I said, "Lord Yahweh, forgive, I beg you! How can Jacob stand? He is so small!" **3** Yahweh was sorry concerning this; "It shall not be," said Yahweh.

4 This is what *the Lord* Yahweh showed me: Behold, he was calling for a 'shower of fire'[3] — *the Lord Yahweh*[4]; it devoured the great deep and began to eat[5] up the land. **5** Then I said, "O Lord Yahweh, cease, I beg you! How can Jacob stand? He is so small!"

6 Yahweh was sorry concerning this; "This also shall not be," said *the Lord* Yahweh.

---

1. See the discussion of 1:8. In a considerable part of the LXX tradition, this title is not found in vv. 1, 4, 6, 7; 8:1; presumably was not appropriated until fairly late in connection with Amos' intercession (vv. 2, 5).

2. The MT uses an obviously circumstantial formulation, and with a verb form (*whyh*) which normally designates the future (so LXX) or repetition, which does not fit the context. Wolff, in loc., in analogy to v. 4b, plausibly suggests a simple *wĕkillâ* as the earlier text; cf. n. 5. Attempts at interpreting the MT can be found in Gese, "Komposition," 76n3; T. Seidl, *BN* 37 (1987): 129–38 (durative understanding; the semantic character of the verb *klh* piel, "complete," militates against this); and H.-J. Stipp, "w' = hayā für nichtiterative Vergangenheit? Zu syntaktischen Modernisierungen im masoretischen Jeremiabuch," in *Text, Methode und Grammatik: Festschrift W. Richter,* ed. G. Walter et al. (St. Ottilien: EOS, 1991), 521–48; 541f.

3. MT ("to contend with fire [for a judgment by fire, so NRSV]," whereby the preposition *b* with the verb *rîb* refers to the trial opponent) probably arose through false word division from *lirbîb 'ēš* (Hillers, "Amos 7:14 and Ancient Parallels," *CBQ* 26 [1964]: 221–25, and Wolff, 292f.). This substantive, otherwise attested in the plural only six times in the Old Testament, is attested in the singular in Ugaritic (*rbb* and *rb*); this may also explain the feminine usage in Amos 7:4: *rb* together with *ṭl* ("dew") forms the elements of the name of one of Baal's daughters: "the dewlike, born-of-rain." The MT might have originated under the influence of the oracles against the nations (cf. J. Limburg, "Amos 7:4: A Judgment with Fire?" *CBQ* 35 [1973]: 346–49).

4. The divine name, which seems disruptive and appended here (the same applies to the prepositioned "Lord" as was said in note 1) probably originally belonged to v. 7a, where it surprisingly is absent in the MT.

5. The intended change in time between v. 4bα (narrative time) and 4bβ (perfect consecutive) focuses on the fact that the first event has concluded and the second has not (Rudolph).

7 This is what '*the Lord* Yahweh'[6] showed me: Behold, he—*the Lord*—was standing on a wall of tin, with tin in his hand. 8 And Yahweh said to me, "Amos, what do you see?" And I said, "Tin." Then the Lord said, "See, I am setting tin in the midst of my people Israel; I can no longer pass them by (and spare them)."

8:1 This is what *the Lord* Yahweh showed me: Behold, there was a basket of summer fruit (*qāyiṣ*). 2 He said, "Amos, what do you see?" And I said, "A basket of summer fruit." Then Yahweh said to me, "The end (*qēṣ*) has come upon my people Israel; I can no longer pass them by (and spare them)."

Bibliography: W. Beyerlin, *Bleilot, Brecheisen oder was sonst? Revision einer Amos-Vision*, OBO 81 (Freiburg, Switzerland: Universitätsverlag; Göttingen: Vandenhoeck & Ruprecht, 1988); J. Jeremias, "Völkersprüche und Visionsberichte im Amosbuch," in *Hosea und Amos*, 157–71; H. G. M. Williamson, "The Prophet and the Plumb-Line: A Redaction-Critical Study of Amos VII," *OTS* 26 (1990): 101–22.

It was not just Amos who received visions. In several prophetic books, the superscription to the various transmitted prophetic sayings already speaks of a "vision" (Isa. 1:1; Obad. 1; Nahum 1:1; cf. the attendant verb ["see"] in Amos 1:1; Hab. 1:1). One is surprised to find how little distinction is made between hearing and seeing in Old Testament prophecy. The circumstances both of word reception as well as of such visions—circumstances of such concern to earlier scholarship (see below)—play virtually no role at all. All emphasis is on what is heard, or on the words received during the vision as an interpretation of what is seen. Here, Amos' visions differ in a number of ways from those of other prophets:

1. Amos is God's immediate partner and is addressed by God directly ("Amos, what do you see?" 7:8; 8:2). No interpretative angel steps in—as in the later visions of Zechariah and Daniel—to interpret some mysterious occurrence.

2. Nowhere in these visions does Amos receive any commission for proclamation. Hence one cannot without further examination characterize Amos' visions as "call" visions. Rather, they represent first of all extremely personal and private experiences whose content by no means automatically suggests that they be passed on to others, nor certainly publicized. This emerges especially from the fact that no mention is made of Israel's sin even though it is clearly presupposed throughout.

3. From a literary perspective, the first four visions are quite consciously and artistically structured in pairs, something shown especially by the twice-

6. Cf. note 4.

identical "results" of the visions (withdrawal of the catastrophe in 7:3, 6; end of forbearance in 7:8; 8:2), as well as by their progression (annihilating catastrophe here, wordplay in need of interpretation there). Although Amos apparently did experience each of these visions separately, probably with longer periods of time between (as suggested by their seasonal allusions[7]), he did not write them down separately, but rather portrayed them in retrospect in their mutual relationships with one another. It is self-evident that each vision may be interpreted only together with its partner. Neither, however, are the two pairs of visions intended to (nor should they) be read merely in and for themselves, but rather only in their proper sequence (with the fifth and final vision as their culmination and goal; only for the sake of better overall clarity will it be treated separately here). For the third and fourth visions emphatically bring to an end an act of God ("I can no longer pass by," 7:8; 8:2) which the first two visions portray virtually *in actu*.[8] In a word: Amos' visions are intended to be read as a sequence of events, as a path along which God has led the prophet; they presuppose that this path has already been traversed, and thus portray it in retrospect. The text does not—nor does it intend to—give any access to Amos' individual experiences; it is utterly silent concerning any feelings the prophet may have had during and after any given individual vision.[9]

4. This structuring in pairs of the first four visions draws attention within the text to the decisive turning point at which Amos' prophetic intervention fundamentally changed. What was initially possible for him in the first two visions, namely, through intercession to have Israel's punishment withdrawn or at least delayed, is denied him beginning with the third vision. Amos had to learn that there are limits to divine patience, that is, that Israel's sin can reach proportions allowing no more room for this patience. This changes the prophet's function in a fundamental way. Whereas at the beginning he was a mediator between Yahweh and Israel insofar as he possessed knowledge of God's plans for Israel, and yet at the same time could influence these plans to Israel's advantage, his

7. In the oldest Palestinian calendar, discovered in 1908 in Gezer and coming from the tenth century B.C.E., the terms "late growth" from the first vision and "summer fruit" from the fourth vision occur as names of "months" referring to the third and eighth (or final) agricultural period; cf. note 31 below.

8. These considerations show compellingly that Amos 7:9–17 and 8:3–14, which interrupt the sequence of the third and fourth or the fourth and fifth visions, were inserted by a later hand into the cycle of visions and are intended as a commentary to that cycle. Cf. the introduction to the present commentary as well as Jeremias, loc. cit., 46f.

9. When in the decades around the two World Wars scholars inquired primarily concerning prophets' experiences and circumstances (e.g., G. Hölscher, *Die Profeten: Untersuchungen zur Religionsgeschichte Israels* [Leipzig: Hinrichs, 1914]; F. Häussermann, *Wortempfang und Symbol in der alttestamentlichen Prophetie*, BZAW 58 [Giessen: Töpelmann, 1932]; I. P. Seierstad, *Die Offenbarungserlebnisse der Propheten Amos, Jesaja und Jeremia* [Oslo: J. Dybwad, 1946]), this line of thinking actually went against the intention of the texts rather than concurrent with them.

own capacity is radically altered beginning with the third vision. It is curtailed insofar as Amos no longer has the opportunity for further intercession. It is enhanced insofar as Amos now moves completely to the side of Yahweh; Yahweh now speaks through him (and no longer through numerous other representatives of religious institutions; cf. 7:10–17), and Amos' words will from now on be the direct words of God (cf. Amos 3:8). The first understanding of prophecy was the one familiar to Amos' contemporaries; the second, associated with the harsh prediction of "Israel's end," was completely new. Hence it is by no means accidental that all the visions beginning with the third have received long commentaries (7:9ff.; 8:3ff.; 9:5ff.), while the first two visions did not need such an interpretation.

This simultaneously discloses the meaning behind making the visions public. Their intention is to show Amos' readers how he changed from the messenger of divine patience to the messenger of relentless divine judgment; put differently, they serve to legitimize the prophetic message of judgment against Israel. They attest how little Amos actually wanted to be the kind of messenger of disaster these visions forced him to become, and how he struggled to the maximum against this new determination of his function. On the other hand, they attest that Israel is not yet lost simply by incurring guilt, but rather only when God himself prevents its prophet from fighting against God's plan of annihilation through the power of intercession.

5. The visionary accounts in the book of Amos stand at the end of the book rather than at the beginning (cf. Jer. 1:11ff.; Ezek. 1:4ff.; Zech. 1:7ff.). This positioning seems astonishing at first, particularly since all the other texts in the book of Amos already presuppose the new understanding of the task of Yahweh's prophet mediated by these visions. This is explicitly the case in Amos 1–2 insofar as the stereotypical, harsh statement from the divine discourse, "for three transgressions of . . . and for four I will not revoke it (i.e., the catastrophe)," already formulates, as it were, the insight gained from the visionary accounts; it is implicitly the case in Amos 3–6 insofar as these chapters consistently describe the "end of Israel" (fourth vision, Amos 8:2). If the book of Amos were following an even incipiently biographical outline, the visionary accounts would have to stand at the beginning of the book. The most likely explanation for their position at the end of the book is that according to the logic of the book itself, Israel's enormous sin must first be presented (in chaps. 2–6) before Yahweh's inaccessibility to prophetic intercession and thus Amos' own new function become comprehensible.

[7:1–6] The first pair of visions clearly exhibits parallel structure, the second vision intensifying the first. In the initial statements, Yahweh is the subject: (1) emphatically in the identical introduction to the vision, so that the reader is prepared not for one of Amos' experiences, but rather for a presumption on the part of God, (so also in the third and fourth visions), then (2) as the initiator of some horrible occurrence (devastation of crops or land). With almost verbatim congruence, there now follows (3) Amos' spontaneous intercession for Israel with identical reasoning, and—again identical—(4) a change in God's will as its consequence, then (5) in conclusion his assurance not to actualize the event just viewed.

Both visions exhibit an analogous progression from God's plan for catastrophe to its revocation. Yet while the catastrophe actually viewed is varied with increasing intensification, Amos' intercession and God's reaction to it remain virtually identical for the sake of impressing themselves on the reader all the more forcefully. In the arc from the initial vision of catastrophe to its divine revocation, the decisive emphasis is on *Amos' intercession,* which elicits a change in God's will.

For the Old Testament, God does not represent some rigid element of fate, but rather can be influenced. For that purpose, the people of God had the great figures of its past (esp. Moses and Samuel; cf. Jer. 15:1) and, after them, its prophets. In the case of Moses, later tradents emphasized the possibility of influencing God so strongly that God himself occasionally must entreat Moses: "now let me alone, so that my wrath may burn hot against them . . . " (Ex. 32:10; cf. Deut. 9:14; Ps. 106:23). According to this view, Moses "so to speak must first release the people for punishment,"[10] otherwise God is incapable of acting. Because of their capacity for intercession, the prophets were solicited for prayer and intercession by individual Israelites especially in cases of illness (e.g., 1 Kings 14:1ff.; 2 Kings 1:2ff.; 8:8ff.), or by representatives of the people in times of national calamity (e.g., 2 Kings 19:2; 22:12; Jer. 21:1; 37:3).[11] This has occasionally prompted the assumption that the first two visions indicate that at least at the beginning, Amos was active in some official prophetic capacity at the court or temple.[12] However, since the

---

10. J. Scharbert, *Heilsmittler im Alten Testament und Alten Orient,* Quaestiones disputatae 23/24 (Freiburg: Herder, 1964), 97; cf. L. Perlitt, "Mose als Prophet," *EvT* 31 (1971): 588–608, and finally also E. Aurelius, *Der Fürbitter Israels: Eine Studie zum Mosebild im Alten Testament,* CB.OT 27 (Stockholm: Almqvist & Wiksell, 1988).

11. Cf. esp. C. Westermann, "Die Begriffe für Fragen und Suchen im Alten Testament," *Kerygma und Dogma* 6 (1960): 2–30; repr. in *Gesammelte Studien,* TB Neudrucke und Berichte aus dem 20. Jahrhundert, 24, 55 Altes Testament; vol. 2 (Munich: Kaiser, 1974), 162–90; J. Jeremias, *Kultprophetie,* 140ff.

12. So esp. E. Würthwein, "Amos-Studien," 86ff.; similarly, though without the aforementioned temporal distinction, also A. H. J. Gunneweg, "Erwägungen zu Am 7,14," *ZTK* 57 (1960): 1–16; 8ff; repr. in *Sola Scriptura: Beiträge zu Exegese und Hermeneutik des Alten Testaments,* vol. 1 (Göttingen: Vandenhoeck & Ruprecht, 1983), 9–24, 16ff.; H. Graf Reventlow, *Amt,* 30ff.

first two visions involve a spontaneous objection to a devastating vision, this conclusion is by no means particularly evident. None of the transmitted sayings of Amos fits into any such separate early period.

The inner logic of what is reported is of decisive significance for Amos' intercession and for an understanding of its success. First, Amos does not ask for milder punishment, as if hoping that Israel itself might change in some fundamental way—when in v. 2 the prophet asks for forgiveness, he knows that God's anticipated punishment of Israel is appropriate; hence he, like God, takes Israel's capital guilt as his point of departure. Rather, he asks only for God's sympathy. "Jacob" could not withstand God's blows, could not survive. The prophet is obviously avoiding the name "Israel," whose ambiguity (as a designation both for the people of God and for the state) characterizes both superscriptions to the middle section of the present book of Amos (3:1; 5:1). For Amos and his followers in the book of Amos (cf. esp. 9:8b), "Jacob" never refers to the state, but rather always to that entity which is totally focused and dependent on God; Jacob is, after all, "small," that is, diminutive, powerless, and thus incapable of life without the help and care of its God, who has taken up with the weak.[13] When God hears the name "Jacob," he can only relent—where the visions describe the end of the divine patience, God later speaks in a more detached fashion about "my people Israel" (7:8; 8:2), and finally about "all of them" (9:1). It is the name of Jacob with all its attendant associations that brings success to the intercession, not any appeal to God's righteousness.

Second, what Amos experiences about the success of this intercession is not simply that God, as Amos has asked, forgives Israel's sin such that this sin might cease to exist and lose its power. As the cycle of visions on the whole presupposes, the advanced and ruthless exercise of power by the strong in Israel (cf., e.g., 2:6–8) renders impossible any such action on God's part. We hear rather that God breathes a deep sigh of relief (so the basic meaning of the root *nḥm* in the niphal, "be sorry, rue") by relenting—for the sake of "Jacob"—from his plan to bring Israel to ruin. Amos manages to change God's will, and God allows Israel to survive. According to the first visions, then, Israel is living, despite its capital guilt, solely on the basis of God's pity; God cannot bring it upon himself to destroy "little Jacob," and thus relents from his (justified!) plans for destruction. The closest substantive parallel to this unusual statement is Hos. 11:8f. Later, Israel confesses in several instances that only through God's change of heart in its favor has it managed to survive at

---

13. For detailed argumentation, cf. J. Jeremias, "Jakob im Amosbuch," in *Hosea und Amos,* 257ff.

all; this change illustrates God's most extreme possibility for sparing his people—a people that has surrendered itself to death—even though actual forgiveness is no longer possible.[14]

The intensification of the two visions of disaster presupposes the unspoken intensification of Israel's guilt, and obviously intends to bring to expression the most extreme peril. The first vision shows how the entire late growth of grain and livestock feed is destroyed in April by the dreaded locust swarm (cf. Joel 1); this already represents a catastrophe for human beings because it involves the destruction of what for a long time will be the last available growth[15]; since after May it does not rain again in Palestine for six months, that growth cannot be replaced. From that perspective, Amos' intercession, "How can Jacob stand," is only too comprehensible for readers in the land of the Bible. This applies to an even greater extent to the second vision, which uses mythical language and conceptions as an intensification. The "great deep" devoured by fire is the cosmic ocean nourishing the earth with water from below (Gen. 7:11; 49:25, et passim), without which all springs would dry up. It is uncertain whether this "shower of fire" evokes associations with the fate of Sodom and Gomorrah, or even with more far-reaching allusions to Hittite myths or Hesiod's *Theogony,* as Hillers and Wolff suggest.[16] Yet even if the reference is only to an extreme version of normal occurrences in nature—an extreme drought, prompted perhaps by the hot southeast winds in May causing the water table to fall and the ground to crack[17]—this still represents a threat Palestinian farmers simply could not survive. Their fields, and with them the basis of their existence, would be destroyed. Amos' objection accordingly becomes more desperate, but also more disheartened; he no longer dares to ask for forgiveness as in v. 2, but rather only for an end to the

14. Cf. the extensive discussion in J. Jeremias, *Die Reue Gottes: Aspekte alttestamentlicher Gottesvorstellung,* BibS(N) 65 (Neukirchen-Vluyn: Neukirchener Verlag, 1975; 2d ed., 1995), 40ff., 75ff.

15. At the end of v. 1, this is probably what the aside (of a later redactor) intends to say regarding the king's privileged access to the harvest. Scholars have not yet determined exactly the nature of this temporally prior harvest, which is referenced with an extremely unusual designation. Even a scholar as familiar with the land as G. Dalman vacillates, thinking first of wild growth (*Arbeit und Sitte,* 1/2.411f.), and later—probably correctly—of the green cut of barley, i.e., that cut made before the barley then put forth a second time as late growth for the actual harvest (letter to Karl Budde, in "Zu Text und Auslegung des Buches Amos," *JBL* 44 [1925]: 67n8; *Arbeit und Sitte,* 6.178, 213).

16. Loc. cit. (note 3).

17. Dalman, *Arbeit und Sitte,* 1/2.320; H. Weippert, "Amos—seine Bilder," 23f. Cf. esp. the drought described in Joel 1:18f., which follows a plague of locusts and is similarly caused by a "devouring fire."

horrible vision ("cease," "desist"). In this way, he once again prompts a change in God's will, and saves Israel.

[7:7–8; 8:1–2] Despite its long interruption in the present text (7:9–16), the second pair of visions is, like the first, clearly structured as parallel. As already in the first pair of visions, Yahweh is identified emphatically at the beginning as the initiator of the two visions; the visions themselves, however, consist not, as in 7:1–6, in a catastrophic event, but rather in a static picture in need of interpretation. After each initial image, God asks Amos, "Amos, what do you see?"; Amos' subsequent, catchphrase summary of the picture guides the reader's attention to the central element of the vision. Only God's own interpretation of the picture, in a play on words, then discloses unequivocally the disastrous meaning of the vision; each concluding summation is formulated with emphatically identical wording.

In the third and fourth vision, then, as in the first pair of visions, a dialogue takes place between God and prophet. This one, however, has a fundamentally different character. Whereas the first two visions portray the successful application of the prophet's authoritative intercession and its influence on God, such an application is inconceivable in the third and fourth visions. Here Amos must go to God's school, so to speak, and must undergo a learning process whose result is that he, Amos, must identify and call forth the disaster God then describes more specifically. Accordingly, the conclusion reached by the second pair of visions constitutes the most extreme contrast conceivable to that of the first. The former told us: "This (i.e., the catastrophe) shall not be, said Yahweh" (v. 3; cf. v. 6). We now hear: "I can no longer pass them by (and spare them)" (7:8; 8:2). The experience of the first two visions is definitively brought to an end with the third and fourth.

[7:7–8] The details of the *third* vision, however, are difficult to interpret precisely, since the keyword *'ănāk* dominates the passage. This substantive is used four times here, yet does not otherwise occur in the Old Testament, and is a loanword from the Akkadian.

> Several attempts at understanding this word stand over against one another.[18] The interpretation common since the Middle Ages understands *'ănāk* as "lead," and the expression itself as an abbreviated description of a lead plummet. The meaning of the vision would then be that through the metaphor of a wall, God as the builder examines Israel anew regarding its usability, with a negative result. Specialized philological investigations, however, have shown that *an(n)āku* in Akkadian refers not

---

18. Williamson, loc. cit., 105ff., presents an extremely careful summation of the interpretive attempts made during recent decades.

primarily to lead, but rather to tin.[19] In that case, however, the vision cannot be referring to any process of examination;[20] it is far more likely that "tin" is to be understood *pars pro toto* as a reference to weapons, since it was used almost exclusively as an alloy of bronze from which weapons were made. It was a far more precious element than copper, even though the latter was used for alloying in at least a sixfold quantity. This was the case especially in Palestine, since copper could be mined here, whereas all tin had to be imported, presumably by way of Cyprus.[21]

The definition "tin" for *'ănāk,* and the meaning "weapons" by extension, are as a matter of fact quite plausible for the concluding divine discourse; its announcement, "See, I am setting tin in the midst of my people Israel," clearly exhibits the character of threat, signaling as it does that Israel will no longer be spared and that the divine patience has run out. The following verse fits remarkably well with this understanding, since as a bridge to the narrative of Amaziah in vv. 10–17 it speaks of God "rising (against the house of Jeroboam) with the sword" (v. 9). This apparently represents a more specific interpretation of the "tin in the midst of Israel," even though the circle of those so affected is narrowed from the people of God to the leaders of the state. One might also compare here the personified sword in the final vision (9:4; cf. 9:1).

These weapons, directed at Israel's center, then constitute an effective contrast

---

19. Cf. esp. B. Landsberger, "Tin and Lead," *JNES* 24 (1965): 285–96 (with bibliography). He is followed by the *Chicago Assyrian Dictionary* and, for Amos 7—in part with additional argumentation—by G. Brunet, "La vision de l'étain, réinterprétation d'Amos 7:7–9," *VT* 16 (1966): 387–95; W. L. Holladay, "Once More, *'ănak* = `tin,'* Amos 7:7–8," *VT* 20 (1970): 492–94; J. Ouellette, "Le mur d'étain dans Amos, VII, 7–9," *RB* 80 (1973): 321–31; C. van Leeuwen, "Quelques problèmes de traduction dans les visions d'Amos," *Übersetzung und Deutung: Studien zu dem Alten Testament und seiner Umwelt: Festschrift A. R. Hulst* (Nijkerk: Callenbach, 1977), 103–12; G. Bartczek, *Prophetie und Vermittlung,* Europäische Hochschulschriften, Reihe XXIII, Theologie 120 (Frankfurt am Main: Peter Lang, 1980), 119f.; H. Gese, "Komposition," 80f.; Hayes, 204f. More recently, this view has been thoroughly reinforced by W. Beyerlin, loc. cit., 18ff., as well as—picking up critically on his work—by C. Uehlinger, "Der Herr auf der Zinnmauer: Zur dritten Amos-Vision (Am. VII 7–8)," *BN* 48 (1989): 89–104, and K. Baltzer, "Bild und Wort: Erwägungen zu der Vision des Amos in Am 7,7–9," in *Text, Methode und Grammatik: Festschrift W. Richter,* ed. G. Walter et al. (St. Ottilien: EOS, 1991), 11–16 (unfortunately, a different view is taken by the most recent dictionaries, *HAL* and Gesenius [18th ed.; ed. by R. Meyer and H. Donner; first installment 1987], s.v., who do not even recognize the problem). These authors thus return to a suspicion expressed long ago by A. Condamin, "Le prétendu 'fil à plomb' de la vision d'Amos," *RB* 9 (1900): 586–94. During the postbiblical period—long before the Middle Ages and its understanding as "lead plummet"—the two metals were often confused; cf., e.g., Brunet, loc. cit., 391n3; Williamson, loc. cit., 111. This makes the interpetation of the great Jewish exegetes of the Middle Ages easily understandable.

20. Despite the compromise suggestion of Williamson, ibid., 111f.

21. R. Maddin, T. S. Wheeler, and J. D. Muhly, "Tin in the Ancient Near East," *Expedition* 19/2 (1977): 35–47.

to the initial vision of the "wall of tin." The sense of this word association has been predetermined by traditio-historical factors. It by no means intends to draw attention to the pure metal's softness and thereby to the vulnerability and use-lessness of the wall, as has occasionally been suggested[22]; "tin in God's hand" would already hardly allow such an association. Rather, ancient translators have long shown the correct way by rendering this metal as adamant (so LXX, Sym-machus, Peshitta), an extremely hard iron, steel, or diamond. Analogously, the prophet Jeremiah is made into a "bronze wall" (Jer. 1:18; 15:20), and Ezekiel into an "iron wall" (Ezek. 4:3). The image of the bronze or iron (city) wall symbol-izes protection and security not only in these particular prophetic texts, but out-side the Bible as well, especially in Egyptian texts and in classical antiquity. Thus, for example, does the Pharaoh of the Exodus, Ramses II, extol himself: "Do you not know that I am your iron wall?" And the vassal king Abimilki of Tyre refers to the Pharaoh, his lord, as a "bronze wall, erected for 'me'(?)."[23]

Now, however, the prophet sees Yahweh "standing *on* the wall of tin" (not "next" to it, as emerges from the identical terminology in 9:1). This statement is not intended as an amplification of the protective function of the wall, as Bey-erlin (46f.) suggests; rather, this image (in analogy to 9:1, where Yahweh stands "on the altar" in order to destroy the temple) anticipates a devastating act of God that destroys all security.[24] God is, after all, already holding the "tin in his hand," which he will soon "set in the midst of my people." He has become a warrior against Israel (cf. Amos 2:13–16); in view of this, all attempts at gain-ing protection are from the very outset doomed to failure. Expressed differ-ently: The same power that Israel has until now experienced as protection ("wall of tin"), it now experiences — and with the same intensity — as destruc-tion ("Yahweh standing on the wall with tin in his hand").

Yet why is this notion expressed in the vision in so complicated a fashion and with such an uncommon term? In my opinion, only one answer is conceivable: As is the case in the following vision with the wordplay between *qayiṣ*, "summer fruit," and *qēṣ*, "end," so also are related words supposed to resonate in the unusual term *'ănāk*. One popular suggestion is *'ănāhâ*, "sigh, groan, moan" ("See, I am set-

---

22. Landsberger, loc. cit., 287; similarly Ouellette, loc. cit. Cf. the persuasive criticism of Williamson, loc. cit., 105–7.

23. Ouelette, loc. cit., 324f., nn. 22–23. Further examples of this sort have been collected by A. Alt, "Hic murus ahencus esto," *ZDMG* 86 (1933): 33–48. Cf. recently S. Herrmann, "Die Herkunft der 'ehernen Mauer,'" *Altes Testament und christliche Verkündigung: Festschrift A. H. J. Gunneweg* (Stuttgart: W. Kohlhammer, 1987), 344–52, who tries to demonstrate the traditio-historical origin of such statements in predications of the unshakable city of the sun-god; cf. also the classical examples in Gese, loc. cit., 80f., n. 18. For Amos' contemporaries, the background to this image of the "wall of tin" may possibly also include the (greatly intensified) custom of reen-forcing the upper parts of towers of citadel walls with shields, as attested by Assyrian illustrations of the conquest of Lachish (e.g., s.v. "Stadtanlage," *BRL*, 498).

24. Esp. Uehlinger, loc. cit., 94ff., has demonstrated this persuasively drawing on both lin-guistic and iconographic materials.

ting a groan in the midst of my people Israel").[25] Both linguistically and substantively, however, a more likely wordplay involves *ʾānōkî*, "I,"[26] since this particular wordplay is already attested in Akkadian, whence the term *ʾănāk* was appropriated,[27] and is explicated more specifically in the interpretative divine oracle. This divine oracle directs attention very quickly from the weapon in God's hand, symbolized by the tin, to God himself.[28] God's announcement, "I can no longer pass them (i.e., Israel) by (and spare them) (*ʿābar lě*) varies an expression used earlier by God in the book of Amos, though without negation and with a different preposition: "I will pass through the midst of you" (*ʿābar bě*, 5:17). Where that happens, where God enters "into the midst of his (guilty) people Israel," no rescue is possible; lamentation for the dead breaks out everywhere (5:16f.). At the same time, the conclusion ("I can no longer . . . ") makes it clear that ultimately, the protective "wall of tin" was God's own protection, protection not only against external enemies, but above all against himself, since he cannot bear, and indeed intends to punish, injustice and violence toward the weak among his people.

Hence the third vision forces the reader to progress from the association of a city protected by God, via the metaphor of war in which God is the attacker, to the notion of an encounter with God resulting in death. God's patience with his sinful people is at an end. Precisely because Israel is and remains "my people" for God (7:8; 8:2), there is a limit to what he can bear.

[8:1–2] The *fourth vision* exhibits the same structure and progression as the third, though with one significant, threefold difference: What is actually seen is no longer (as was the case in all three previous visions) an incipient event (in Hebrew: participle), but rather an object; only in this vision does God himself not appear. It plays itself out while he himself withdraws from the process, and the interpretation of the vision does not use the future (7:3, 6), nor the *futurum instans* for the immediate future (7:8), but rather the perfect.[29] What is seen *is* already a reality without Israel having realized it.

25. F. Horst, "Die Visionsschilderungen der alttestamentlichen Propheten," *EvT* 20 (1960): 193–205, 201; Ouellette, loc. cit., 329; Gese, loc. cit., 81f.

26. So esp. F. Praetorius, "Bermerkungen zu Amos," *ZAW* 35 (1915): 23. He offers a double translation: "See, I am setting the I (previously rendered more freely: see, I am setting myself) in the midst of my people Israel." Cf. R. B. Coote, *Amos among the Prophets*, 92f.; Williamson, loc. cit., 117f., n. 69, and esp. Baltzer, loc. cit. (n. 19).

27. In the Ishtar hymn, col. 41, lines 23–24: *anāku anāku anāk siparri [anāku]* , "Tin am I, the tin of bronze [am I]," cited after A. Falkenstein, "Sumerische religiöse Texte," *ZA* 56 [N.S. 22] (1964): 76; cf. Beyerlin, loc. cit., 28f.; Baltzer, loc. cit., 14.

28. Rudolph, in loc., who rejects the wordplay for grammatical reasons, does nonetheless recognize correctly that the essential change between the second and third vision is "that Yahweh himself now sets about actualizing his work of destruction: the plagues he earlier sent could yet be thwarted . . . " (236).

29. Word order militates against any (theoretically possible) understanding of the verb as a participle ("the end is in the coming"). Cf. also the word's history of influence within the Old Testament in Ezek. 7; Lam. 4:18; Gen. 6:13 (Priestly); Dan. 8:17.

The object Amos perceives in this vision evokes the most varied associations. Initially, the basket of fruit is a symbol of the year's foremost time of joy, the time in which Israel celebrated its main festival, the festival of wine and oil, of figs and pomegranates, the festival of thanksgiving for the precious gifts of the land, the festival of free-flowing jubilation and dancing. Yet—just as in the third vision—as soon as Amos is prompted to utter and identify what he has seen, the reader becomes aware of other things as well. Harvest, which this fruit basket represents, is in prophecy also a symbol of judgment, as is already shown by the image of the fully laden and teetering harvest cart in Amos 2:13. Late Old Testament prophecy is full of examples of this notion, one in which the *tertium comparationis* is usually the ingathering of sheaves; perhaps Amos was the first to use the image of harvest as a metaphor for judgment.[30] In any case, the wordplay characterizing this vision—*qayiṣ* (from the root *qyṣ*, "to be hot"), "summer fruit," and *qēṣ* (from the root *qṣṣ*, "cut off"), "end"—is more than a purely fortuitous, original linguistic association. We do not even know whether during Amos' time the orthography and pronunciation of the two words were not identical, such that contemporary readers would possibly always have heard the two meanings together.[31] In any case, these two nouns were also related much more closely in substance for readers at that time than are the terms "harvest" and "judgment" in English; moreover, for people in the ancient Orient, a thing's name yet contained the secret of its essence in a much different fashion than, for example, was the case in classical antiquity, and certainly for us today.

However that may be, the interpretive divine oracle defines unequivocally what is viewed, and does so in the harshest conceivable manner. Here an even more gruesome change occurs in the fourth vision than in the third: from the notion of the festival to the idea of destruction. If God is no longer able to spare Israel, then the people of God are not only—as previously already—ripe for "harvest," but have now come to their "end." After all, for a long time they have been living (a) despite their own sin, and (b) only because God has spared them (cf. the analogous idea in Hos. 11:8f.). Because God's patience has run out, Israel's "harvest" and "end" are not events in a distant future, but rather have already commenced. Through the third and fourth visions, Amos has become a prophet of death. The final vision shows how this "end" will take place.

---

30. On the basis of such considerations, some have also considered translating "harvest basket" in Amos 8:1f., thinking then of an empty basket (H. Weippert, "Amos—seine Bilder," 24; E. Zenger, "Die eigentliche Botschaft des Amos," in E. Schillebeeckx, ed., *Mystik und Politik: Festschrift J. B. Metz* [Mainz: Matthias-Grünewald, 1988], 394–406, 399f.).

31. In the famous Gezer Calendar from the tenth century B.C.E., the final month is called *qṣ*, which can mean both "month of summer fruit" as well as "final month," and perhaps both together; cf. B. Rathjen, "A Critical Note on Amos 8:1–2," *JBL* 83 (1964): 416f.

Amos Is Prohibited from Speaking
Amos 7:9–17

8 . . . Then the Lord said, "See, I am setting tin in the midst of my people Israel; I can no longer pass them by (and spare them).

9 The high places of Isaac shall be made desolate,
and the sanctuaries of Israel shall be laid waste,
and I will rise against the house of Jeroboam with the sword."

10 Then Amaziah, the priest of Bethel, sent to King Jeroboam of Israel, saying, "Amos has conspired against you in the very center of the house of Israel; the land is not able to bear all his words. 11 For thus Amos has said: 'Jeroboam shall die by the sword, and Israel must go into exile away from his land.'" 12 And Amaziah said to Amos, "O seer, go, flee away to the land of Judah, eat your bread there, and prophesy there; 13 but you can no longer prophesy at Bethel, for it is the king's sanctuary, and it is a temple of the kingdom." 14 Then Amos answered Amaziah, "Although I (was)[1] no prophet, nor member of a prophetic guild,[2] but rather a herdsman, and a dresser of sycamore trees, 15 Yahweh took me from following the flock, and Yahweh said to me, 'Go, prophesy to my people Israel.' 16 But now hear the word of Yahweh. Because you say, 'Do not prophesy[3] against Israel, and do not vilify[3] the house of Isaac,' 17 therefore thus says Yahweh:

'Your wife shall become a prostitute in the city,[4]
and your sons and your daughters shall fall by the sword,
and your land shall be parceled out by line;
you yourself shall die in an unclean land,
and Israel must go into exile away from its land.'"

---

1. Regarding the rendering of the nominal clause as a dependent clause, cf. R. Bach, "Erwägungen zu Amos 7,14," in J. Jeremias and L. Perlitt, eds., *Die Botschaft und die Boten: Festschrift H. W. Wolff* (Neukirchen-Vluyn: Neukirchener Verlag, 1981), 203–16, 212f.

2. Since in the two sentences "I (was) no prophet" and "I (was) no member of a prophetic guild" the second sentence offers a partial statement of the more comprehensive first one, the connective *wĕ* is to be understood explicatively ("i.e."); cf. *G–K*[28], 154n1b, as well as the examples in E. Vogt, "Waw explicative in Amos 7:14," *ExpTim* 68 (1956/57): 301f., and Rudolph, in loc. This need not be translated in English.

3. Both instances attest an amplified negation of the imperative (so-called prohibitive) as in the commandments; cf. *G–K*[28], 107o; 109c; 152b;, cf. also the appropriation of the form in 2:12.

4. Following Symmachus, passive vocalization is occasionally suggested: " . . . will be treated like a prostitute." The other versions, however, follow the MT.

8:2b . . . Then Yahweh said to me, "The end has come upon my people Israel; I can no longer pass them by (and spare them)."

Bibliography: A. J. Bjørndalen, "Erwägungen zur Zukunft des Amazja und Israels nach der Überlieferung Am 7,10–17," in R. Albertz et al., eds., *Werden und Wirken des Alten Testaments: Festschrift C. Westermann* (Göttingen: Vandenhoeck & Ruprecht, 1980), 236–51; H. Utzschneider, "Die Amazjaerzählung (Am 7,10–17) zwischen Literatur und Historie," *BN* 41 (1988): 76–101.

Amos 7:10–17, the only narrative (of a disciple?) concerning the prophet himself in the book of Amos, is the best-known individual text in the book; numerous specialized studies even today testify to the special interest exegetes have in this text.[5] It has, however, often been misunderstood in two respects. Earlier scholarship (Marti, Sellin, A. Weiser [1929], and others) tried to understand the text biographically, and several contemporary exegetes still follow this tradition (e.g., Watts, Hammershaimb, Andersen-Freedman). Support has been drawn, for example, from the fact that the narrative enters rather abruptly, from which scholars have concluded the presence of an earlier, larger narrative context. Such an interpretation, however, is already rendered less persuasive by the fact that the reader does not even learn of the decisive consequences following for the prophet Amos from this dispute with the priest Amaziah; although exegetes expect as a logical consequence of the text that the prophet might return to the Southern Kingdom (Weiser; Wolff; Rudolph), be deported to the Southern Kingdom (Kapelrud; Amsler; R. R. Wilson, *Prophecy and Society in Ancient Israel* [Philadelphia: Fortress, 1980], 270), or die a martyr's death in Bethel (Herntrich and Ackroyd following the Christian *Vitae Prophetarum*), and so on, the text itself says nothing of any of this. And it certainly says nothing about whether Amos had already been in Bethel more frequently, had prophesied there at an important festival, how the king reacted to Amaziah's news, and so on. The text is oriented rather toward the divine oracle at the end and toward the preceding divine oracle of Amos himself; otherwise, it limits information to the circumstances of these divine oracles necessary for the reader's own understanding. Even this information consists

---

5. In addition to the works of Bjørndalen and Utzschneider already mentioned, cf. recently esp. G. M. Tucker, "Prophetic Authenticity: A Form-Critical Study of Amos 7:10–17," *Int* 27 (1973): 423–37; P. R. Ackroyd, "A Judgment Narrative Between Kings and Chronicles? An Approach to Amos 7:9–17," in G. W. Coats and B. O. Long, eds., *Canon and Authority: Essays in Old Testament Religion and Theology* (Philadelphia: Fortress, 1977), 71–87; R. Bach, loc. cit.; C. Hardmeier, "Alttestamentliche Exegese und linguistische Erzählforschung: Grundfragen der Erzähltextinterpretation am Beispiel von Amos 7,10–17*," *WD* N.S. 18 (1985): 49–71. The authors quoted here also variously adduce earlier scholarship, among which I would like to emphasize esp. the contributions of Rowley, "Was Amos a Nabi?" in *Festschrift O. Eissfeldt* (Halle a. d. S.: Max Niemeyer, 1947), 191–98, Würthwein ("Amos-Studien," *ZAW* 1949/50), and Smend ("Das Nein des Amos," *EvT* 23 [1963]: 404–23).

almost exclusively only in words (of the priest Amaziah) and citations (Wolff correctly recalls what are known as the apophthegmata of the Gospels).

A second and even more widespread misunderstanding is that the narrative is usually interpreted as an individual text, with scholars arguing that it in all likelihood ended up in its present position by chance. Verses 10–17, however, are linked in so many ways to their context that the narrative cannot be fully understood without that context. This interconnection applies both to the end of the preceding third vision ("in the midst of my people Israel," 7:8b / "in the very center of the house of Israel," 7:10b; "I can no longer . . . ," 7:8b / "you can no longer . . . ," 7:13a) as well as to the end of the following fourth vision (" . . . upon [to] my people Israel," 8:2b / " . . . to my people Israel," 7:15b; "I can no longer . . . ," 8:2b / "you can no longer . . . ," 7:13a); yet it applies even more to the transition verse 9 (cf. the "the high places of Isaac" there with the "house of Isaac" in v. 16—the name Isaac does not otherwise occur in the book of Amos; cf. also the "sanctuaries of Israel" in v. 9 with the "king's sanctuary" in v. 13, and the "house of Jeroboam," which will end by "the sword," with v. 11a). H. Utzschneider has performed the service of disclosing all these connections with exceptional clarity. It is by no means an accident, and even less a sign of the redactors' incompetence, that the narrative comprising Amos 7:10–17 interrupts the originally paired set of visions in 7:7f. and 8:1f. Rather, it stands between the third and fourth visions in order to show later readers why Amos' intercession, which in the first and second visions was yet successful, is silent beginning with the third vision, and why it is no longer able to dissuade God from carrying out his acts of disaster. The visionary accounts themselves do not indicate at which point God's patience in bearing with his sinful people runs out. In the earliest book of Amos, chaps. 1–6 as a whole served this purpose.

The encounter between the priest Amaziah and the prophet Amos is portrayed in two sections of almost equal length. Each of the two opponents speaks once (vv. 10–13, 14–17), albeit both of them in a complex discourse nexus in which the discourse direction changes (in the case of Amaziah) or in which different speakers are mentioned and cited (in the case of Amos). The complexity of these discourses derives from the fact that the two dialogue partners are not really being portrayed in their mutual reactions to the actual course of this dispute, but rather in connection with the authority in whose name and commission they are acting in the first place. The priest of the royal sanctuary in Bethel is presented to the reader first in his official function; as is his duty, he sends a message to his state superior, the king, before turning to Amos. Analogously, Amos is presented first in relation to his superior, God, before he turns with his divine oracle to Amaziah. Moreover, both speakers cite their dialogue partner either literally or substantively to their respective superiors (vv. 11, 16). Through these artistic devices, the narrator manages from the very beginning to juxtapose—in the figures of the priest

Amaziah and the prophet Amos—state interest on the one hand, and the divine will on the other.

[7:10] The considerable extent to which the narrator understands Amaziah as a representative of the state is shown by the first term in the latter's official message to the king. Amos' prophecy is considered from a purely political perspective as "conspiracy" against the state or against its highest representative. In the books of Kings, this term generally refers to coups and revolutions (or attempts at such) against current rulers, among which the revolution of Jehu (2 Kings 9:14; 10:9) was of the most serious consequences.[6] Hence according to Amaziah, the king Jeroboam II[7] is in the utmost danger if he continues to allow Amos to engage in revolutionary activity. The emphasis in this warning falls on the place, whereby the unusual formulation is clearly alluding to the third vision (7:8). Just as in the latter Yahweh became a mortal threat "in the midst of my people Israel," so also, according to Amaziah, does Amos become a mortal threat for Jeroboam "in the very center of the house of Israel." The difference between the two formulations is that in the first case, the election ("my people") is threatened, and in the second the state ("house of Israel"; cf. the discussion of 5:1). This underscores the enormous difference from the very outset in the perspectives of God and of Amaziah. Yet the conclusions they draw are again analogous. The third vision shows the end of the divine patience: "I can no longer (pass them by and spare them)." The Amaziah narrative shows the end of the state's patience: The official state high priest stipulates for the prophet, "You can no longer (prophesy at Bethel)" (v. 13); the altered formulation in his message to the king earlier was "The land (i.e., the territory of the state) is not able to bear all his words," with the image of an overflowing vessel constituting the background to this language. Here, however, the logic of the narrative within the context of the cycle of visions becomes clear: Wherever king and priest as representatives of the state determine the degree to which both they and their subjects are to accept the word of God—a word on which their very existence and authority does, after all, depend—God himself stipulates the end of this state, which is no longer acceptable to him.

[7:11] This basic idea is developed step by step in what follows. In the summary of Amos' message, emphatically attributed back to Amos himself (Amos himself sees it differently, vv. 16f.), it is noteworthy on the one hand that not a word is said concerning any sin on Israel's part; that is, nowhere does it become clear that the prophetic oracle is aiming at eliciting insight; on the other hand, the variously attested announcement of Israel's exile (cf. 4:3; 5:5, 27; 6:7) is accompanied by the prediction—attested nowhere else in the book of Amos—of Jeroboam's death, and again without any reasons. The interests of the state clearly step anew into the foreground.

---

6. Cf. the material and its discussion in Ackroyd, loc. cit., 77f.

7. The apposition "the king of Israel" shows clearly that this text is directed at Judean readers.

[**7:12–13**] In this context, the priest's advice to Amos, whom he strikingly addresses as "seer" (cf. 1:1) rather than "prophet" (cf. v. 14),[8] to flee to his native Judah, which is nearby, is hardly an expression of a conflict regarding authority (Wolff); rather, it is an attempt to eliminate as quickly as possible this threat to the state. Amaziah is concerned not with punishing Amos, but with political stability for the Northern Kingdom of Israel. Just as the Jerusalem high priest was to oversee "any madman who plays the prophet" (Jer. 29:26), so also was Amaziah as high priest in Bethel to do the same. As the agent of the king, it was his duty to determine what was said at the state and royal sanctuary. Neither Amos' profession nor his legitimate professional income is to be jeopardized (v. 12b); in Bethel (and in the attendant state territory: v. 16), however, his words—especially those against the king—are intolerable.

[**7:14–15**] Amos' response in vv. 14f. begins with a double counter. The twice-repeated "not . . . I" (v. 14a) is countered by the positive statement "but rather . . . I" (v. 14b) on the one hand, and by the "(but) Yahweh . . . " (v. 15) on the other, which acquires even more weight through its change of subject. This conceptual sequence must be kept in mind when we consider the old point of contention, namely, whether the nominal clauses without verbs in v. 14 are to be translated in the present ("I am no prophet") or past ("I was no prophet"); this question extends back to the very beginning of biblical exegesis and still has not been resolved.[9] Syntactically, the understanding in past time seems more likely, and was thus chosen by the LXX and Peshitta (the Vulgate takes a different view); this derives from the fact that the continuation ("[but] Yahweh took me . . ") is formulated in past narrative time, albeit in distinction to the preceding v. 13. The substantive difference is that in an understanding of v. 14 as present time, Amos rejects the title of prophet while by contrast claiming prophetic activity in v. 15; in an understanding as past time, Amos is usually considered to be rejecting the title of prophet only for the past, not for the present. The wording, however, by no means definitively allows this determination. The two explicative possibilities do come considerably closer if one recognizes that the second sentence member in v. 14 ("no member of a prophetic guild") is not intended to offer any additional statement, but rather a more precise delineation of the extremely comprehensive first one.[10] This also

---

8. A "seer" is set apart primarily by special personal gifts (cf., e.g., 1 Sam. 9), not by any institutional function (cf. v. 14). Is the narrator trying through the priest's form of address to allude to Amos' visions?

9. Wolff and Rudolph, in loc., enumerate less likely solutions (Driver and others: interrogative without interrogative particle; Cohen and others: different interpretations of *lō'*, "not." in the first two sentences).

10. Concerning the wide semantic sphere of the title "prophet," cf., e.g., J. Jeremias, "*nābî'* Prophet," *THAT* 2.7–26; H. P. Müller, "*nābî*," *ThWAT*, vol. 5 (Stuttgart: W. Kohlhammer, 1984), 140–63. Verse 14 does not suggest any restriction of the term to cult prophets, around which the discussion revolved in the 1950s and 1960s.

allows a more precise understanding of the firm exegetical point of departure mentioned at the beginning, namely, the opposition between v. 14a and vv. 14b, 15. Amos points out over against Amaziah that he has not undergone any training as a prophet of the sort attested for us with the same terminology ("pupils of prophets," "member of a prophetic company") in the Elisha-narratives (2 Kings 2:3, 5; 4:1; 6:1; 9:1, et passim) and in 1 Kings 20:35; rather, he owes his prophetic activity to God's unexpected intervention in his daily life as a farmer. This is what obliged him to step forward as a prophet in the Northern Kingdom (concerning the coercive nature of this commission, cf. 3:8). This clarification implies two things. First, by drawing attention to his agricultural existence, Amos is emphasizing his economic independence. Prophetic activity offers him no economic support such that the priest, by prohibiting him from prophesying in Bethel, might cause him financial distress. He has at his disposal both larger livestock (the singular *bôqēr* is denominated from the common word *bāqār,* "oxen") as well as small livestock, unless the expression, "take from following the sheep" (used similarly in reference to David, 2 Sam. 7:8), is merely proverbial.[11] He also dresses sycamore figs, which prosper in the warm climate of the Jordan depression, toward which his hometown Tekoa is oriented; the fruit is ripened and brought to a higher degree of sweetness by means of regular scratching or slitting, as is still done today in some locales.[12] For this purpose, the Targum understands Amos as owning property in the Shephelah. In any case, he did have access to different sources of income.

A much more essential element than this clarification of Amos' economic independence, however, is the emphasis on the authority of his prophetic activity: "Not I . . " (v. 14), "but rather Yahweh . . . " (v. 15). This elevates the narrated conflict to the level at which it belongs. It is not Amaziah and Amos who are involved in this conflict, but rather Jeroboam II (or the state) and Yahweh. As little as Amos desired this prophetic activity, or even prepared himself for it professionally, just as little can he determine where he will step forward with it. In the name of the state, the priest forbids Amos from speaking at the state sanctuary, and thus in actuality tries to forbid God from speaking and acting with regard to his own people. The priest's order, "go, flee away . . . " (v. 12) is countered by God's commission, "go, prophesy to my people Israel . . . " (v. 15).

---

11. Cf. H. Schult, "Amos 7,15a und die Legitimation des Aussenseiters," in *Probleme biblischer Theologie: Festschrift G. von Rad,* ed. H. W. Wolff (Munich: Kaiser, 1971), 462–78, who nonetheless does defend the historicity of this information (475f.). Amos 1:1 also supports this; cf. the extensive discussion in H.-J. Stoebe, "Der Prophet Amos und sein bürgerlicher Beruf," *WD* N.S. 5 (1957): 160–81; S. Segert, "Zur Bedeutung des Wortes *nōqēd,*" in *Hebräische Wortforschung: Festschrift Walter Baumgartner,* VTSup 16 (1967): 279–83.

12. The process and purpose of this procedure is thoroughly explained by J. Galil, "An Ancient Technique for Ripening Sycamore Fruit in East-Mediterranean Countries," *Economic Botany* 22 (1968): 178–90; 188f.

[**7:16**] Verse 16 shows this opposition even more sharply: "You say, 'Do *not* prophesy . . . ' " (cf. v. 13). Amaziah's (formally intensified; cf. note 3) prohibition doubly restricts and misunderstands the divine commission. Although Amos was sent "to" Israel, to "speak to it," Amaziah turns this into activity "against" Israel (v. 16); more importantly yet, although God sent Amos "to my people Israel" (cf. 7:8 and 8:2 in the visions), Amaziah knows only state terminology: "Do not vilify the house of Isaac."[13]

[**7:17**] Accordingly, it is no longer Amos, but rather God who now answers Amaziah; Amaziah was, after all, once *his* priest, while now he is merely an organ of the state trying to obstruct God's unpleasant words. For just that reason, he will experience its truth personally. The sentences of disaster against him are intended as intensifications, and initially pick up on the ancient oriental imprecatory tradition (Wolff). The public shame of one's wife (probably by enemies), the violent death of one's children (cf. vv. 9, 11), and the loss of one's property—already an indication of exile—are merely the prelude to the harshest conceivable fate for a priest: death "on unclean ground," that is, in a land far from God and without any possible cultic contact with God (cf. more precisely Hos. 9:3ff.). Yet even this harsh fate is merely one example of the experience waiting for all Israel. Hence at the conclusion, Amos' oracle from v. 11b is emphatically repeated with exactly the same wording, except that now it is attributed to its real initiator, God.[14] The priest who for the sake of state stability wanted to forbid Amos from speaking, will experience personally and in all its severity the truth of the prophetic word of God. God's patience with his people, however, runs out once and for all (7:8; 8:2) where that people not only becomes permanently guilty toward him, but also, through the organs of its state, obstructs him from speaking—that is, from pointing out its culpability—through its prophets. Without the demonstrations of sin provided by its prophets (and without their intercession, 7:1–6), Israel is irrevocably lost. From the retrospective of the text, this means that the people of God would long ago have perished had it had no prophets.

13. The word rendered by "vilify (preach, so NRSV)" originally refers to the "slavering, dripping" speech of the ecstatic; during Amos' time (cf. esp. Micah 2:6), it refers to the passionate engagement for something. The use of the term "Isaac" is as yet unexplained; outside Amos 7:9, 16, the Old Testament never uses this term parallel with Israel, and never as a reference to the Northern Kingdom. Rudolph, 237n3, enumerates the various solutions suggested. One should probably follow Wolff, *Amos' geistige Heimat,* 54f. (see also ET, *Amos the Prophet*), who suggests that the striking double mention of Beer-sheba (5:5; 8:14) in the book of Amos should be viewed in connection with this linguistic usage, since Beer-sheba is firmly associated with the Isaac-tradition in Genesis (esp. chap. 26). The polemic in 5:5 and 8:14, however, is clearly later and hardly preexilic.

14. Cf. the terminologically identical confirmation of this announcement's actualization in the Deuteronomistic history: 2 Kings 17:23 for the Northern Kingdom, 2 Kings 25:21 for the Southern Kingdom. Concerning the history of influence of Amos 7:10–17 as a whole, cf. the much-discussed chapter 1 Kings 13.

[7:9] The purpose of the narrative in Amos 7:10–17 is to ground and explain the third vision. To that end, a poetic verse functioning as a hinge has been inserted with v. 9 between the visionary account and the narrative. Its intention is to render more precise the general pronouncement "I can no longer pass them by (and spare them)" in v. 8 by picking up and generalizing in an anticipatory fashion (or by altering) the terminology of the narrative. It speaks about the end of the "house of Jeroboam" instead of about the death of Jeroboam (v. 11; Jeroboam II had perhaps already died a natural death), about the plural "sanctuaries of Israel" instead of about the sanctuary in Bethel (v. 13), and about the "high places of Isaac" instead of about the "house of Isaac (v. 16; see above)." The meaning of this procedure emerges when one notes how strongly this connective verse links Amos' ideas with those of Hosea. Within the book of Amos, only Amos 7:9 mentions "high places"; only v. 9 distinguishes state cultic sites ("sanctuaries") from local cultic sites ("high places"); only v. 9 predicts disaster for a dynasty; and above all, only v. 9 mentions kingship and cultic sites, politics and the cult in the same breath (cf. v. 11). By contrast, Hosea attests all these things several times: Worship at the high places is the central theme in 4:4ff., and especially in 4:11ff.; the state sanctuaries are the central theme in 8:4ff., 10:5ff., and 13:2, each time in connection with the theme of kingship; and 1:4 already mentions the dynasty of Jehu. Apparently, the tradents of the book of Amos establish this connection between the words of Amos and Hosea to impress upon readers that one must consider the prophetic voices of both Amos and Hosea together to comprehend the entire measure of Israel's sin, as well as the limits of the divine patience about which the third vision (Amos 7:8) spoke. The narrative already available in 7:10–17 had anticipated this development insofar as its announcement of the loss of the land (vv. 11, 17) touched on one of Hosea's central themes. Ultimately, the beginnings of the development resulting in the book of the Minor Prophets lie concealed in this association of the two prophetic books.[15] Temporally, the fall of the Northern Kingdom in 722/21 is clearly presupposed, and presumably is already several decades past, since the Amaziah-narrative already anticipated in v. 9 was also not formulated until long after the fall of Samaria.[16]

---

15. Cf. J. Jeremias, "Die Anfänge des Dodekapropheton," in *Hosea und Amos,* 34ff.

16. Utzschneider, loc. cit., 98ff. Cf. the conclusive demonstration in Williamson, loc. cit. (with bibliography concerning the visions), 116–21, that Amos 7:10–17 stands extremely close to the slightly younger Deuteronomistic theology.

Explications of the End
Amos 8:3–14

2b ... Then Yahweh said to me, "The end has come upon my people
Israel;
I can no longer pass them by (and spare them).

3 The singers[1] of the palace shall be wailing in that day,"
says the Lord Yahweh;
"the dead bodies shall be many, cast out in every place. Be silent!"

4 Hear this, you that trample on the needy,[2]
and want to bring to ruin the poor of the land,[3] saying,[4]

5 "When will the new moon be over so that we may sell grain;
and the sabbath, so that we may offer wheat for sale?[5]
We will make the ephah small, and the shekel great,
and practice deceit with false balances,

6 buying the poor for silver
and the needy for a pair of sandals,
and selling the sweepings of the wheat."[6]

7 Yahweh has sworn by the pride of Jacob:
Surely I will never forget any of their deeds.

8 *Shall not the land tremble on this account,*
and everyone mourn who lives in it,
and all of it rise like 'the Nile,'[7]
and be tossed about[8] and sink again[7] like the Nile of Egypt?

---

1. Instead of *šîrôt*, "songs" (the plural is otherwise always masculine in the Old Testament; cf. here v. 10), one generally reads *šārôt*, "(female) singers" (or *śārôt*, "princesses"). In that case, however, *hêkāl* is referring to the royal palace; by contrast, female singers are never attested in connection with the temple. If with Gordis and Hayes one reads *šûrôt*, "walls" (cf. LXX: the ceiling of a room), the reference would more likely be—under the influence of 9:11ff.—to temple walls.

2. Cf. note 2 concerning 2:7.

3. Literally: " ... and that with the intention of putting an end to the poor of the land." Concerning the function of the copula before infinitive constructs, cf. *G–K*[28], 114p. The form of the infinitive hiphil is contracted (*G–K*[28], section 53q).

4. The first word in v. 5 probably yet belongs poetically to v. 4 (Gese, loc. cit. [see bibliography], 61).

5. Literally "open (the sack, etc., of) corn/grain."

6. Verse 6b is an addendum stylistically interrupting the framework, since it offers neither infinitives (like vv. 4b, 5b, 6a) nor final clauses (like v. 5a).

7. Concerning the original reading, cf. the parallel verse 9:5 and *BHS*.

8. This metrically superfluous verb is absent in the LXX as well as in the parallel verse 9:5.

9 *On that day, says the Lord Yahweh,*
   I will make the sun go down at noon,
   and darken the earth in broad daylight.

10 *I will turn your feasts into mourning,*
   and all your songs into lamentation;
   I will bring sackcloth on all loins,
   and baldness on every head;
   I will make it like the mourning for an only son
   and the end of it like a bitter day.

11 *Days are surely coming, says the Lord Yahweh,*
   when I will send a famine on the land;
   not a famine of bread, or a thirst for water,
   but of hearing the words⁹ of Yahweh.

12 *They shall stagger from sea to sea,*
   and from north to east they shall run to and fro,
   seeking the word of Yahweh,
   but they shall not find it.

13 *In that day*
   the beautiful young women and the young men
   shall faint for thirst.

14 *Those who swear by Ashimah¹⁰ of Samaria,*
   and say, "As your god lives, O Dan,"
   and, "As the power¹⁰ of Beer-sheba lives" —
   they shall fall, and never rise again.

Bibliography: H. Gese, "Amos 8,4–8: Der kosmische Frevel händlerischer Habgier," in V. Fritz, K.-F. Pohlmann, and H.-C. Schmitt, eds., *Prophet und Prophetenbuch: Festschrift O. Kaiser,* BZAW 185 (Berlin/New York: W. de Gruyter, 1989), 59–72; J. Jeremias, "Am 8,4–7—ein Kommentar zu 2:6f.," in *Hosea und Amos,* 231–43; G. Fleischer, *Menschenverkäufer,* 174–200.

Amos 8:3–14 offers a commentary on 8:1f.; that is, this section tries to make comprehensible for its readers the enigmatically brief, harsh announcement of the fourth vision ("the end has come upon my people Israel"); it does this through a renewed, concise demonstration of culpability (vv. 4–7, 14) and through a description of the deadly "end" itself (vv. 3, 8–14). Differently than in the narrative 7:10–17, it does not pick up on the conceptuality of the vision itself; rather, it cites Amos' preceding words—something every careful reader easily notices—simultaneously combining them with others of his words, and in every case extrapolating beyond their initial meaning. Although Amos'

9. The majority of versions reads the singular in accomodation to v. 12.
10. Cf. the commentary.

tradents already chose a similar course in 6:8–11, 8:3–14 belongs to a considerably later period (its oldest parts date at earliest to the time of Jeremiah,[11] its
latest to the exilic and postexilic period). This becomes quite evident even before any consideration of content, since in almost all partial sections (except in
v. 8 and in the younger vv. 11f., which cite the plague series from 4:6ff.), the
citations of earlier words of Amos are artificially organized such that first an allusion is made to the verses that stand later; that is, the ideas are reversed. In
vv. 3 and 7, serving as a framework for the accusation in vv. 4–6, first 6:9f. are
cited, and then 6:8. In vv. 4–6 themselves, first 2:7, and then 2:6 are cited; in
vv. 9f. and 13f., both of which allude to Amos 5, first vv. 16f., 18–20 are cited
in vv. 9f., and then 5:2 in 8:13f.

Yet another formal indicator supports the assumption of later provenance.
Amos 8:3–14 is characterized by a plethora of organizational framing formulae occurring only rarely in the preceding chapters, but then with increasing frequency during the late period of prophecy; two of these framing formulae are
taken up again in the latest part of the book of Amos (9:11–15) with reference
to 8:11, 13. The expanded divine oracular formula ("says the Lord Yahweh")
is attested only twice in the rest of the book of Amos (3:13; 4:5), but then three
times in rapid succession in 8:3–14 (vv. 3, 9, 11); the same applies to the common framing formula "in that day" (otherwise only in 2:16; later in 9:11; here
in 8:3, 9, 13). To this can be added the more extensive formula "the time is
surely coming" in v. 11, occurring previously only in 4:2 (and later in 9:13). In
this way, vv. 9f., 11f., and 13f. are formally clearly separated from vv. 3–8 (or
vv. 3, 4–7, 8). As will be shown, what is involved here is a successive redactional continuation of vv. 3–8.

[8:3] Verse 3 provides a bridge between the visionary account and the commentary, and is modeled formally after the analogous transitional verse following the third vision (7:9; perfect consecutive, moreover: masculine form
with feminine subject)[12]; it employs a framing formula ("in that day"; cf. vv. 9,
13; 9:11) of the sort extremely frequent in prophecy in cases of redactional con-
tinuations of older texts.[13] It strikes up two themes for what follows. First, all
gaiety disappears and is transformed into lament, even within the sphere of the
royal palace, the paradigmatic locus of the celebration of festivals; this constitutes a prelude to the thematic material of v. 10a. Second, it picks up ideas from
6:10, with its reference (1) to the accumulation of corpses for which funeral per-
sonnel is no longer available—the catchword "cast" may be clarifying the fate

---

11. Cf. A. Weiser, *Profetie*, 26ff.; I. Willi-Plein, *Schriftexegese*, 49; J. Jeremias, loc. cit.

12. Substantively, mention of the royal palace provides a loose connection with the mention
(one singular in the book of Amos) of the "house of Jeroboam" in 7:9; cf. Weiser, ibid., 25.

13. Cf. P. A. Munch, *The Expression Bajjôm Hāhū': Is It an Eschatological terminus technicus?* (Oslo: J. Dybwad, 1936).

of Samaria's women (4:3)—and then (2) to the powerless attempt to defend oneself against God's deadly nearness through silence, as is required in worship services in the presence of the holy (cf. the discussion of 6:10); this constitutes a prelude to v. 10b and vv. 13f. Verse 3 is linked with vv. 4–8, specifically with v. 7, through the allusion to 6:10; v. 7 picks up just as emphatically on 6:8.

The Destruction of the Poor
(8:4–7[8])

The commentarial character of vv. 4ff. is already apparent in its introduction. That is, the summons "hear this" is not directed toward what follows, since vv. 4–6 exclusively provide more specific characterizations of the listeners or readers being addressed in the vocative, or more precisely: seek to disclose their intentions; rather, the summons is directed backward to the "end of Israel" (v. 2) and to the accumulation of corpses (v. 3). This is also why the divine oath in v. 7 does not, as otherwise in Amos, contain any announcement of chastisement (cf. 4:2; 6:8), but rather only the assurance that God will always remember the deeds of the guilty; after all, in vv. 2 and 3 the punishment itself has already long become unsurpassably harsh. Verse 4 never introduced an independent saying; vv. 4f. seek rather, as a written text, to make the relentless finality of the fourth vision completely clear to later readers by referring to a measure of guilt rendering impossible in principle the kind of forgiveness Amos was yet able to solicit from God in the first visions (7:1–6). What is this guilt?

In contradistinction to all the other accusatory texts in the book of Amos, vv. 4–6 do not refer primarily to deeds of the guilty (such is the case only initially in v. 4a with its participle cited from 2:7), but rather to their plans and most secret intentions; to this end, the original text uses a long, uninterrupted chain of infinitives extending to v. 6 that can hardly be imitated in translation. At the beginning (v. 4a) and end of this series (v. 6), Amos 2:7 and 2:6 are cited with only slight variation,[14] while the middle verses framed in this way, namely, 4b–5, introduce a completely new theme into the book of Amos: deceit in commerce, through which the traditional concepts are now interpreted. This brings to substantive expression the fact that vv. 4–6 are to be understood as an in-

---

14. The citatory character becomes clear in both passages esp. from two features: (1) The formulations of 2:7 and 2:6 are picked up verbatim (most evidently in the unusual orthography of the first verb in v. 4); (2) in the Hebrew, the appropriated characterizations of the poor (twice *'ebyôn; 'ănāwîm, dallîm*), though rendered in part in a new position, are yet taken in exactly the same previous case, such that in 8:4 and 8:6 the singular and plural are juxtaposed in *parallelismus membrorum* in an extremely unusual fashion. Moreover, 8:6 maintains the distinction between prepositions in 2:6 even though the distinction itself becomes substantively meaningless.

separable unit, not as a summation of different individual transgressions as in the older reference text 2:6–8.

The concerns of vv. 4–6 are accordingly completely different from those of the earlier text of Amos in 2:6–8. The latter used accusations involving the various spheres of life to demonstrate in an exemplary fashion how much greater was Israel's sin than that of its neighbors, as corrupt as the latter may well have been. Amos 8:4–6 grounds the "end of Israel" with a single, albeit wholly grievous, sin.

[**8:4**] Verse 4b indicates the nature of this sin in the manner of a superscription with an extremely artificial wordplay on the sabbath (*lašbît,* "bring to an end/to ruin, remove"); vv. 5f. then explicate this more fully. According to v. 4b, violence toward the "poor" as cited from 2:7 (mentioned as a guiding category in the singular at the beginning in v. 4a and in conclusion in v. 6) involves the methodical destruction of the independent existence of small farmers and tradespeople. Reference to them as "needy" (*'ănāwîm*) recalls for later readers the language of the psalms; the "needy, poor, afflicted" stand especially close to God, and can count on his help because they cannot help themselves (cf. Pss. 22:25, 27 [24, 26E]; 34:3 [2E]; 37:11; 69:33 [32E], et passim).

[**8:5**] The means to such annihilation of a person's existence are enumerated in v. 5, which formulates independently of Amos 2:6f. Here the traditional wisdom theme of deceptive weights (cf. Prov. 11:1; 16:11; 20:10, 23, et passim[15]) is immediately presented in three variations: (1) a reduction in the volume-measure for goods sold (one ephah was about forty liters); (2) enlargement of the weight-stones for silver (one shekel was about 11.5 grams; coins were not used until the Persian period); and finally (3) manipulation of scales through a distortion of the beams. This theme is then associated with the problem of sanctification of holy days: Greedy merchants, unable to rest or rejoice on holidays, lose not only one full day of profit per month because of the day of the new moon (cf. 1 Sam. 20:5; 2 Kings 4:23; Hos. 2:13 [11E]; Isa. 1:13, et passim)—whose exact holiday character is not known more precisely—they also lose one day a week because of the sabbath, on which the bearing of any burdens (Jer. 17:21ff.) and all trade (Neh. 13:15ff.) were forbidden.[16] This sort of commercial deception was bitterly contested both within the wisdom tradition and, especially, during the age of Jeremiah (Deut. 25:13–15; Micah 6:9ff.), from which this text, too, most likely dates.

[**8:6**] In Amos 8:4–6, however, it is only a means to an end, which v. 6 then presents by picking up and varying 2:6.[17] The "ruin of the poor" (v. 4b) comes

15. Cf. the examples in Wolff, in loc.; idem, *Amos' geistige Heimat,* 42f. (see also ET, *Amos the Prophet*).

16. One recently popular thesis is that during Amos' time, the sabbath had the character of a monthly festival of the full moon; cf. Fleischer, loc. cit., 190ff., with bibliography.

17. By declaring v. 6a to be a gloss, Gese, loc. cit., 62, robs the conceptual progression of vv. 4–7 of its goal.

about through their inability to pay back even a trifling debt ("for a pair of sandals")[18]; those ruined through such deceptive commerce—with the help of the
money taken from them through such business deception (*b instrumentalis*)—
fall into economic dependence on the merchants, either in the form of debt slavery or in the form of an obligation to pay dues. To that end, they are "bought"
by the creditors. This significant alteration of the original in 2:6 ("sell") shows
that 8:6 is no longer concerned with the problem of debt slavery in the technical sense; this is rather a case of figurative meaning. Neither does the occasion
of purchase play any role now (in 2:6, "the righteous" are sold), since the means
to such "purchase" are falsified measures, weights, and scales.[19] Though one
might perceive the contempt for human beings to be stronger in Amos 2:6–8,
the intensification in 8:4–6 consists in the fact that the numerous infinitives disclose a methodical, multilayered strategy through which human beings become
disposable goods for other human beings as a means of increasing wealth.

[8:7] The weight of this sin is amplified to a virtually unsurpassable degree
through the solemn divine oath. This oath guarantees that God will continually be mindful of this sin; that is, the sins will be recalled in full when the perpetrators themselves are punished (cf. Isa. 22:14).[20] This verse is highly
unusual, and indeed even unique insofar as God does not—as in all other instances in prophecy—swear by himself or by his own holiness, by his name,
by his right hand, and so on, but rather by the *gā'ôn* of Jacob. This peculiarity
is incomprehensible without the reference to 6:8. There, too, Yahweh swears,
but he swears *by* his own life *in the face of* the *gā'ôn* of Jacob, referring to Israel's self-confident "pride" or "arrogance," which Yahweh "hates" and "ab-
hors." Yahweh cannot swear *by* this "arrogance" as he otherwise does when
swearing by himself, even though several exegetes since J. Wellhausen have
attempted such an interpretation. Rather, the term "*gā'ôn* of Jacob" contains a
wordplay, since outside the book of Amos the term refers to the "majesty of
Jacob," that is, to Israel's land (Ps. 47:5 [4E]; Nahum 2:3 [2E]), itself an expression of the "majesty of God," that is, of his kingship.[21] This generates a

18. R. Kessler, "Die angeblichen Kornhändler von Am VIII 4–7," *VT* 39 (1989): 13–22, 20,
considers whether the pair of sandals might be mentioned as a loan pledge.

19. It is only against the syntax of the verse that Wolff, in loc., finds in v. 5 and v. 6 two separate
reproofs, and Rudolph, in loc., even finds two different groups of persons involved in the two verses
(grain and slave traders). Substantive considerations also militate against this separation; cf. esp. R.
Kessler, loc. cit., and earlier M. Krause, "Soziale Kritik" (1972), 33–39; B. Lang, "Sklaven und Unfreie im Buch Amos," *VT* 31 (1981): 482–88. Lang mentions an interesting parallel from an Alalakh-
text in which the verb "buy" is similarly used to express the appropriation of an insolvent debtor (484).
I have collected together (loc. cit., 241f.) Old Testament parallels for the "buying" of several people.

20. By contrast, cf. petitions in the Psalter such as "Do not remember the sins of my youth"
(Ps. 25:7).

21. Cf. the detailed argumentation in J. Jeremias, "Jakob im Amosbuch," in *Hosea und Amos*,
257ff.

profound, albeit extremely artificial, irony which is already the expression of nascent scribal erudition: Yahweh swears "by the pride of Jacob," that is, by his world dominion for the benefit of Israel, dominion which the people of God, by absurdly overestimating their own potential, distort into "arrogance" and thereby forfeit once and for all; indeed, they will now experience it personally as judgment.

[8:8] Verse 8 leaves this divine discourse. It is a bridge that on the one hand draws the conclusions from the preceding material, and on the other provides a transition to the cosmic perspective of the following verses. The sin God holds on to programmatically has universal effects extending even into the sphere of nature. The initial "on this account" in v. 8 refers not to the divine oath (Rudolph), but rather, as in analogous rhetorical questions (Jer. 5:9, 29; 9:8 [9E]; Isa. 57:6), to the gravity of sin. Substantive parallels to such sin causing the earth to become sterile can be found beginning with the prophecy of the seventh century (Hab. 3:17; Jer. 3:3; 12:4; 23:10; Hos. 4:3, et passim). When the community of the people of God collapses, the world order, including nature and all human beings (Hos. 4:3 enumerates animals separately), are drawn into the catastrophe. The verb in the second half of the verse scintillates semantically: In reference to human beings, *'ābal* means to "mourn"; in reference to natural phenomena (cf. 1:2), it means to "dry up." "Mourning" is thus the manner in which human beings experience the failure of nature's powers of blessing; it is not a matter of feeling.[22] Amos 8:8 reformulates this traditional notion (similarly Nahum 1:5) into a reference to an earthquake. This interprets the earthquake mentioned in the superscription 1:1 (cf. 2:13; 9:1) retrospectively as a cosmic event; it does so by picking up on 2:13, where the same sin as in 8:4–6 is punished with an earthquake, and in anticipation of 9:5a, from which 8:8a is presumably drawing.[23] This is presumably also the purpose served by the peculiar comparison between the earthquake and the gradual rising and falling of the Nile, which the verb "be tossed about" (added by later redactors; absent in LXX and the parallel verse 9:5) apparently would like to understand from the thematic perspective of the battle of chaos. Amos 8:8b in its own turn is then cited almost verbatim in the last hymnic section of the book of Amos (9:5f.). This inclusion allows the cosmic conceptual horizon to be maintained for all the intervening verses. At the same time, it already alludes in an anticipatory fashion to the cosmic consequences of the destruction of the temple (9:1ff.).

---

22. Cf. the bibliography in note 1 to Amos 1:1f.

23. So the majority of (esp. earlier) exegetes. Concerning the supporting argumentation, cf. esp. F. Crüsemann, *Studien zur Formgeschichte von Hymnus und Danklied,* WMANT 32 (Neukirchen-Vluyn: Neukirchener Verlag, 1969), 101f., and J. Jeremias, *Hosea und Amos,* 193ff. Wolff, in loc., and Gese, loc. cit., 64ff., consider the dependency to be reversed.

Transformed Joy
(8:9–10)

Verses 9f. carry this notion forward with a formula typical of redactional con-
tinuations in prophecy (cf. v. 3). It is by no means certain whether v. 9 is alluding to the experience of a solar eclipse as an ominous portent, as has
frequently been suggested[24]; it is just as conceivable that the notion of the dark
"day of Yahweh" (5:18–20) led to this formulation. What is essential for this
text is that the "transformation" (*hpk* as in 4:11; 5:7, 8; 6:12) of joy to lamentation within the human experiential sphere is associated with cosmic changes.
The twice-mentioned "mourning," replacing the "festivals" (5:21), carries forward the "mourning" for the devastated world and failing nature from v. 8. Here
the silent songs allude to v. 3, the striking up of lamentations to 5:1f., and the
lamentation and mourning rites[25] to 5:16f.; v. 10b then intensifies these appropriated ideas by transferring them into the most personal experiential sphere
(mourning for an only child).

Hunger for God's Word
(8:11–12)

Verses 11f. introduce the new theme of nascent hunger for Yahweh's word
with a transitional formula ("days are surely coming") common especially in
the book of Jeremiah (fifteen occurrences); here in the book of Amos, it may
be alluding to 4:2. These verses pick up on the content of the narrative in
7:10–17, in which Amos is forbidden to speak, and presuppose that narrative—just as do, analogously, 2:11f. and 9:10. In addition, they are probably
also presupposing the (exilic) series of plagues in 4:6ff. insofar as the ideas of
hunger and thirst (4:6–8) are transferred here so consciously, with the emphatic assertion—as in 4:6ff.—that this hunger does not simply come about in
some arbitrary fashion, but rather is sent by God himself; furthermore, an unusual term may have been appropriated from 4:8 with the verb *nw'*, "stagger,
reel" (in the sense of "wander about aimlessly"). Verses 11f. are in all likelihood also presupposing the Deuteronomic declaration that human beings do
not live "from bread alone," but rather "by every word that comes from the

---

24. This presupposition has also prompted some to use 8:9 to date the book of Amos; cf. J. A.
Soggin, "Das Erdbeben von Amos 1:1 und die Chronologie der Könige Ussia und Jotham von
Juda," *ZAW* 82 (1970): 117–21; F. R. Stephenson, "Astronomical Verification and Dating of Old
Testament Passages Referring to Solar Eclipses," *PEQ* 107 (1975): 107–20.

25. Concerning the mourning rites of wearing sackcloth and cutting one's hair, cf. E. Kutsch,
"'Trauerbräuche' und 'Selbstminderungsriten' im Alten Testament," *Kleine Schriften zum Alten
Testament*, BZAW 168 (Berlin: Töpelmann, 1986), 81ff.

mouth of Yahweh" (Deut. 8:3; cf. 30:15)[26]; similarly, the formulation "hearing the words of Yahweh" is characteristic for the same period, specifically for the Jeremiah narratives (Jer. 36:11; 37:2; 43:1; so Wolff). Above all, however, they presuppose that the readers no longer dispute the fact that the words of Amos and of the other prophets of judgment were God's own words (cf. the Deuteronomistic verses 2:11f. and 3:7); for Jerusalem, however, this was the case only after the catastrophe came, that is, during the exile. This true word of God is ultimately one (singular in v. 12), even though it consists of many individual words (plural in v. 11).

The intention of this text is to warn and to entice. The generation of the exile should not consider itself rescued merely because it survived the destruction of Jerusalem and of the land; rather, it is rescued only if at least now, after God's judgment, it takes seriously Amos' word of God. For this generation, too, there may be a "too late," when God himself withdraws his word. For the generation of the exile, this prospect is just as devastating as the announcement of the destruction of cultic sites was for previous generations (9:1ff.; cf. 5:5f.; 3:14). This is why vv. 11f. were presumably once positioned quite consciously immediately before the concluding vision in 9:1ff.; they would make it quite clear to generations after 587/6 that the people of God would lose all contact with God—and thus be irrevocably lost—not just with the destruction of the Jerusalem temple, but rather with the withdrawal of the prophetic word. In rendering this idea, v. 12 uses the language of Hosea ("seek—not find"; cf. Hos. 5:6, 15); the geographical terms cover the entire breadth of the earth ("from sea to sea" as in Ps. 72:8 and Zech. 9:10),[27] or—with the directions north and east— the distribution of the dispersed population of exiles (Maag, Wolff).

The Fall of the Apostates
(8:13–14)

The most recent redactional continuation of the text, again introduced by the formula "in that day" (vv. 3, 9), provides the most obvious and simultaneously the most superficial allusion to Amos himself; it picks up literally the metaphorical language of the lamentation in 5:2 (the fall of the "maiden Israel"), transfers it to reality, and allows it to frame the entire statement of the two verses (vv. 13a + 14b). The appropriation of the theme "thirst" at the end of v. 13 also provides an extremely external continuation of vv. 11f. In these verses, the

26. Cf. in this regard L. Perlitt, "Wovon der Mensch lebt (Dtn 8,3b)," in L. Perlitt and J. Jeremias, eds., *Die Botschaft und die Boten: Festschrift H. W. Wolff* (Neukirchen-Vluyn: Neukirchener Verlag, 1981), 403–26. Just as in Deut. 8:3b "the gift of the law . . . is already God's gift of life as such" (ibid., 412), so also in Amos 8:11f. the prophetic word.

27. There is no evidence for the occasionally suggested understanding of this as a smaller area (from the Mediterranean to the Dead Sea: Harper, Rudolph).

young women and men represent the seemingly unrestricted, full vitality of life that is suddenly snatched away. The real emphasis of the verses, however, is actually on the accusations of v. 14a, directed probably at the mixed population that arose in the Northern Kingdom after the fall of Samaria and about whose influence on Judah during the early-postexilic period the book of Nehemiah speaks (3:33ff. [4:1ff.E], et passim). The oaths mentioned in v. 14a are intended as confessions, and in this context are juxtaposed with Yahweh's own oath in v. 7. The formula "as god x lives" appeals to the power of the deity, which is why the Old Testament always understands oaths to foreign gods as a breach of the first commandment (Deut. 6:12f.; Jer. 5:7; 12:16; Zeph. 1:5, et passim).[28]

Strikingly, however, only in the middle example, that is, in the case of Dan, does the Masoretic Text mention a deity; in the case of Samaria, the "sin of Samaria" at most enciphers such mention, and in the case of Beer-sheba the "pilgrimage to Beer-sheba" mentions such not at all. Since the beginning of religio-historical inquiry in Old Testament scholarship, exegetes have suspected that names of gods originally occupied both places. H. M. Barstad[29] most recently offered a thorough presentation of the thesis that in both passages, the Masoretes either consciously defused the traditional consonantal text or unconsciously misunderstood it; J. A. Soggin followed him in his own commentary. In that case, the "Ashimah of Samaria"[30] would be a deity which, according to 2 Kings 17:30 (a verse that perhaps also strongly influenced Amos 5:26), was introduced in Samaria by colonists from Hamath after the fall of the Northern Kingdom, a deity whose male counterpart is attested later in the Jewish colony in Elephantine under the name "Ashema-bethel" and who perhaps lived on in the Phoenician Eshmun. The "power of Beer-sheba"[31] would be a characterization of the deity sought out by inhabitants of the Northern Kingdom on their pilgrimage deep into the south of Judah at the edge of the Negeb—such a pilgrimage is indeed already attested for the readers of the book of Amos in Amos 5:5.[32] With

---

28. Cf. F. Horst, "Der Eid im Alten Testament," *EvT* 17 (1957): 366–84; also in idem, *Gottes Recht: Studien zum Recht im Alten Testament,* ed. Hans Walter Wolff; TB 12 (Munich: Kaiser, 1961), 292–314. For this reason, the masoretes vocalized the oath to foreign gods artificially with different vowels than those in the oath to Yahweh.

29. "The Deities of Am 8,14," in idem, *Religious Polemics,* 143–201.

30. The orthography '*šmt* would hardly indicate a construct state (Barstad, 164f.), but more likely an old ending (Soggin).

31. The term *drkt* is attested several times in Ugaritic in reference to divine dominion; the LXX reads "the god." Barstad critically discusses other suggested solutions (conjecture to *dwdk,* "your beloved," or *drk,* as "your pantheon"), loc. cit., 192f. Cf. also Wolff and Rudolph, in loc.

32. Whereas the pilgrimage in 5:4f. stood in opposition to "seeking God," so here in opposition to hearing the prophetic word (vv. 11f.). The reality of such pilgrimages is attested by inscriptions from Kuntillet 'Ajrud, situated far to the south of Beer-sheba, where the divine names "Yahweh of Samaria" and "Yahweh of Teman" (a region in Edom) occur next to one another. Cf. J. Emerton, "New Light on Israelite Religion: The Implications of the Inscriptions from Kuntillet 'Ajrud," *ZAW* 94 (1982): 2–20.

respect to Judean Beer-sheba as well, this would argue that the Samaritans were not worshiping Israel's God, Yahweh. A bilingual (Aramaic and Greek) consecratory inscription from the Hellenistic period has thrown light on the textually inoffensive divine name in the middle oath, "your god, Dan"; the Greek text of this inscription, found during excavations at Tell Dan (= Tell el-Qâdī), reads *theoi toi en Danois,* "to the god in Dan."[33] This shows that later as well, the deity worshiped in Dan without any personal name was designated through reference to the famous sanctuary; above all, however, it shows that unlike in Bethel, which Josiah desecrated, cultic continuity was maintained for centuries in Dan. For Amos 8:14, it is a continuity of apostasy from Yahweh. Dan and Beer-sheba, as in the frequent formula "from Dan to Beer-sheba," are presumably mentioned as the northernmost and southernmost points of culpability, which is thus presented as all-encompassing. As in 2:4 and 5:26, later redactors here retroactively supply that particular reproof they found most lacking in the book of Amos: the worship of foreign gods; it was with this reproof above all others that they sought to explain the fall of the state of Israel (and Judah).

The Fifth Vision: God on the Altar Amos 9:1–6

9:1 I saw the Lord standing on the altar, and he said:
'I will' strike[1] the capitals until the thresholds shake,
The lives of all of them 'will end' in 'quaking';[2]
and what is left of them I will kill with the sword;
not one of them shall flee away,

---

33. Cf. A. Biran, "'To the God who is in Dan,'" in idem, ed., *Temples and High Places in Biblical Times* (Jerusalem: Nelson Glueck School of Biblical Archaeology of Hebrew Union College–Jewish Institute of Religion, 1981), 142–51.

1. The imperative *hk,* "strike," arose perhaps from an infinitive absolute *hkh* (so Duhm and many followers); the following word begins again with *h.* Concerning the problem of content, cf. the commentary.

2. MT ("and end their life on the head") has been transmitted incorrectly; the suggestions for emendation are numerous (cf. Wolff, Rudolph). In any case, *bṣʿ* does not mean—so the usual translation—"shatter," but rather "cut off," and with human beings as its object (esp. in the piel) always means "to cut off (life's thread)," "kill"; so already—correctly—A. B. Ehrlich, *Randglossen V,* 253. The first word is most likely to be vocalized with Rudolph as a passive participle *ūběṣu'im;* the second is perhaps to be read with Volz, Weiser, and others, as *běra'aš.*

not one of them shall escape.

2   Though they dig into Sheol,
    from there shall my hand take them;
    though they climb up to heaven,
    from there I will bring them down.
3   Though they hide themselves on the top of Carmel,
    from there I will search out and take them;
    and though they hide *from my sight* at the bottom of the sea,
    there I will command the serpent, and it shall bite them.
4   And though they go into captivity in front of their enemies,
    there I will command the sword, and it shall kill them;
    and I will fix my eyes on them
    for harm and not for good.

5   *(But the Lord, Yahweh of hosts,)*
    he who touches the earth and it teeters,[3]
    and all who live in it mourn,
    (and all of it rises like the Nile,
    and sinks again, like the Nile of Egypt;)
6   *who builds his 'upper chambers'*[4] *in the heavens,*
    and founds his vault above the earth;
    who calls for the waters of the sea,
    and pours them out upon the surface of the earth—
    Yahweh is his name.[5]

Bibliography: J. Ouellette, "The Shaking of the Thresholds in Amos 9:1," *HUCA* 43 (1972): 23–27; J. Jeremias, "Das unzugängliche Heiligtum: Zur letzten Vision des Amos (Am 9,1–4) (1993)," in *Hosea und Amos*, 244–265.

[9:1–4] The fifth and final vision stands alone and without any parallel vision; because it differs from the preceding visions in a number of ways, scholars have variously separated it from the literary context of the first four visions[6] (the present commentary does so only for the sake of overview). In

3. The mixed vocalization of the Masoretes possibly intends to offer two readings (present or past); cf. Rudolph.

4. The uncertain objects in v. 6a must be interpreted from the perspective of the unequivocal verbs. Here, then, the term *m'lh*, usually meaning "step, stair," either has the meaning of *'lyh*, "upper floor, chambers" (Hammershaimb, van Gelderen), or has been spelled incorrectly from the latter. The second object (literally: "something fitted/bound together") must have an otherwise unattested architectural meaning.

5. V. 5aα$_1$ and v. 5b possibly represent later fills in the hymn: At the beginning, a solemn divine predicate is added to frame the refrain; later, expressions from 8:8 are added.

6. Esp. Maag, *Text*, 46f.; Reventlow, *Amt*, 49f.; Willi-Plein, *Schriftexegese*, 48; Koch, *Amos: Teil 2*, 86; Hayes, 216.

so doing, however, scholars overlook how strongly the oracles against the nations and the visionary accounts constitute parallel compositions variously culminating in the fifth and final member.[7] Like the Israel-strophe in 2:6ff., so also do 9:1ff. involve a conscious and intensified transformation of the preceding, well-defined forms.

The vision begins such that the prophet is now the immediate subject of what is seen; there is no more talk about God initiating this for him. The coercion attaching to this vision is implied by this abbreviation; what is then seen is as a matter of fact neither a disaster nor any symbol such as in the previous visions, but rather God himself, moreover at an unusual place. With a conscious intensification of the third vision, God now stands on the altar—not "next to" it, as one might also translate, in which case one would be importing priestly associations into the picture (cf. 1 Kings 13:1), associations inconceivable in the parallel 7:7. Every reader already suspects here that this altar will enjoy as little duration as did the wall of tin on which God was standing according to 7:7; thus God will shatter not only the protective power of the state, which ultimately was merely God's own protection, but also Israel's very relationship with God. Surprisingly, there now follows no dialogue between God and the prophet as in the previous visions, no objection from the prophet, and no divine inquiry concerning what is viewed that might reveal the meaning of the vision beyond the prophet's own answer. Neither mode of prophetic participation in the vision is needed any longer. The time has long passed when intercession might be possible, and after 7:7, the vision of 9:1 is in no way ambiguous or in need of interpretation. In his following announcement of disaster, God merely presents the horrible consequences. In this announcement, there is no more talk of "my people Israel" as in 7:8 and 8:2; it speaks rather from the most extreme distance about "all of them." The "end of my people Israel" (8:2) has already occurred.

[9:1a] An understanding of the final vision is admittedly hampered by the fact that its beginning has obviously been transmitted erroneously. According to the MT, an unnamed person—who can hardly be anyone other than the prophet (a heavenly messenger, which has also been suggested, would have needed an introduction)—receives the commission to strike the temple at its (column) capitals such that it shakes, and to kill the people in the sanctuary area ("all of them"). Such a commission would be without parallel in the Old Testament, and might at most be understood as a symbolic act (so Graf Reventlow, who, to be sure, presumes this interpretation applies only to the first imperative). This solution, however, can hardly be considered, since prophets' symbolic acts are otherwise always accompanied by an interpretation, which is

7. Cf. the detailed argumentation in J. Jeremias, "Völkersprüche und Visionsberichte im Amosbuch," in *Hosea und Amos*, 157ff., carrying forward observations made by Weiser (*Profetie*), Wolff, and Gese ("Komposition").

precisely what is missing here (Rudolph). Hence almost all exegetes correctly assume that originally Yahweh was the logical subject of the disputed verbs; in the present text, he is already such in the announcement of the slaying. The brevity of the description of what is seen does remain rather peculiar compared with God's long discourse; many exegetes (including Wolff) have thus assumed the presence of more extensive textual corruption, and have included the blow to the capitals as part of the vision. It is more likely, however, that in God's discourse the fate of the temple and that of human beings are to be presented as inextricably bound together.

The key to understanding the vision resides in precisely this connection between the shaking of the temple and the broadly explicated, irrevocable predicament of human beings. Following J. Wellhausen, this connection has usually been understood with typically western logic such that the disintegrating temple with its collapsing roof would crush the assembled crowd. Yet this does not really accord with the fact that nowhere is the alleged collapse of the temple portrayed; instead, the shaking of the thresholds is peculiarly emphasized. Nor does it accord with the fact that judged by the standards of the Jerusalem temple, only the priests would have been in the building in the first place, with the crowd out in its forecourts. Above all, however, it does not accord with the fact that what follows (vv. 1b–4) employs completely different notions about the death of these people, notions among which the double statement—framing the entirety—about death by the sword (vv. 1a, 4a) is particularly noticeable. Wolff, however, has already observed that the shaking of the thresholds resulting from the disintegrating columns suggests a reference to the columns flanking those thresholds. Moreover, we know of no other (non-wooden) columns in connection with the Jerusalem temple, with which we are familiar for the Old Testament period only from the construction account in 1 Kings 6–8. In that case, however, something decisive must be involved in this quaking of the threshold. But what?

The closest parallel (and aid to understanding) is Isaiah's famous vision in which the thresholds quake along with the pivots of the temple doors (recessed to the side) before the holiness of the world's king when he approaches Israel's impenitence (Isa. 6:4). Isaiah 6 reveals more clearly than does Amos 9:1 that this sanctuary possesses cosmic dimensions; the reader's eye is continually guided back and forth between the heavenly temple (God's throne; singing seraphim) and the earthly temple (hem of the heavenly king; atonement of the prophet), since according to the ancient oriental conception of the world this does not really involve two sacred places, but rather only dimensions of God's *one* dwelling place, the one to which the heavenly and earthly congregations simultaneously shout in joy.[8] This is why the temple gates are called "gates of eternity" in Ps. 24:7, 9: They belong to the world of God and participate both

---

8. Cf. the excellent essay by M. Metzger, "Himmlische und irdische Wohnstatt Jahwes," *UF* 2 (1970): 139–58.

in its holiness and in its unshakable stability.[9] Only God himself, as the founder of that sanctuary, can ever shake those gates (cf. Amos 9:6). Where he indeed does this, the world itself comes unhinged, since its own stability rests on the stability of the temple (in Ps. 93, cf. vv. 1f. with vv. 4f.). Whether such notions from the Jerusalem temple on the whole apply in full or merely in part to Bethel as well, it is certain that God's standing on the altar, along with his stroke against the temple columns, possesses cosmic significance for Israel insofar as it means the end of all contact with God as well as the end of asylum, that is, of all protection with God.[10] This latter consideration explains why in what follows, metaphors of war determine the train of thought as in the third vision, evoking images of the irrevocable ruin of every individual person. For Amos, a world without any contact with God is a lost world.

[9:1b–4a] This is not, however, a world from which God has withdrawn, but rather a world full of God's pernicious presence; since the third vision (7:7f.), he has, after all, become Israel's enemy. No one can escape him, a notion inculcated with almost fatiguing intensity in what follows. First of all, a stylistic form which H. Gese calls "irreal synchoresis"[11] brings to double expression in a seemingly illogical fashion that "all of them" will perish in the quaking of the temple, but then nonetheless insists that "what is left of them" will be delivered over expressly to the divine sword. It becomes clear that every exception is to be excluded, and that the temple-quaking and the following war belong together as a single event in which the former is the cause, the latter the consequence (cf. 2:13–16). Nonetheless, thereafter positive sentences emphasize thetically once again the impossibility of any flight, and finally the form of the priamel already familiar from chap. 2 demonstrates the same thesis with negative sentences in (again, five) examples. Unlike 2:14–16, these examples do not involve the exceptional possibilities of powerful persons in war, but rather carry forward the vision's cosmic perspective in adducing the farthest conceivable possibilities of flight, whereby the text makes no distinction between geographical (top of Carmel, bottom of the sea) and cosmic (heaven, underworld) remoteness. The geographical terms are also characterized by mythic connotations: In Egypt, the mountain peak is the locus of the rising sun, the sea the locus of the setting sun.[12] Here we notice the proximity of this imagery to

9. Cf. O. Keel, *The Symbolism of the Biblical World*, trans. T. J. Hallett (New York: Seabury, 1978), 171f.

10. The interpretation of the fifth vision in 3:14 esp. alludes to the temple as a place of asylum; at the same time, this interpretation shows that later redactors also sought the unnamed site of the sanctuary in Bethel.

11. H. Gese, "Kleine Beiträge zum Verständnis des Amosbuches," *VT* 12 (1962): 436f.

12. Keel, loc. cit., 23f. From the prebiblical period, we can compare the famous parallel to v. 2 in Amarna Letter no. 264 (J. A. Knudtzon, ed., *Die El-Amarna-Tafeln I* [Leipzig: Hinrichs, 1915], 826f.): "When we climb up to heaven, when we go down to the earth, our head is in your hands."

Ps. 139:8ff., which is considerably younger than Amos 9.[13] In each instance, a highest high (in Amos 9: heaven and the peak of Carmel) is juxtaposed with a lowest low (in Amos 9: the realm of the dead and the bottom of the sea). The cosmic significance of the temple corresponds to the cosmic effects of God's disasters in a world without the temple. For both Amos and his tradents, God's power is limitless, extending even into the underworld, which Psalm 88 presents as separate from God[14]; its instruments are mythical powers which traditionally were considered to be anti-divine powers of chaos ("serpent"; cf. Isa. 27:1; Job 26:13).

This train of thought, however, is not finished until the priamel, in a final intensification, reaches the sphere of history. It repeats on a smaller scale (as do also 2:14–16) the number "five" of the visions (and of the older oracles against the nations), including the device allowing two conceptual pairs (underworld/heaven, peak of Carmel/bottom of the sea) to lead to an isolated final member. It speaks of a war in which all the Israelites, without exception, are killed (cf. the framing reappropriation of the expression "killing with the sword" from v. 1), such that not even the exile about which Amos threateningly spoke in several instances (5:27; 6:7; 7:11, 17) offers a chance of at least physical survival.

[9:4b] With a concise summary, the visionary accounts conclude. The older—that is, preexilic—book of Amos presumably once also ended here. God's gaze upon Israel, a gaze that once led to the deliverance of the oppressed from Egypt (Ex. 3:7, 9), is now fixed upon them "for harm" instead of "for good." With that, Israel is irrevocably lost. In the book of Amos, terminology resonates back to the admonition in 5:14f. to seek "the good" rather than "evil," an admonition accompanied by the famous "perhaps" of God's compassion.[15] From the perspective of the older book's end, it now proves to be its real center.

---

13. The occasionally suspected growth traces within 9:2–4 (P. Weimar, "Der Schluss des Amos-Buches; ein Beitrag zur Redaktionsgeschichte des Amos-Buches," *BN* 16 [1981]: 66f., with bibliography) can linguistically hardly be traced back to influences from Ps. 139. Verses 3–4a are more likely conceivable as an addendum, since they use imagery from Amos (cf. 5:19) anew and announce the (Babylonian) exile in familiar language. Yet E.-J. Waschke is acting precipitately when on the basis of such observations he then immediately dismisses Amos as the author of the fifth vision as a whole ("Die fünfte Vision des Amosbuches (9,1–4)—Eine Nachinterpretation," *ZAW* 106 [1994]: 434–45). He pays sufficient attention neither to the tradition history of the vision (Ouellette, Jeremias; see the bibliography) nor to the interpretation of the vision in 9:8–10 and 3:13f.

14. In this regard, cf. W. Herrmann, "Jahwes Triumph über Mot," *UF* 11 (1979): 371–77.

15. Cf. the analogous idea in Hosea: "Israel has spurned the good"—"Your calf is rejected, O Samaria" (Hos. 8:3, 5).

The Concluding Doxology
(9:5–6)

As in 4:13 and 5:8(f.), the generation that had experienced the destruction of Jerusalem and the exile responded to Amos' final vision with what is known as a judgment-doxology (cf. the excursus to 4:13). Together with the introductory hymn in 1:2, 9:5f. constitutes an artistic literary framework for the book of Amos in its exilic form. Unlike 4:13 and 5:8(f.), however, the concluding doxology in 9:5f. is different insofar as it does not follow imperatives (4:12; 5:4f., 14f.), but rather Yahweh's unsurpassably harsh acts of judgment in the final vision. The consciously ambiguous nuances of the first doxologies thus give way to unequivocalness. At the same time, in 9:5f. it becomes even clearer than before how consciously the hymnic statements were chosen for their respective contexts.

[9:5] First of all, v. 5 expands the quaking of the temple thresholds from v. 1 to include all the earth; it traces that quaking back to Yahweh's own mighty acts, and like 1:2 describes these in the traditional language of theophany portrayals.[16] Yahweh need merely extend his hand, and the earth trembles. As in 1:2, the verb "mourn" (*'bl*) is alluding to the consequences of this quaking, namely, the withdrawal of blessing, though now no longer from nature, but from all humankind.

[9:6] The concluding v. 6 emphasizes even more clearly the cosmic perspective in its extremely daring commentary on and continuation of vv. 1–4. In the Old Testament, God normally "founds" (*ysd*) the earth or Zion with its sanctuary. This usage is now transferred in a highly unusual fashion[17] to the stability of the heavenly sanctuary, a sanctuary which—in an even more unusual fashion—is "founded above (*'al*) the earth." This says more and something different than the rather harmless assertion that heaven rests upon the earth. Rather, the earth is otherwise founded "above the seas" and "above the rivers" so that it might defy all the dangers surrounding it (Ps. 24:2; cf. Ps. 104:3). In that case, Amos 9:6 can hardly be saying anything other than that the palace of the world ruler (cf. the concluding, emphatic "Yahweh is his name") continues to endure even when that ruler desecrates his own temple on earth and rejects his people

16. Cf. J. Jeremias, *Theophanie*, WMANT 10, 2d ed. (Neukirchen-Vluyn: Neukirchener Verlag, 1977), 21f., and esp. Ps. 104:32: "who looks on the earth and it trembles, who touches the mountains and they smoke." The doxology closely recalls Ps. 104 in other ways as well; cf. Ps. 104:3a, 13a. The two combined readings of the Masoretes (see note 3 above) probably intend to say that although such acts of God have already been experienced in part in the past earthquake (Amos 1:1) and in the destruction of Bethel and Jerusalem, their full realization is yet to come.

17. A distant substantive parallel can be found only in 2 Sam. 22:8 (differently in Ps. 18:8 [7E]!).

(9:1–4). The final statement ("who calls for the waters of the sea"), already familiar from 5:8, alludes in this context to the Flood.[18]

Hence it is extremely likely that the dark conclusion to the exilic book of Amos is associating the fifth vision not only with the destruction of the sanctuary in Bethel and its faulty worship (the polemical divine predication "the Lord, Yahweh of hosts," positioned at the beginning of the hymn, especially supports this, picking up as it does on 3:13 and 4:13), but also with the destruction of the Jerusalem temple. It is not God's powerlessness, but rather precisely the limitless power of the heavenly ruler that comes to expression there, such that this very destruction leads the exilic congregation, one submitting to God's judgment, to praise his name. A more essential observation, however, is that the doxologies in the book of Amos must be understood in their close relation to one another. In substance, this means that Amos 9:1–6 is not to be read as the irrevocable conclusion to God's path with his people, but rather as the most extreme experience of God conceivable, one that is to prompt those rescued from the catastrophe to seek the true God, the God who yet inquires concerning his people even when their guilt has reached proportions rendering his most extreme judgment unavoidable.

Prospect:
The Change in Fortune
Amos 9:7–15

9:7 *Are you not like the Cushites to me, O people of Israel? says Yahweh.*
Did I not bring Israel up from the land of Egypt,
and the Philistines from Caphtor and the Arameans from Kir?

8 *Behold, the eyes of the Lord Yahweh are upon the sinful kingdom,*
and I will destroy it from the face of the earth
—except that I will by no means[1] destroy the house of Jacob, says
Yahweh.

---

18. This is why the Masoretes vocalized the *verbum finitum* in v. 6b as a narrative; concerning its interpretation, cf. W. Gross, *Verbform und Funktion*, ATSAT 1 (St. Ottilien: EOS, 1976), 103f.

1. Concerning the unusual position of the negation before an amplifying infinitive absolute, cf. *G–K[28]*, 113v. Wolff shows that, as in Gen. 3:4, misunderstandings within a preceding statement are to be disputed (344). H. Gese has with good reason taken issue with the usual translation, "but I will not utterly destroy the house of Jacob" ("Das Problem von Amos 9,7," in A. H. J. Gunneweg and O. Kaiser, eds., *Textgemäss: Aufsätze und Beiträge zur Hermeneutik des Alten Testaments: Festschrift E. Würthwein* [Göttingen: Vandenhoeck & Ruprecht, 1979], 37f., n. 13).

9 *For lo, I will command, and shake the house of Israel [among all the nations]*
   as one shakes with a sieve, but no pebble[2] shall fall to the ground.

10 *All the sinners of my people shall die by the sword, who say: "You will not let evil overtake us[3] or meet us".[4]*

11 *On that day*
   I will raise up the booth of David that is fallen,[5]
   and repair 'its' breaches, and raise up 'its'[6] ruins,
   and rebuild it as in the days of old;

12 *in order that they may possess the remnant of Edom*
   and all the nations upon whom my name has been called,
   says Yahweh, who will do this.

13 *Behold, the time is surely coming, says Yahweh,*
   when the one who plows shall approach the one who reaps,
   and the treader of grapes the one who sows the seed;
   the mountains shall drip sweet wine,
   and all the hills shall melt.[7]

14 *I will turn the fortunes of my people Israel,*
   and they shall rebuild ruined cities and inhabit them;
   they shall plant vineyards and drink their wine,
   and they shall make gardens and eat their fruit.

15 *I will plant them upon their land,*
   and they shall never again be plucked up
   out of the land that I have given them,
   says Yahweh your God.

Bibliography: U. Kellermann, "Der Amosschluss als Stimme deuteronomistischer Heilshoffnung," *EvT* 29 (1969): 169–83; P. Weimar, "Der Schluss des Amos-Buches: Ein Beitrag zur Redaktionsgeschichte des Amos-Buches," *BN* 16 (1981): 60–100; J. Nogalski, *Literary Precursors to the Book of the Twelve*, BZAW 217 (Berlin/New York: W. de Gruyter, 1993), 97–122.

2. Concerning the alternative interpretative possibility of *ṣĕrôr* as "stone" or "little stone, pebble," cf. *HAL*, 987.

3. Literally: "around us, round about us," expressing the idea of being surrounded (Wolff).

4. The versions and numerous modern exegetes alter the verbs slightly (see *BHS*) such that the subject is "evil": "Evil shall not overtake or meet us." Yet this sooner weakens the reproach compared with the MT, which presupposes that the guilty in Amos' saying already know the word of Yahweh.

5. The context requires a preterite understanding of the participle (which in Hebrew is timeless in and of itself); the alternative would be "shoddy."

6. Concerning the meaning of the different suffixes in the MT, cf. Nogalski (see the bibliography to the text), 106. In context, the reference is in each case to the "booth of David"; cf. LXX.

7. Concerning this understanding of the verb, cf. the commentary.

The concluding section presupposes the exilic book of Amos (Amos 1:1–9:6), is intended as its complementary completion, and was not added to the book of Amos until the postexilic period. It is rich in formulaic elements (cf. the threefold use of the divine oracular formula in vv. 7, 8, 12; the three-fold call to attention, "behold, for lo," introducing a new idea in vv. 8, 9, 13; the opening expressions taken from chap. 8 in vv. 11 and 13; the solemn con-cluding formula in v. 15) and consists of three parts that originated succes-sively. As the initial questions in v. 7 show, 9:7–10 reflect a discussion—more exactly, a discussion concerning the fifth and final vision, since vv. 8–10 are full of allusions to formulations from 9:1–4 (cf.the reference to "Yahweh's eyes" in v. 8 with v. 4;[8] cf. Yahweh's "command" in v. 9 with vv. 3 and 4; cf. the "sword" in v. 10a with v. 1; cf. the "harm" or "evil" in v. 10b with v. 4; and in addition to all this, cf. the name of Jacob in v. 8b with 7:3, 6). The discus-sion addresses the double question whether Amos' unsurpassably harsh oracle can claim any validity at all (v. 7), and if so, for whom. Verses 8–10 respond to the latter question with the notion of the judgment of purification.

The clearly younger promises concerning the reestablishment of the "booth of David" (v. 11) and the change in the people's fortune (vv. 14–15) already presuppose the purified congregation and employ themes that are connected much more loosely with Amos' message. As in vv. 8, 9f., first the kingdom, and then the people are addressed. Both promises allude in this way to the older book of Amos such that the announcements of disaster (e.g., 5:11 or 9:8) are turned into their opposites. Amos 9:11, 14f. are connected with the preceding section 9:7–10 particularly through the theme of the land (vv. 8, 15), though here, too, v. 8 announces disaster, and v. 15, by contrast, salvation.

Finally, at an even later date, v. 12 and v. 13 add to the text two verses whose horizon is no longer that of the book of Amos alone, but rather of the larger book of the Twelve Prophets; their intention is to link the book of Amos with the preceding and following books of Joel and Obadiah.

The Judgment of Purification
(9:7–10)

[9:7] Recent scholarship usually isolates the divine oracle in v. 7 from its con-text and interprets it as an especially characteristic individual saying of the prophet, analogous to Amos 3:2, a verse that similarly was considered to be an individual saying with a similar theme (an argument against the popular belief in election as absolute protection from catastrophe). For Amos 9:7, such a possibility cannot be excluded for the oral stage, and in view of 1:3–8, which

---

8. In this case, the allusion is taken so seriously that it causes a brief (only v. 8aα) abandon-ment of the divine discourse, which otherwise characterizes the entire context.

presumably presupposes Amos 9:7 in its juxtaposition of Arameans and Philistines, this is even quite likely.[9] The double question in v. 7, however, taken in and for itself, can be given extremely varying interpretations, and to that extent has been subject to a certain interpretative arbitrariness whenever the contextual aid to understanding offered by the book of Amos itself is dismissed. Hence v. 7, for example, has recently also been understood as a salvific oracle of a later redactor seeking to encourage the disheartened people of God in exile regarding God's possibilities — already variously attested in history — for turning his people's fortunes.[10] In both cases, the presumed dialogue situation lying behind the questions had to be reconstructed from the questions themselves. Such a procedure is, of course, burdened by a high degree of uncertainty.

Moreover, it runs contrary to the biblical text. The dialogue context of v. 7 is precisely indicated in the text by the preceding fifth and final vision and by the following response verses 8–10, which continually refer back to this vision.[11] Verse 7 then presupposes the argumentation against the content of the final vision — namely, the irrevocable ruin of the people of God as a whole — based on reference back to Israel's election. Verse 7 itself does not deny Israel's founding experience with God during the liberation from Egypt, and expresses this in the usual confessional language attested largely in younger texts (cf. merely 2:10); but it aligns it with analogous experiences among neighboring peoples. Given the sense of the provocative question, it can hardly be an accident that with the Philistines and Arameans it is precisely Israel's archenemies from the past and from Amos' own present (cf. the commentary to 1:3–8) who are adduced. The origin of the Philistines, a group of historically powerful, so-called "sea peoples," who conquered large parts of Palestine in the second half of the second millennium B.C.E., and who among other things put an end to the high empire of the Hittites, is presented as being in the western Aegean (Caphtor is probably Crete).[12] The Arameans, who are also linked to Israel's own beginnings, came by way of the marginal zones of the Syrian-Arabian desert into the area of modern Syria (the unknown location of Kir, which is also mentioned in 1:5, is usually sought far to the east because of Isa. 22:6, where it appears

9. Cf. Wolff, in loc. V. Fritz, "Die Fremdvölkersprüche des Amos," *VT* 37 (1987): 26–38, is drawing precipitate conclusions by adducing Gese (see note 1 above) in abruptly declaring 9:7 to be Deuteronomistic, and thus 1:3–5 to be later than Amos (though inconsistently to be pre-Deuteronomistic).

10. So R. B. Coote, *Amos among the Prophets,* 117–20.

11. Even despite the aforementioned stylistic change in v. 8aα, the formal connection between v. 7 and vv. 8ff. is extremely close; cf. Wolff, 345f., and Gese, loc. cit., 34f., 37f.

12. Cf. Zeph. 2:5; Ezek. 25:16, and the Ugaritic *kptr.* LXX, Targum, the Peshitta, and the Vulgate all think of the southern coast of Asia Minor ("Cappadocia"), a location still occasionally advocated today; cf., e.g., G. A. Wainwright, "Caphtor—Cappadocia," *VT* 6 (1956): 199–210.

next to Elam). The relativization of the idea of election is expressed even more forcefully in v. 7a, which because of the offensive content briefly addresses Israel directly and is introduced emphatically as divine discourse. From the perspective of Palestine, the inhabitants of Cush, encompassing geographically modern Ethiopia and the southern Sudan, were the southernmost, most distant, and at the same time—because of their skin color—the strangest people with whom one came into contact (cf. Isa. 18:1f.). Hence Luther's translation "are you not like the Moors to me . . . ?" thus renders precisely what is meant: Israel stands before God without "any historical claim," or without "the summons to a historical provision,"[13] that is, without any special privileges allowing it to sin at will because of some guarantee of forgiveness; God is the Lord of the world, and not Israel's national deity.

[**9:8–10**] Verses 8–10, which introduce the idea of a divine judgment of purification, show why Israel's election was relativized in this way in v. 7. All three verses are clearly to be read together; this is made clear by the parallel beginnings of v. 8 and vv. 9f. ("behold," "for lo") on the one hand, and by the use of the same term for sin in v. 8a and v. 10a on the other, and finally also by the aforementioned shared allusions to the fifth vision. Together, v. 8 and vv. 9f. demonstrate that there are two forms of sin that cannot possibly be compensated by the election of the people of God. For those who fall under either category, the statements of the fifth vision apply in all their severity, albeit—and here the accents are characteristically posited differently than in vv. 1–4 with Amos himself—only for them. They do not apply to the new salvific community.

[**9:8**] Verse 8 refers first of all to the sin of the state, toward which God first directs his "eyes" (v. 8, picking up on v. 4). Whenever God "sees," he then acts either for good (he rescues, e.g., from distress, Ex. 3:7, 9) or for harm. In the book of Amos, the assertion that the state as such is Israel's hotbed of sin is made only by the younger narrative of the dispute between the priest Amaziah and Amos (Amos 7:10–17), a dispute juxtaposing in a fundamental fashion the word of the state's representative and that of Yahweh. The expression "from the face of the earth" (Amos 7:11, 17: "away from his land") is also alluding to Amos 7:11, 17.[14] The announcement of the destruction of the kingdom anticipates a time in which the people of God as a community will live without the apparent support of the state—support which in reality

---

13. M. Buber, *The Prophetic Faith* (New York: Harper & Row, 1960), 99.

14. This assumption is supported by the observation that the expression "die by the sword" in v. 10a is alluding to 7:11b (and 7:9). Failure to recognize these literary connections (and the further connection with 1 Kings 13:34 to be discussed) has often resulted in v. 8a—even quite recently (cf., e.g., K. Koenen, *Heil den Gerechten—Unheil den Sündern! Ein Beitrag zur Theologie der Prophetenbücher,* BZAW 229 [Berlin/New York: W. de Gruyter, 1994], 11f.)—being erroneously referred to the people of Israel as a whole.

represents acute danger. Here the language of v. 8 shows that the verse itself is already formulated from the perspective of the postexilic community; that is, it looks back at the destruction of Jerusalem and is referring the fifth vision to the end of the Davidic rulers. For the middle line of v. 8 is a quote from 1 Kings 13:34, whence also presumably the term for sin (root *ḥṭ'*) has been borrowed, connecting v. 8 with v. 10 and yet otherwise occurring only a single time in the book of Amos (5:12). 1 Kings 13:33f., however, is actually an exilic-Deuteronomistic interpretation of an older narrative involving a prophetic oracle disregarded by King Jeroboam (I). It is this disobedience of the state toward the prophetic word of God ("the sin of the house of Jeroboam," 1 Kings 13:34) which in 1 Kings 13 (as well as according to Amos 7) leads to the violent death of the king (v. 11) or of his entire dynasty (v. 9); this king is once again named Jeroboam (II), so that the connection was self-evident for readers at that time. Amos 9:8 generalizes texts which at first refer only to the Northern Kingdom: The destruction of Samaria and of Jerusalem has shown that God is in a general fashion about to bring to an end the state as an institution of his people[15]; for in both the Southern and Northern Kingdom, the state has disregarded his messengers or even forbidden them from speaking (cf. 2:11f.; 7:10–17).

Yet vv. 8–10 are by no means restricted to retrospective. Verses 8b–10 are rather concerned with the question of what kind of entity, after the fall of Jerusalem, might be God's partner, and who can belong to it. Verse 8b wants first to avoid the misunderstanding that the existence of the people of God as such ceases along with that of the state,[16] and introduces "house of Jacob" (cf. 3:13) as the new name of the new people of God (picking up on Amos 7:2, 5; cf. 8:7). With one possible exception (Ps. 114:1), this term is always used outside the book of Amos in reference to Judah, and stands "with particular significance wherever the old announcement of judgment is revoked and reinterpreted by a message of salvation."[17] The term has been chosen for Amos 9:8 because—in contrast to the "house of Jeroboam," though also to the "house of Israel" (v. 9)—"there is no danger of its being misunderstood in a political sense."[18]

---

15. Here the verb "destroy, exterminate, eradicate" may consciously be alluding to the fate of the Amorites in 2:9, while the more far-reaching expression "eradicate from the face of the earth" evokes associations with the Flood Narrative (Nogalski, loc. cit., 102).

16. This restrictive character, expressed by the same verb as in v. 8a, has often resulted in v. 8b being viewed as an addendum. This view, however, would leave in abeyance the "for" at the beginning of v. 9 linking the sin of v. 8 with that of vv. 9f. "Verses 9f. provide the reasoning for v. 8b, not for 8a" (Rudolph, 276).

17. L. Perlitt, *Bundestheologie im Alten Testament*, WMANT 36 (Neukirchen-Vluyn: Neukirchener Verlag, 1969), 170.

18. H.-J. Zobel, "ya'ăqōḇ/ya'ăqôḇ," *TDOT*, vol. 6 (Grand Rapids: Eerdmans, 1990), 204; cf. J. Jeremias, "Jakob im Amosbuch," in *Hosea und Amos,* 257ff.

[9–10] Verses 9f. make it clear that this "house of Jacob," however, is not simply identical with those who were rescued from the state catastrophe, but rather emerges from an evaluation process which God's order sets into motion (and which later redactors identified with the exile through the addendum "among all the nations," which disrupts the poetic structure[19]). This process is compared with a sieve that retains even small impurities (cf. Sir. 27:4) while permitting good materials (grain or meal) to fall through. Verse 10 shows that essentially Amos' own divine oracle of disaster is intended as a "sieve," that is, as an instrument of evaluation. Whoever after the fall of Jerusalem still treats this divine oracle as thoughtlessly as did the contemporaries of Isaiah (Isa. 5:19) or Micah (Micah 3:11)—to whom a loose allusion is made (cf. also Amos 6:3)—is just as lost as the disobedient state. For the renewal of the remaining "house of Jacob," however, the book of Amos must remain the only, unchangeable standard toward which all life is oriented. The "house of Jacob" and the prophetic word belong *per definitionem* inextricably together; this is why the book of Amos is absolutely vital for the "house of Jacob." When this, the only essential precondition, is fulfilled, God will also actualize his old promises for the remaining "house of Jacob" purified through judgment.

New Kingdom of David and
Commencement of the Time of Salvation (9:11–15)

Two units have been amalgamated within the older material of vv. 11–15 and introduced with formulae (vv. 11a, 13a) that—in reverse sequence—correspond to 8:11, 13 and have presumably been appropriated thence to produce an effective contrast. The first picks up on the David tradition, the second links this with the notion of the turn of fortune and the secured existence of the people of God. In contradistinction to vv. 7–10, neither of these units picks up Deuteronomistic themes, alluding rather to older prophetic sayings already available. Together with the altered object of interest and the specifically Judean perspective, these observations suggest that vv. 11–15 originated later than vv. 7–10 and are intended as a continuation of these verses. Within vv. 11–15, verses 12 and 13 with their wide literary horizon are to be separated yet again, as already mentioned.

[9:11] Verse 11 apparently wants to avoid the usual reference to the "house," that is, to the dynasty of David (so the Targum) by using the unique metaphor of the collapsed "booth of David"—this verb is normally used in reference to stumbling human beings and has probably been selected as an antithesis to 5:2 ("fallen . . . is maiden Israel"); now this booth is to be

---

19. This addendum significantly alters the train of thought: Now the exiles are those saved in the evaluation process (Rudolph).

"raised up again" (picking up terminology from 5:2 yet again). This avoidance of "house" was presumably prompted by two considerations. First, the juxtaposition in v. 8 of the "sinful kingdom" that will be destroyed on the one hand, and the "house of Jacob" that survives (in part) on the other, did not exactly make any robust political promises; second, at the time of this oracle probably only a few members of the Davidic dynasty were still even alive. The dual image of the breaches of the booth that can yet be repaired, and of the ruins that are to be rebuilt, however, shows that this is referring not to a booth with a roof of branches, but rather to an especially simple edifice not yet deserving the name "house." This certainly is not laying the foundation for any new national consciousness or, especially, for a state with any military power. In any event, however, v. 11 is to be read in connection with v. 8. According to v. 11, the surviving "house of Jacob" will not remain without any political form at all; it will not, however, involve a "sinful kingdom" as in the past that disregards the words of God's messengers out of misled self-confidence. Rather, it will be an edifice of David "as in the days of old." This refers to God's time, that is, it alludes to God's ideal beginnings with the Davidic dynasty (cf. 2 Sam 7) before the sin of God's kings thwarted God's plans.

[9:12] To be sure, v. 12 is not focusing on David's original relationship with God (cf., e.g., Isa. 11:1f.), as one might expect on the basis of v. 8. The focus is rather on the sphere of rule of the Davidides; this takes place in a stylistically striking, abrupt transition from poetry to prose, and from the third-person feminine singular to the third-person masculine plural with no mention of a new subject. This stylistic break and thematic shift are complemented by yet another consideration showing that v. 12 is younger than v. 11. Verse 12 is focusing apparently on those nations and boundaries that constituted David's kingdom, since God mentions nations "upon whom my name has been called." This announcement of name is referring to a legal act through which something passes into the possession of the person making the announcement.[20] Among these nations, however, only Edom is emphasized by name, the kinship nation which during and after the destruction of Jerusalem had behaved with particular hostility toward Judah to its own advantage (occupation of the entire southern part of Judah). Yet the unique expression "remnant of Edom" is used here; this can only mean that in the meantime, Edom in its own turn had lost large parts of its original possessions, something that beginning with the fifth century B.C.E. did indeed occur as a result of the influx of Arab tribes.[21]

In the older text, this promise ends solemnly with Yahweh obligating

---

20. Cf. K. Galling, "Die Ausrufung des Namens als Rechtsakt in Israel," *TLZ* 81 (1956): 65–70.

21. M. Weippert, "Edom und Israel," *TRE* 9 (1982): 296.

himself ("who will do this"), perhaps in opposition to the threat in 4:12 ("because I will do this to you").

[9:13] With the introductory formula of 8:11, the concluding section looks to the more distant future; at that time, and as a result of the proper kingship willed by God, not only will the fate of human beings change and be fulfilled (vv. 14f.), but also that of nature (v. 13). The connection between righteous kingship and fertile nature is broadly attested in the ancient Orient[22]; in the Old Testament, this conception is most clearly evident in Psalm 72. In this view, the alterations in nature are always related to human beings; in Amos 9:13, the melting of the mountains—as the parallel statement shows—serves to open up even the last bare patches of land to the overflowing fruitfulness, making possible a completely new harvest of grapes. This is presumably an intensifying allusion to the promise of blessing in the Holiness Code in Lev. 26:5a: "Your threshing shall approach the vintage, and the vintage shall approach the sowing." This is referring to "such a rich yield that the threshing of the corn [prior to the long summer drought] will last on till grape-gathering begins [after this long dry period]. This in its turn, with the pressing and making of oil and wine, will go on so long that it will soon be time to think once more of sowing the new crops."[23] Without the summer drought, or without its effects, there will be no more poverty. (Concerning the allusions to Joel 4:18 [3:18E], see the discussion below.)

[9:14] In the older text, v. 14 followed immediately upon v. 11 (with the concluding formula from v. 12b). Both verses are more reserved in their expectations of salvation; both deal with the rebuilding of something that has been destroyed; both refer to their themes programmatically at the beginning (rebuilding the booth of David, or the turn in the fate of the people of God) and then develop the content of that theme. In contradistinction to v. 13, vv. 14f. are not yet concerned with portraying a salvific period surpassing all previous human experience, but rather only with the fundamental change in the fate of the people of God from distress to salvation. As a reference to this change, postexilic theology coined a *terminus technicus* (literally probably: "to turn the turn"; the majority of versions translates: "to turn the imprisonment"),[24] refer-

---

22. Rudolph correctly refers esp. to L. Dürr, *Ursprung und Ausbau der israelitisch-jüdischen Heilandserwartung* (Berlin: Schwetschke & Söhne, 1925).

23. M. Noth, *Leviticus: A Commentary*, trans. J. E. Anderson, OTL (Philadelphia: Westminster, 1965), 198. In Amos 9:13, the imagery in the first member is analogous insofar as the long summer dry period lies between the plowing after the first autumnal rain (in October) and the preceding grain harvest (in April/May); the second member in 9:13 is substantively identical with Lev. 26:5.

24. Cf. the balanced discussion of scholarship in *HAL*, vol. 4 (1990), 1289f. Perhaps the verb *šûb* is alluding antithetically here to the same verb in 2:4, 6: "for the . . . transgressions of Judah/Israel I will not revoke it (the punishment)" (Coote, *Amos among the Prophets*, 112).

ring not to a restitution of earlier conditions (so the majority of exegetes), but rather to a *restitutio in integrum* in the sense that Yahweh's true plan with Israel can finally be realized. God's goal with Israel is not the destruction of cities and of cultivated land such as that characterizing the reality of the period when these verses were composed, nor such as that which was interpreted for the readers as the fulfillment of Amos' oracle of judgment. God intends rather to render possible again the kind of normal, uninterrupted daily life in which meaningful activity is commensurate with its anticipated result (cf. Isa. 65: 21f.). The real intention of these moderate statements of hope becomes comprehensible only when read against the background of Amos 5:11 as a revocation of the divine curse (on which the younger portrayal of the blessed age in v. 13 could then seamlessly pick up).

[9:15] Following Hos. 2:25 [23E]; 14:6–9 [5–8E]; Jer. 2:21; etc., v. 15 finds in the notion of planting a new nuance that takes the idea a bit further: Not only vineyards, but also the people of God themselves can be "planted." The goal of the metaphor resides in the abiding and unthreatened quality of the change in fortune. The emphatic "never again" ("and they shall never again be plucked up out of their land") is probably being used antithetically to the "no longer" of the third and fourth visions ("I can no longer pass them by [and spare them]", 7:8; 8:2), whereby the verb "pluck out" stands in the tradition of Jeremiah's imagery (Jer. 1:10; 24:6, et passim). The verse—and with it the entire book of Amos— concludes solemnly by recalling the gift of the land, a gift concerning which God once again gives binding assurance; here God is reassuringly called "your God" in language drawn from that of individual trust. This address is directed to the community; in contrast to the sinful state, which is "eradicated from the earth" (v. 8), that community is told that the exile will remain a one-time experience never again to be repeated. In connection with the analogous assurance, Isa. 54:7 cites God's self-obligation from Genesis 8–9, namely, that despite the enduring sin of human beings, he will never again cause such a flood. God limits further his own possibilities for chastisement in favor of his people. In submission to the seriousness of Amos' words (vv. 8–10), it has since then been able to rely on the "never again" of this revocation in God's salvific plan.

[9:12–13] Verses 12 and 13, on which we have already commented, intensify the promises of the older verses; unlike vv. 11, 14f., they are focused not only on the entire book of Amos as such (and, as the tradents' numerous allusions show, on the slightly older book of Hosea[25]), but also, as J. Nogalski has recently and persuasively shown,[26] on the book of the Twelve Prophets. Verse 12 picks up the theme of the small book of Obadiah and constructs a bridge to it; v. 13 provides a link back to Joel 4:18 and thereby simultaneously a closure

---

25. Cf. the introduction to this commentary.
26. Loc. cit., 104ff.

with the beginning of the present book in Amos 1:2, which in its own turn alludes to Joel 4:16. We do not need to address the difficult problem of the priority of these connections in order to see clearly that these relationships are to prevent the reader of the book of Amos from reading it in isolation. This device assumes that the reader has the perseverance to consider the book of Amos together with the other prophetic books comprising the Twelve Prophets. That reader should read the book of Amos with the seriousness of Amos 9:9f., according to which the deliverance or ruin of the individual depends on that person's reading of the book. At the same time, however, the reader should know that Amos' own witnessing voice belongs together with the other witnessing voices in the book of the Twelve Prophets. Only in relationship to one another and together with one another do these voices constitute the word of God opening up Israel's future.

INDEX OF SCRIPTURE